Y0-ABJ-519

CHRONICLE OF 20TH CENTURY MURDER
Volume II: 1939–1992

A fascinating chronology of the most shocking
and historically significant murder cases
of our time.

Don't miss the first volume of this essential
true-crime reference,

CHRONICLE OF 20TH CENTURY MURDER
Volume I: 1900–1938

by Brian Lane

Available from Berkley Books

BRIAN LANE's true crime volumes include the series
The Murder Club Guides. He is coauthor of
The Encyclopedia of Serial Killers, which was praised by
The Criminologist as "indispensable."

Berkley Books by Brian Lane

CHRONICLE OF 20TH CENTURY MURDER
VOLUME I: 1900–1938

CHRONICLE OF 20TH CENTURY MURDER
VOLUME II: 1939–1992

CHRONICLE OF
20th CENTURY
MURDER

VOLUME II: 1939–1992

BRIAN LANE

BERKLEY BOOKS, NEW YORK

The publishers wish to thank the following organizations for permission to use cover art photos: photo of Aileen Wuornos courtesy UPI/Bettman; photo of Jack Henry Abbott courtesy UPI/Bettman; photo of electric chair courtesy Archive Photos; photo of Ruth Ellis courtesy UPI/Bettman; photo of Lyle and Erik Menendez courtesy UPI/Bettman; photo of Elizabeth Short ("The Black Dahlia") and mother courtesy UPI/Bettman; photo of Mark Gary Gilmore courtesy UPI/Bettman.

CHRONICLE OF 20th CENTURY MURDER
VOLUME II: 1939–1992

A Berkley Book / published by arrangement with
the author

PRINTING HISTORY
Virgin Publishing edition published 1993
Berkley edition / July 1995

All rights reserved.
Copyright © 1993, 1995 by Brian Lane.
This book may not be reproduced in whole or in part,
by mimeograph or any other means, without permission.
For information address: The Berkley Publishing Group,
200 Madison Avenue, New York, New York 10016.

ISBN: 0-425-14832-7

BERKLEY®
Berkley Books are published by The Berkley Publishing Group,
200 Madison Avenue, New York, New York 10016.
BERKLEY and the "B" design
are trademarks belonging to Berkley Publishing Corporation.

PRINTED IN THE UNITED STATES OF AMERICA

10 9 8 7 6 5 4 3 2 1

Chronological Index

Introduction

This book began its existence as an innocent attempt to answer a deceptively simple question. As a crime historian with a weakness for showing off, I have often engaged—wisely or not—in public discussion on the nature of Crime; and in particular its inter-reaction with the society that it feeds off. In other words, the debate as to whether Crime reflects its own time. Like many simple questions, the answer to it is as complex as can be—or, rather, there are several answers: "No," "Maybe" and "Yes."

Take the "No" answer first: the proposition that there is nothing, philosophically at least, to distinguish the crime of one age from that of another.

A QUESTION OF MOTIVE

Fundamental to all crime—though in the course of this book we are mainly concerned with homicide—is *motive*. Let nobody tell you there is any such thing as a motiveless murder.

The misconception has arisen because it is customary to classify murder according to the relationship between the killer and the victim—that the victim owned something coveted by the killer, perhaps; or had come into conflict with him; or had proved an unfaithful spouse; and so on. However, with certain types of murder—particularly those categorised as "serial" murders—the crime is *apparently* random and without purpose. In fact what has happened is that the motive is so deeply locked into the killer's inner psyche that the victim need only be one of a *type*—an elderly woman, a child, a priest . . .

Further complications arise when a killer's impaired logic fails to *correctly* identify members of his target group, resulting in a quasi-random selection.

It follows that if all murderers have a motive, then there must be a way of categorising those motives; and there is. The remarkable fact is that all murders fall into one or another of only six categories of motive. I should add here that the present author lays no claim to this revelation. It was first proposed in print by that doyenne of true-crime writers, Miss F. Tennyson Jesse, in her *Murder and Its Motives* (1924). According to Miss Tennyson Jesse the six classes are Gain, Jealousy, Revenge, Elimination, Lust and Conviction.

But such single-word concepts are at best only a convenience, because many crimes will traverse categories, or be motivated by more than one emotion. An advanced understanding of the criminal mind made possible by the rapid development of psychology has enabled us to embroider this list of motives with silks of richer colours and deeper shades.

The world has lost count of its psychopaths and psychotics, those madmen throughout history who have slaughtered with no discernible reason—no gain, no lust; cold, calculating killers. Killers like the fanatical Nazi sympathiser Joseph Franklin who shot dead mixed-race couples; like Harvey Carignan who was acting as an "instrument of God," killing to rid the world of sin, and Herbert Mullin, whose "voices" told him that only through bloodshed could he avert a cataclysmic earthquake which would destroy California.

But all these "visionaries," these "missionaries" who accept a self-imposed responsibility for improving the quality of life and ridding society of its "undesirable" elements, have one, basic, all-encompassing *motive*—that of Conviction. A deep and abiding belief in their own rightness that transcends socially acceptable behaviour and even the law.

I would like to propose just one small change to the existing sextet of universal motives and add a seventh. As the result of a need to discover some means of combating the seemingly unrestrained escalation of serial murder—particularly in the United States—criminologists and forensic psychiatrists have been exploring methods of identifying individuals who may be predisposed to deviant behaviour. One section of this programme has been concerned with compiling lists of behaviour patterns common to known serial killers, another part with categorising their specific motivations. Although the vast majority fit comfortably into the traditional six (with Lust being predominant), a small minority exhibit a newly identified motive. Labelled Thrill killers, they display many of the characteristics of Lust killers, but what distinguishes thrill killing is that although sexual abuse *may* take place, the motive is not sexual gratification but the desire for an experience, or "thrill." Quite simply, the *act* of killing is its own reward.

This is a useful addition, because it also helps to absorb those rare murders which prove to be the exceptions to the "rule of six"—cases such as Frederick Field, who strangled prostitute Beatrice Sutton because, he claimed, he was "browned off." He later confessed that he had also been browned off a couple of years earlier when he murdered Norah Upchurch.

And so, to return to the original question armed with our seven motives, it can be seen that the *roots* of murder have remained unchanged throughout times, culture and geography, from the "first" murder by Cain of his brother Abel (a classic case of Jealousy) to, say, the depredations of Jeffrey Dahmer, the serial cannibal whose killing pattern was determined by sexual lust. Thus, in one sense—that of the persistence of motive—crimes are not a product of their time so much as a result of unchangeable aspects of human nature.

MAKING THE WORLD A SMALLER PLACE

Despite the clear truth of the "No" answer in purely academic terms, it tends to lack colour and fails to take account of seminal events and discoveries in human history which have inevitably imposed themselves on the progress and pattern of crime, law and law enforcement.

This is the area in which we find the "Maybe" answer, because there is no denying that the development of stable agricultural societies out of small nomadic hunting groups led to the acquisition of land and possessions which might prove attractive to less scrupulous and less hard-working neighbours.

And with the increased vulnerability the first "policeman" would have been mobilised—members of the group who would take turns as watchmen to fend off or warn of the approach of danger. Means also became established by custom of dealing with crimes and indiscretions committed *within* the group or tribe, with the effect of rationalising the relationship between crime and punishment. The system of English law (and that adopted by other parts of the world which fell under English colonisation, including America) derived from Anglo-Saxon tribal customs which, with some systematisation in 1250, still provide the basis for the Common Law.

Another far-reaching influence on the pattern of international crime was the availability of firearms made general by the American gun manufacturer Samuel Colt with the introduction of a range of revolvers, from the "Walker" in 1847 to the ironically named "Peacemaker" around 1873 (and still in production today). Lethal, accurate over far greater distances than any previous weapons, guns enabled killings to be carried out with less chance of observation. Guns also introduced the possibility of multiple killing—after all, a spear could kill only one person at a time, a Colt "equaliser" six!

The use of gaslight to illuminate city streets was introduced to Britain in the early decades of the nineteenth century, with a consequent reduction in the activities of footpads, who until then had infested every dark corner like vermin. The organisation of a regular police force resulted, if not in fewer crimes, then at least in a greater likelihood of a felon being brought to book—or in most cases brought to the gallows. In England the task of thief-taking had been in the hands of what scant team of watchmen could be mustered by the parish—and a rag-bag lot they generally were; senile, simple, or downright criminous, the watchmen were often little better than the villains they were paid to catch. The legendary Bow Street Runners were formed by magistrate and novelist Henry Fielding in 1749, and they gave way to the permanent police force established by Robert Peel's government—in 1829 in London, and throughout the country by 1956. In the United States the first state police force—the Texas Rangers—came into being in 1835, though it was not until 1907 that a proposal was adopted for a detective agency with federal powers; in July of the following year the Federal Bureau of Investigation was founded.

Latterly, the advent of mass communication such as the telegraph and telephone, and rapid transport by railway and motor car added their own spicing to the melting pot of society's crime and crime detection.

What is most notable in an overview of criminal history, then, is that while minor changes in the *method* of committing acts of homicide have resulted from scientific and technological developments—the gun, for example, or modern poisons—the crimes themselves remain a fairly stable result of *motive*. Where the greatest changes have resulted from the development of society over the centuries is in the *detection* of crime and in the treatment of offenders. The law-enforcement agencies now have an unprecedented range of sophisticated scientific wizardry to add to their arsenal of weapons against the criminal; and if the crook has increased his mobility with motor vehicles, then the police are increasingly taking to the air in helicopters. As police forces internationally are making the criminal's world a smaller place, powerful computers are brought in to manipulate information with a speed and accuracy never dreamed of when Scotland Yard formed its first Murder Squad in 1907.

However, this is the point at which the debate either stops—with the possibility that broad changes in the pattern of crime *may* have resulted from social progress—or moves on to a consideration of the "Yes" answer.

MURDER IN THE TWENTIETH CENTURY

Colin Wilson, in his estimable work *Casebook of Crime*, suggests that "murder has not really come into its own until the twentieth century. Our age could be called the age of murder . . ." A study of Crime, and particularly the crime of homicide, reveals that as at no time before, murder in this present century has become immensely varied, and murderers increasingly idiosyncratic. We begin to see the question "Does Crime reflect the society in which it occurs?" in a different light. In the twentieth century at least, the answer is "yes."

Although certain tentative steps had already been taken in the scientific detection of crime during earlier centuries, the period from the last decade of Queen Victoria's reign to the present has seen a previously unimaginable escalation in the fight against serious crime—from the test to distinguish human from other animal blood discovered by the German biologist Paul Uhlenhuth in 1900, to the development by Professor Alec Jeffreys in England of digitalised DNA profiling in the early 1990s. New techniques of scientific analysis were enabling the law-enforcement agencies throughout the world to fully exploit a vital principle first propounded by Edmond Locard of the University of Lyon in 1910. The theory states simply that a criminal will always carry away with him some trace from the scene of his crime, and leave some trace of his presence behind. This has become the very foundation of forensic science. The practicalities of policing were also being addressed—the bobby's bike was being supplemented by motor vehicles for fast response to crimes by detectives alerted via the newly invented wireless.

Another feature of homicide in the twentieth century has been the growing number of "celebrity" murders. It is true, of course, that every age has had its famous cases. But for all that, the chronicler of the eighteenth, or even the nineteenth centuries would be hard put to find a truly notorious case for every decade, let alone every year. As for the twentieth century, the task of selection has at times been overwhelming, so great is the available material; and so the journey through the century's zoo of human monsters which lies ahead is an essentially subjective choice.

Frequently the relevance of cases will be that they do act as a mirror to the times, but the escalation of crime and its detection in the twentieth century has also been punctuated by what crime writers like to call "classics" and criminologists refer to as "landmarks." Whichever title we choose to use, these are the cases that have endured not necessarily because they are of scientific, legal or social importance but because, often unaccountably, they have entered popular mythology—crimes such as those of Harry Thaw and Bonnie and Clyde, Dennis Nilsen, and mad Charlie Manson.

THE WAR YEARS (1939-1950)

By 1935 the storm that was about to break over Europe for the second time in a quarter-century was gathering over Germany. Adolf Hitler had taken over as Chancellor of the German Reich in January 1933. Two months later Josef Goebbels, as Minister of Public Enlightenment, was denouncing the "Jewish vampires." Jews were forbidden to marry Germans and were barred from public office. In 1937 Hitler was joined by the Italian fascist leader Benito Mussolini in a show of strength at a massive floodlit rally in Berlin, and having worked their way through the world's literature, the Nazis next began to destroy "unGerman" art. Soon they would be destroying non-German people too. The German Army marched into Czechoslovakia in October 1938; three months later the British Home Office began to deliver air-raid shelters to private homes throughout London. Following France and Britain's official declaration of war on 3 September 1939, the Nazis invaded Poland. Once more the world was in the grip of a destructive war from which no winners would emerge—only greater or lesser losers.

The Second World War can be blamed for many things, but it cannot be said that it created any great escalation in civilian violence. In fact the reverse was generally true—the old principle of comradeship in adversity counter-acting the frustrations of wartime privation. For those impressed by statistics the British murder rates for the period were: 1939, 135; 1940, 115; 1941, 135; 1942, 159; 1943, 120; 1944, 95; 1945, 141. In fact with few exceptions, the same old murders were being committed for the same old motives—the only difference being that some of the killers wore uniform.

Of course the war did help in some ways—bomb-damaged buildings became the last resting places of several wartime murder victims. The darkness imposed by the blackout may have been used to advantage by a number of murderers; it certainly made crime easy for Gordon Cummins, "The Wartime Jack the Ripper."

The war also brought the people of Britain into contact with the visiting US forces. Some of them, like the Walter Mitty GI Karl Hulten, did little for international relations. Hulten, with English-born Betty Jones, acted out their own Bonnie and Clyde fantasy on the streets of London. In France the war helped Dr. Marcel Petiot to explain away the pile of dismembered corpses in his basement—Nazi collaborators, he told the men from the Sureté, assassinated by the Resistance fighters and entrusted to Petiot to dispose of. However preposterous the story sounds, at the time the good doctor escaped with a pat on the back!

By August 1945 the war was over; once again humankind was the only loser. But this time a horror more wicked even than the 55 million slain in the theatres of war; a new and terrible weapon, capable of unimaginable destruction, had been loosed on the world. We had just entered the age of the atom bomb.

THE ROCK 'N' ROLL YEARS (1951-1960)

Despite the Shadow of the Bomb, and the continuation of post-war rationing, the world was beginning to look forward to the future with optimism; after all, perhaps *this* had been the War to End Wars!

Technology developed as part of the struggle for military supremacy began to make itself useful in the civilian field. And nowhere was this more instantly apparent than in the manufacture of passenger aircraft. In July 1949, almost before the last echo of the last gun had died away, the De Havilland company flew their new Comet, the world's first jet airliner. 1949 was also the year Albert Guay planned to commit the perfect murder by planting a bomb on the Quebec Airways DC-3 on which his wife was travelling.

England was following the United States in the growing demand for consumer goods, and television was creeping into more and more of the nation's living-rooms. The police were not slow to exploit the immediacy of the medium in seeking assistance with tracking down suspects.

But above all the 1950s would be remembered as the Rock 'n' Roll Years—the age of the Juvenile Delinquent, the Teddy Boy; the decade teenagers were invented. A generation was being fed rebellion from a succession of films such as *Blackboard Jungle* and *Rock Around the Clock*, and was aping the sullen aggression of James Dean's *Rebel Without a Cause* and the leather-clad Marlon Brando.

Guns were also beginning to play a part in the activities of London's underworld. As if nothing had been learned from

Chicago and the 1930s, this became the age of the gangster London-style, with an escalation of violent gangland activity surrounding the Kray twins in East London and the Richardsons south of the Thames. It was in this climate of increasing aggression that Ruth Ellis gunned down her faithless lover on a North London street. Although she would almost certainly have been able to plead diminished responsibility in today's courts, Ruth was convicted of murder and, on 13 July 1955, became the last woman to be hanged in Britain.

It was increasingly clear that a kind of lawlessness was here to stay as the 1950s made way for the 1960s and 70s.

THE AGE OF VIOLENCE (1961-1970)

As a decade, the 1960s was a period characterised by opposites. Youth had grown confident enough to recognise its own collective strength, and nowhere was this more apparent than in America. While half the nation's youth seemed content with the power of flowers, others were engaged in using power of a very different kind in Vietnam, producing a generation of young men returning from a pointless and seemingly endless conflict, already battle-weary "veterans" at the age of 22. Ironically members of both these extremes fell prey to a drug culture that was to spread its evil and suffering over the following thirty years—the hippies to "expand" their minds, the vets to deaden their minds to the horrors of war. "Love and Peace" may have been the benign battle colours that welcomed the dawn of the Age of Aquarius, but it was rapidly developing into the Age of Violence. A new kind of madness seemed to strike: the assassination of another American President on the open street, and the assassination of his assassin, followed shortly by the senseless murder of Dr. Martin Luther King and, unbelievably, just two months later, the gunning down of the late President's brother. In Britain at least, it seemed that sanity was prevailing when an Act of Parliament abolished capital punishment for murder. Less than nine months later the retentionist lobby's worst fears seemed to have been realised—three policemen were shot dead on the streets of London by a gang of petty crooks. The criminals were arming themselves for their own war; and they were prepared to kill. In the Age of Violence the gun became the equaliser for the forces of disorder.

EMERGENCE OF THE SERIAL KILLER (1970-1979)

It is quite obvious that what we call "serial" murder was not "invented" in the 1970s—indeed, the stereotype sado-sexual serial killer was Jack the Ripper whose reign of terror took place in the autumn of 1888. However, what did emerge in the United States in the 1970s was the *identification* of this new and increasingly prevalent *type* of murderer: one who kills randomly and without apparent motive. An awareness of the need to make some positive effort to analyse and combat this baffling phenomenon coincided with the establishment in the early 1970s of the FBI's National Academy at Quantico, where senior instructors founded what was called the Behavioral Science Unit. In response to the virtual impossibility of applying the time-honoured techniques of homicide investigation to some of the cases before them, FBI agents began work on a system of "psychological profiling" which would use the disciplines of the behavioural scientist, the psychologist, and the psychiatrist to help analyse evidence, both tangible and intuitive, collected by officers at the scene of the crime. The profile is built by the careful analysis of elements such as victim traits, witness reports and the method and location of the killings. The profile attempts to indicate physical and psychological characteristics resulting in a "portrait" of the suspect and his behaviour patterns. For obvious reasons a considerable element of intuitive guesswork is involved, and no law-enforcement officer would dismiss a suspect from his investigation simply because he did not fit the profile. However, profiling has proved increasingly accurate in narrowing the field of inquiry.

THE SLAUGHTER CONTINUES (1980-1992)

The violence did not go away; it never does. The predominance of multicide which had begun with such household names as "Son of Sam," Ted Bundy and the "Boston Strangler" during the last half of the 1970s, escalated to epidemic proportions in the following decade. One study published in 1991 listed upwards of 50 serial killers active during the 1980s in the United States alone. In 1990 an "unofficial" estimate suggested that in America as many as 5,000 people a year could be the victims of serial killers. In Britain the pattern was being repeated. In 1980 Peter Sutcliffe was arrested after a reign of terror lasting five years during which, as the "Yorkshire Ripper," he had murdered thirteen women. Michael Ryan went on a shooting spree in the small English town of Hungerford in 1987, leaving fourteen people dead before turning the gun on himself; and at the University of Montreal, Marc Lepine cut down fourteen women in a hail of gunfire because he "hated feminists."

But at least in the 1980s Britain was able to lead the world in a revolutionary new scientific technique that could make the positive identification of criminals accurate beyond dispute: DNA profiling. It was in 1986 that "genetic fingerprinting" was successful for the first time in convicting a savage double killer.

As for the 1990s, it is too early to tell. Certainly the curse of the serial killer persists, with seemingly ever greater excesses—like the cannibalism of Jeffrey Dahmer and Andrei Chikatilo. Patterns of crime can only be assessed in retrospect. One thing is certain: homicide statistics always rise . . .

CHRONICLE OF
20th CENTURY
MURDER

VOLUME II: 1939–1992

1939

UNITED KINGDOM
THE MURDER OF
PAMELA COVENTRY

A severe test of the practice of identification through body secretions. A cigarette end found at the scene of the murder was saliva-matched with a suspect's cigarette; unfortunately the man proved to be a "non-secretor," one of only fourteen per cent of the population whose blood type cannot be revealed by their other body secretions.

The case started, as so many of its kind do, with a missing child report. After lunch on 18 February 1939, eleven-year-old Pamela Coventry set off from her home in Coronation Drive, Hornchurch, to meet some friends on their way to a dancing class. The friends hung around until 1:30 and then went on without her. When Pamela failed to return home that night Mrs. Coventry reported her missing, and a police search was launched. However, it was not the police team that found Pamela's body, but a passer-by. She had been stripped but for a petticoat pulled up round her neck, and her legs had been trussed up with electrical flex and string. It fell to Sir Bernard Spilsbury to examine the girl's body, and the experienced eye of the pathologist was soon able to provide Scotland Yard with further valuable clues. Pamela had been sexually assaulted, and the cause of death was manual strangulation. The process of digestion indicated that death had occurred within an hour of Pamela eating her last meal; as she had disappeared shortly after eating lunch, that set the time of her mur-

1

der at between 1:20 and 1:45 p.m., and so she must have been killed close to home. When the victim's legs had been untied, a cigarette-end of the hand-rolled variety was found caught between the thigh and the abdomen. Part of the flex used to tie the legs up to the chest was of a distinctive seven-strand 600-ohm type not manufactured in the previous seven years; the rest was of a common type, as was the green garden twine. Several days after the discovery of the body a number of significant articles were found wrapped up in a copy of the *News Chronicle* dated 11 January: a school badge, some buttons, and a length of flex similar to that used to tie the victim's legs.

The nature of the crime and the discovery of the body on an airfield so close to the child's home suggested to detectives that the killer was a local man, and with information gathered around the district, investigating officers were able to target 28-year-old Leonard Richardson, who lived on Coronation Drive, not far from the Coventry family. At the time of the murder Richardson's wife had been in hospital giving birth to their child, and he was alone in the house, a routine search of which turned up a number of pieces of evidence which were later examined by forensic specialists. For a start there was some garden twine and some flex of the common type used to tie the body; there was also a sequence of copies of the *News Chronicle* from which one issue was missing—that of 11 January. A raincoat hanging in Richardson's hallway bore small spots of human blood on the inside of the sleeve and pocket. Finally, it did not go unnoticed that the bottom of Richardson's garden bordered the airfield; what was more, the wire fence separating them had been pressed down, as though somebody had climbed over at that point.

Mr. Richardson, understandably, denied having anything to do with Pamela Coventry's death; he was, he claimed, at his sister-in-law's house at 1:30 on the afternoon in question, and at work before and after that. Both his relative and his employer supported Richardson's alibi. However, other witnesses were found who claimed to have seen him at his house at 1:15 p.m. Unbelievably, as he sat talking to detectives, Leonard Richardson rolled himself a cigarette.

This, then, was the tangible evidence available to the prosecution when the case came up for committal at the Romford Magistrates' Court, where Leonard Richardson was ordered to stand his trial at the Central Criminal Court. The process opened in March 1939 and Richardson, as we shall see, was most fortunate in his defence team, led by Mr. (later Lord Justice) Winn. He was lucky, because a skilful defence all but annihilated what at first seemed to be evidence—albeit circumstantial—of the most damning kind.

It is worth following an acknowledged master in the field along his own analysis of the evidence. Although he was not directly involved in the case, the redoubtable pathologist Professor Francis Camps subsequently presented a lucid discussion of the evidence in the Richardson case,* from which the following arguments emerge:

The green flex and garden twine: The defence rightly pointed out that although these articles were deemed "similar" to those used to tie the body of Pamela Coventry, they were in such common use that as scientific evidence it was little better than useless. Indeed, the judge himself felt obliged to question why the eminent Home Office Analyst, Dr. Roche Lynch, had been called to present evidence on matters which might more reliably be assessed by experts from the manufacturing industry. Of the special, rarer type of wire used on the body, none was ever found in association with the defendant.

Bloodstains on the raincoat: Again it was Roche Lynch who dealt with this piece of evidence, and again it proved to be rather a red herring—though it must be added that this was not the analyst's fault. Richardson claimed that the stains resulted from a minor injury to his hand, and that could well have been so. If this blood had been the same group as that of the victim, and different from Richardson's, it could be a very damaging clue indeed. The fact was that Sir Bernard Spilsbury had omitted to take a blood sample during autopsy, so Pamela Coventry's group was not known.

The cigarette-end: "Experts" from the tobacco world had already ponderously pronounced that the material found on the body and that rolled up by Leonard Richardson were "iden-

*The Investigation of Murder, F. E. Camps and Richard Barber. Michael Joseph, London, 1966.

tical''; however, in those days when scientific chemical tests such as neutron activation analysis were a way off, the methods were crude to the extent of, as it was described, ''smell after ignition.'' In other words, the burning tobaccos smelt alike. What the defence were able to do was find an expert to demolish the evidence that the cigarette paper around the suspect butt was identical to those in the packet used by Richardson. It was simply not even *possible*, the defence expert insisted; the method of cutting and packing the papers ruled that out. Besides, a random sample of cigarette-ends of the homemade variety were picked up from a factory floor, and despite their different origin all were similar to each other and similar to the cigarette made by Leonard Richardson.

The pressed-down fence: It was undeniable that the fence at the end of Richardson's garden had been pressed down in the centre—just as if a heavy load had been carried over it. What nobody but the defence solicitors bothered to check were the fences of the properties on either side of the Richardsons. Both had been pressed down; both had been pressed down even lower than the Richardsons'. Yet another red herring.

Most of this information came out during the cross-examination of Crown witnesses, and when it came Mr. Winn's turn to present the defence he opened by submitting that the prosecution had not proved its case, and there was, therefore, no case to answer. The judge was not prepared to go quite as far as he was entitled—that is, to instruct the jury to return a formal verdict of not guilty; but he did allow the jury to retire and decide for themselves whether the case should proceed. After deliberation, they returned to court to announce that, on the evidence presented, they would not be able to arrive at a verdict. The case was consequently dismissed and Leonard Richardson released. The murder of Pamela Coventry remains an open case.

UNITED STATES
MURDER BY REQUEST

In a case, so he claimed, of "murder by request," Rodney Greig repeatedly stabbed and then cut the throat of girl-friend Leona Vlught. He subsequently explained to arresting officers that Miss Vlught could see no future for herself and had asked Greig to put her out of her misery. Unwilling to let a good story go ungilded, newsmen reporting the case added that Rodney Greig had also drunk his victim's blood—an accusation which he vigorously denied. Greig was put in the gas chamber at the end of 1939.

1940

MEXICO
ASSASSINATION OF LEON TROTSKY

By order of Josef Stalin, the exiled Russian revolutionary was tracked to his fortress villa in Mexico and killed by a blow to the head with an ice-pick.

While Leon Trotsky, the Russian revolutionary leader exiled by Stalin, was taking refuge in an ostensibly siege-proof villa at Coyoacan, outside Mexico City, he fell victim to the one type of assassin against whom it is all but impossible to guard—a treacherous friend. There had already been one serious attempt on Trotsky's life on 24 May 1940, when a gang of assassins led by the Mexican artist and Stalinist agent David Siqueiros gained entry to the fortress by wearing police uniforms. They strafed the bedroom with machine-gun fire, but miraculously Trotsky and his wife Natalie, who had been hiding under the bed, were unhurt. Prophetically, Trotsky commented: "Fate granted me a reprieve. It will be of short duration." On 20 August 1940 Frank Jackson, a trusted comrade, arrived at the villa to discuss revisions before the publication of a new article by Trotsky. While the two men were alone in the study Jackson drove an ice-pick through Trotsky's skull. When he was taken into custody Jackson was revealed to be Moscow-trained agent Jacques Mornard.

Some years later, Mornard's fingerprints finally proved his real identity as a Spanish Communist activist named Jaime Ramon Mercader; the assassination had, predictably, been ordered by Josef Stalin. Jackson/Mornard/Mercader served twenty years in solitary confinement before being released in 1960. He was given a Czech passport and returned to oblivion behind the ''Iron Curtain,'' where he worked as a radio mechanic.

1941

UNITED KINGDOM
ANTONIO "BABE" MANCINI

Chicago Comes to London. *An unsavoury gangland murder which results in Mancini taking his case first to the Court of Appeal and then to the House of Lords where it becomes a legal cause célèbre.*

It is surprising how many complex legal arguments arise out of sordid backstreet crimes which would otherwise go unremarked by public and criminologist alike. Never was this more apparent than in the case of Mancini. It occurred at the time when Britain, along with much of the rest of the world, was allied in its fight against fascism; it was a period when America's recent gangland experiences with Prohibition and beyond had eventually found its way around the globe via the Hollywood movie boom. US-style gangsters were popping up the world over, and London's share centred around the night clubs, bars and strip joints of Soho. One of these seedy drinking clubs, in Wardour Street, was managed by an equally seedy character named Antonio "Babe" Mancini (they mostly affected these preposterous nicknames in emulation of their gangster heroes across the Atlantic—perhaps Mancini had wanted to be "Baby Face" Nelson. Who knows?). In the early hours of the morning of 1 May 1941 "Babe" Mancini got into a disagreement with a fellow Gangland bit-part player named Harry Distleman (though he preferred "Scarface" Distleman—no doubt after Big Al Capone). The upshot of the argument was that "Babe" stabbed "Scarface" to death.

At his Old Bailey trial before Mr. Justice McNaghten, Mancini pleaded self-defence, but the jury convicted him of murder. And that was about as far as such cases usually got. However, Mancini's attorney took the case to the Court of Criminal Appeal where he argued that by not giving full emphasis to the point in his summing-up, Mr. Justice McNaghten had deprived the jury of the option to find a verdict of manslaughter, and consequently deprived Mancini of the possibility of conviction on a non-capital charge. The appeal was dismissed.

Mr. Hector Hughes KC, defending Mancini, then took the unusual step of applying to the Attorney-General, Sir Donald Somervell, for leave to appeal to the highest court in the land, the House of Lords. In an even more unusual step, Sir Donald granted his fiat to be heard in the Lords. On 2 and 3 October 1941 the evidence was presented to the panel of law lords comprising the Lord Chancellor Viscount Simon, Lord Sankey, Lord Russell of Killowen, Lord Wright and Lord Porter. This time around they considered the defence's complaint that Mr. Justice McNaghten had not adequately instructed the jury on the matter of *provocation*. Mr. Hughes argued that the judge should have made it clear that if the jury felt that the defendant was provoked, or if there was any reasonable doubt about the provocation, then he should be acquitted of the charge of murder. For the Crown, Sir Donald Somervell countered that it was not incumbent upon a judge to advance information on a possible charge of manslaughter unless the evidence before him either raised the issue directly, or left open a possibility of doubt—which did not apply in the case of Mancini.

After a retirement to consider the evidence, the Lord Chancellor delivered their Lordships' judgment on 16 October. Viscount Simon was of the opinion that although Mancini had advanced the defence at his trial that he was obliged to use the knife in self-defence, it was the duty of the judge in his charge to the jury to adequately state any other view of the facts which might reasonably arise out of the evidence presented, and which would reduce the offence to manslaughter. The fact that Mancini's counsel did not stress the alternative case to the jury—which he might feel it difficult to do without prejudicing his main line of defence—did not absolve the judge from the duty to direct the jury to consider the alternative, "if there were material which would justify such a direction." The argument that there was lack of direction on the matter of provocation depended entirely on whether there was evidence in front of the jury which might, if they chose to believe it, be regarded as amounting to *sufficient provocation*. And this is where Mancini's case failed. In order to reduce murder to manslaughter, the provocation would need to have been such as to deprive the person provoked of the power of self-control. The test that had to be applied was what would the effect of that provocation be on a "reasonable" man. His Lordship declared that if the evidence before a jury at the close of a case did not contain material on which a reasonable man could find a verdict of manslaughter rather than murder, it was not a defect in the summing-up that manslaughter was not dealt with. Therefore there was no error of law in Mr. Justice McNaghten's summing-up.

It was a creditable example of the way in which the intrinsic fairness of the English legal system permitted such lengthy and painstaking deliberations to be conducted on behalf of one of society's less upright citizens. Shortly afterwards, however, all avenues of appeal having been explored, "Babe" Mancini kept his appointment with the hangman. [See also 1944, the case of Leonard Holmes.]

UNITED STATES
THE MAN IN THE ATTIC

Theodore Coneys was a 59-year-old vagrant who broke into the home of Philip Peters intending to commit a burglary and instead secretly took up residence in the attic, creeping down for food when Peters was sleeping or out of the house. Coneys had been living in the loft for almost a year when, on one of his forays for sustenance, he woke Peters from his bed and felt obliged to kill him before retreating to his hideaway. It was a puzzled police force that tried to solve the ultimate in "locked room" mysteries. Months later, Theodore Coneys was spotted disappearing into the roof by police officers set to watch the "empty" house after neighbours had reported disturbances. The "Spiderman of Denver," as he became known, was taken into custody and later imprisoned for the murder of Philip Peters.

1942

UNITED KINGDOM
HARRY DOBKIN

Another Victim of the Blitz. *Professor Keith Simpson's early triumph with forensic dentistry was responsible for identifying the near-skeletal remains of Mrs. Rachel Dobkin.*

On 17 July 1942 a workman helping to demolish the badly bomb-damaged Vauxhall Baptist Chapel in Vauxhall Road, Kennington (now Kennington Lane), prised up a stone slab and found beneath it a mummified body. The immediate assumption was that the remains were either of an air-raid victim or had come from the old burial ground underneath the church, which had ceased to be used some fifty years before. When the church had been bombed on 15 October 1940 more than a hundred people had been killed in the conflagration and the area around the chapel had been the target of a number of Luftwaffe raids between that time and March of 1941. Nor was this the first body that the workers had come upon while demolishing the chapel. Nevertheless, routine was followed, and the police were called in, arriving in the persons of Detective Inspectors Hatton and Keeling, and the bones were removed to Southwark Mortuary for examination by the pathologist, Dr. Keith Simpson.

Simpson immediately suspected foul play. In trying to raise the bones, the skull had become detached, and Simpson realised that the head had already been cut from the body. In addition to this, the limbs had been severed at the elbows and knees, flesh had been removed from the face, the lower jaw was missing and the bones were partially burnt. It was obvious that an attempt had been made to disguise the identity of the corpse. Dr. Simpson obtained the permission of the coroner to take the remains back to his laboratory at Guy's Hospital for a more detailed inspection. Returning to the crypt of the church in a vain attempt to find the missing limbs, Simpson noticed a yellowish deposit in the earth, subsequently analysed as slaked lime. This had been used to suppress the smell of putrefaction, but it also had the effect of preventing maggots from destroying the body. Examining the throat and voice box, Simpson detected a blood clot, strongly indicating death due to strangulation.

The next task was to discover the identity of the victim. The body was that of a woman aged between 40 and 50, with dark greying hair, was five feet one inch tall, and had suffered from a fibroid tumour. Time of death was estimated at between twelve and fifteen months prior to discovery. Meanwhile the police had been checking the lists of missing persons, and noted that, fifteen months previously, Mrs. Rachel Dobkin, estranged wife of Harry Dobkin, the fire-watcher at the firm of solicitors next door to the Baptist Chapel at 302 Vauxhall Road, had disappeared. An interview with her sister elicited the information that she was about the right age, with dark greying hair, was about five feet one tall, and had a fibroid tumour. She also gave police the name of Mrs. Dobkin's dentist, Barnett Kopkin of Stoke Newington, who kept meticulous records and was able to describe exactly the residual roots and fillings in her mouth. They matched the upper jaw of the skull. Finally, Miss Mary Newman, the head of the Photography Department at Guy's, superimposed a photograph of the skull on to a photograph of Rachel Dobkin, a technique first used six years earlier in the Buck Ruxton case. The fit was uncanny. The bones found in the crypt were the mortal remains of Mrs. Rachel Dobkin.

Rachel Dubinski had married Harry Dobkin in September 1920, through the traditional Jewish custom of a marriage broker. Within three days they had separated, but unhappily nine months later a baby boy was born. In 1923 Mrs. Dobkin obtained a maintenance order obliging her husband to pay for the upkeep of their child. Dobkin was always a spasmodic

payer, and over the years had been imprisoned several times
for defaulting. In addition, Mrs. Dobkin had unsuccessfully
summonsed him four times for assault. However, it must be
said in mitigation of Dobkin's actions that she habitually pestered him in the street to get her money, and it should be
remembered that she was still demanding cash in 1941 when
the "child" was twenty years old and hardly a dependent.
Dobkin was to hint later that she was also blackmailing him
over some undisclosed indiscretion at work.

On Good Friday, 11 April 1941, Dobkin and his wife had
met in a café in Kingsland Road, Shoreditch, near to where
he lived in Navarino Road, Dalston. They left at 6.30 p.m.
and she was never seen alive again, though he claimed that
she had boarded a number 22 bus to visit her mother. The next
day Rachel's sister reported her missing to the police, implicating Harry Dobkin in the process. Because of the priorities
of war, Dobkin was not interviewed about the disappearance
until 16 April. On the night of the 14th a small fire had broken
out in the ruined cellar of the Baptist Church. This was peculiar, because there had been no air raids and the blaze was
only noticed at 3:23 a.m. by a passing policeman. When the
fire brigade arrived Harry Dobkin was there, pretending to put
it out. He told the constable that the fire had started at 1:30
a.m. and that he hadn't bothered to inform the authorities because there was little danger of the fire spreading. There was
a serious air raid on the next night, so the incident was quickly
forgotten. Dobkin was interviewed twice more about his wife's
disappearance and a description and photograph were circulated by the police, but no further action was taken.

In May 1942, before the body was found, Dobkin had
ceased to be a fire-watcher and was back in Navarino Road.
Three weeks later he was observed by a local policeman entering the Baptist Church in Kennington at 6 a.m. On 26 August, Dobkin was interviewed for the first time by Chief
Inspector Hatton, and escorted to the church cellar, where he
vehemently denied any involvement in his wife's death. He
was then arrested for her murder.

The trial of Harry Dobkin opened at the Old Bailey on 17
November 1942, with Mr. Justice Wrottesley presiding and

Mr. L. A. Byrne prosecuting. Dobkin's counsel, Mr. F. H. Lawton, spent most of his efforts trying vainly to challenge the identification evidence. The prisoner's appearance in the witness box left the jury unimpressed, and it took them only twenty minutes to arrive at a verdict of guilty. Before his execution Dobkin confessed to his wife's murder, claiming that she was always pestering him for money and he wanted to be rid of her for good. On 7 January 1943 Harry Dobkin was hanged in Wandsworth Prison.

AUSTRALIA
"I'M A DR. JEKYLL AND MR. HYDE . . ."

The third death was on 28 May 1942. Gladys Hosking had followed Ivy McLeod and Pauline Thompson in the succession of strangled corpses to be found where they had fallen on the streets around Melbourne. It was also to be the last death, thanks to an observant sentry at the local US Army base who remembered challenging a shaken and dishevelled GI coming into camp late on the night of the murder. The description happened to match that of a young soldier reported for threatening violence to a young woman only a couple of days before; both these descriptions fitted Edward Joseph Leonski, a big Texan who had recently confided to a camp buddy the alarming news that "I'm a Dr. Jekyll and Mr. Hyde! I killed! I killed!" There was not a lot of need to search for incriminating evidence; Leonski provided his own. Sure he had killed these ladies: "It was to get their voices!" He recalled with particular affection that Pauline Thompson had sung to him as he walked her to her home, a soft, sweet voice: "I could feel myself going mad about it." Nutty as a fruit-cake? The court-martial didn't think so, despite the prisoner's own best efforts and a long family history of insanity. The "Singing Strangler,"

(continued)

the ''Melbourne Jack the Ripper,'' was hanged on 19 November 1942, at Pentridge Gaol; it is said that in the hours before execution he sat in his cell singing softly to himself.

1943

UNITED KINGDOM
DENNIS EDMUND LECKEY

The Right to Silence. *In which a single, basic blunder by the judge allows a brutal sex-killer to walk free.*

English law has built into it—and quite rightly so—certain safeguards for the protection of persons accused of committing a crime. One of these fundamental rights—and one currently under threat—is to remain silent; in other words, a suspect is not obliged to say anything that may incriminate him until he has the benefit of legal advice. An extension of this is the right of an accused not to give evidence at his own trial. And it must not be inferred from a prisoner's silence in either of these circumstances that he is making an admission of guilt; and it must certainly never be suggested, either from the Bench or by counsel. Indeed, so strictly is this basic rule applied that any deviation could represent grounds for the verdict being overturned. The case of Dennis Leckey was one such rare example.

In 1943 Caroline Trayler was just eighteen years old, but already a bride of six months, with a husband on active service with the British Forces in North Africa. And like many lively youngsters in her peer group, Caroline was bored; the war which had disrupted English life since 1939 had been going on just too long. She had a part-time job as a cinema usherette, which gave her a small financial independence, but there was little enough in those days of austerity on which to spend her hard-earned wages.

It might have been just another familiar Sunday evening spent with her mother behind the black curtains which kept their modest private lives from the searching eyes of the Luftwaffe's bombers. But this was Whit Sunday, and Caroline Trayler was determined to get some pleasure out of the holiday. As it was she ended up drinking at the Mechanic's Arms, Folkestone. At closing time she left, a little the worse for drink, on the arm of an off-duty soldier. The darkness swallowed them up; Caroline never returned from it.

When her anxious mother reported Caroline's disappearance, the police moved into a now-familiar wartime routine—first search the considerable area of the town's bomb-damaged buildings. Caroline Trayler's body was found four days later in a blitzed shop, and a cursory glance at the body indicated strangulation compounded with violent sexual assault.

The medical examination was undertaken, as it was in so many cases during those war years, by pathologist Dr. Keith Simpson. Simpson's reconstruction suggested that the "rape" almost certainly began with Caroline Trayler's consent—the dirtied state of her calves was consistent with her lying with her legs wide apart and flat on the floor. Whether she changed her mind or found herself in the hands of a sexual sadist we will never know. The bruising around Caroline's throat indicated her killer had tried unsuccessfully to strangle her from the front, then turned her over and completed the job from behind. The pathologist then began the gruesome task of scavenging such clues as the body could offer to the identity of the attacker. Simpson found a half-dozen dark body hairs stuck to Caroline Trayler's thighs; they contrasted sharply with her own auburn colouring and almost certainly came from her killer. The girl's fingernails had become torn and broken during the struggle, and scrapings from the nails contained rusty-brown fibres, in all likelihood from the assailant's clothing. All that was needed now was a suspect to match the clues.

If Dennis Leckey, a serving Artillery gunner, had not gone absent on the day that Caroline's body was found, it is possible that the trail would never have led to him. As it was, the Folkestone police issued a nationwide description and a request for his apprehension. Gunner Leckey was picked up in London ten days later. Formally arrested, Leckey was required to surrender samples of his body hairs which Professor Simpson confirmed matched those left behind during the assault on his victim. Furthermore, the couple had "exchanged" hairs, one of Caroline's being found on Leckey's uniform trousers. The fibre taken from beneath Caroline Trayler's fingernails matched those of his uniform shirt. Not conclusive proof, perhaps, but strong enough evidence with which to bring Dennis Leckey to trial, for the jury to return a verdict of guilty, and for Mr. Justice Singleton to pronounce sentence of death.

At the conclusion of the Leckey trial, in a legal error that was as damaging to the prosecution case as it was inexplicable from so experienced a judge, Sir John Singleton not once but three times in his summing-up gave utterance to the sentiment that the prisoner's reluctance to make a statement to the police at the time of his arrest could be seen as an indication of guilt: "Of course, he is not bound to say anything—but what would you conclude?" he asked the jury. Anyway, it was enough to force the Court of Appeal to overturn the conviction, and allow Dennis Leckey—without dispute the brutal killer of poor Caroline Trayler—to walk free; society had, on this thankfully rare occasion, become victim to its own impeccably fair legal system.

UNITED STATES
JARVIS CATOE

The Case of the Scapegoat. *Jarvis Catoe murdered eight women; for one of these killings an innocent man was jailed for life. Under arrest, Catoe claimed that a diet of pornography and crime books brought on his "spells."*

Savage killer Jarvis Catoe managed to elude detection long enough to murder seven women in Washington and one in New York City; he escaped detection altogether in the case of his first victim, Florence Dancy, when a man named James Smith was wrongly convicted of her murder and jailed for life in 1935.

The regularity of Catoe's killings accelerated after he raped and strangled Josephine Robinson on 1 December 1939. Between September 1940 and January 1941, he killed three more women, all in Washington. Still gathering momentum, on 8 March 1941 25-year-old Rose Simons Abramowitz asked Catoe if he would wax her kitchen floor. Once inside her apartment, Catoe raped and murdered her. Three months later he picked up Jessie Strieff by posing as a cab driver. He drove her to a nearby garage where he raped and killed her, and then dumped the body in another garage several blocks away. Despite an extensive state police presence, and support from the FBI, no arrest was made.

In August 1941, Jarvis Catoe transferred his attentions to New York City where, on the morning of the 4th, he offered 26-year-old Evelyn Anderson a lift in his car, and then strangled her. But by this time his luck had run out, and the wrist watch which Catoe had stolen from Evelyn Anderson finally came into police possession. Catoe had given the watch to his girlfriend as a present, and she in turn had asked her uncle to pawn it.

When Catoe returned to Washington a warrant for his arrest was waiting. Under interrogation, he finally admitted the Strieff and Abramowitz murders and by way of explanation claimed that he suffered from what he called ''spells'' after reading crime stories and pornography. Catoe later confessed to ten rapes and six other murders, including the killing in 1935 of Florence Dancy.

Both Washington and New York laid claim to Jarvis Catoe—New York for the murder of Evelyn Anderson, and Washington for the murder of Rose Abramowitz. In the end he was tried in Washington, though by this time he had retracted his confession, claiming that it had been coerced from him under torture and duress. He was, nevertheless, found guilty and sentenced to death. Jarvis Catoe was executed in January 1943, chanting a hymn as he walked to the death chamber.

1944

UNITED KINGDOM
LEONARD HOLMES

The Case of the Unfaithful Wife. *It was wartime infidelity that forced Holmes to murder his wife, a common enough motive for marital violence during the Second World War, and one which led to the rationalisation of the defence of Provocation.*

Leonard Holmes represents a sad, if by no means uncommon phenomenon of wartime conditions the world over. He was demobilised from the Army in October 1944 after serving King and Country in the still-effervescent Second World War. When he returned to his home in New Ollerton, Nottinghamshire, Holmes discovered that his absence, far from making his wife's heart grow fonder, had given Peggy Ann the opportunity to spread her affections farther afield. It was, therefore, an uneasy homecoming, and matters did not improve over the succeeding weeks. On 19 November the couple were spending the evening drinking at a local public house when, inflamed by drink, Holmes got it into his head that his wife was being too familiar by half with a bunch of RAF men standing at the bar. Once ignited, the flames of the subsequent quarrel continued to rage throughout the evening and on the journey home. When they arrived, Mrs. Holmes, also somewhat the worse for drink, unwisely decided to confess: "If it eases your mind, I *have* been unfaithful to you." There was a brief pause, a silence, before Holmes picked up a hammer and smashed it down on his wife's head; then for good measure he strangled her.

It was, we have observed, a common domestic murder with a common motive—sexual jealousy. Leonard Holmes faced trial and was convicted and sentenced to death at the Nottingham Assizes in February 1945. And there, one might think, the matter would end, with just two more tragic victims of a war that was claiming millions. However, Leonard Holmes was about to become a minor *cause célèbre*.

In the time allotted to him after sentence, Holmes's attorney made application to the Court of Criminal Appeal to overturn the sentence on the grounds that Mr. Justice Charles had instructed the jury that it was not open to them to return a verdict of manslaughter. Presenting their Lordships' judgment, Mr. (later Lord) Justice Wrottesley declared:

> It cannot be too widely known that a person who, after absence for some reason such as service, either suspects already, or discovers on his return, that his wife has been unfaithful during his absence, is not, on that account, a person who may use lethal weapons upon his wife, and, if violence should result in her death, can claim to have suffered such provocation as would reduce the crime from murder to manslaughter.

Clearly the provocation factor was of great importance in a case such as this. As the law stood (and for that matter still stands), in the general run of criminal cases provocation is entitled to be taken into account only in *mitigation*—that is, once a verdict has been reached, the judge, in deciding sentence, is entitled to consider the degree of provocation and adjust the severity of sentence accordingly. However, in charges of murder, provocation amounts to a *legal defence*; it is unlikely to secure a defendant's release, but it could be successful in reducing the charge to manslaughter. This was especially beneficial in days when the death sentence for murder was *mandatory*.

Bearing this in mind, the then Attorney-General, Sir Hartley Shawcross KC, granted permission for Leonard Holmes's case to be referred for appeal before the House of Lords. The matter was argued before Lords Simon, Porter, Simonds and du Parq, with Holmes's counsel contending that provocation by adultery was a matter for the jury to consider, and the Crown submitting that words could never amount to good enough justification for the taking of life—it would be unfortunate, Sir Frank Soskice suggested, if a confession to adultery should be seen as a licence to kill. It was a sentiment endorsed by the Bench, and Lord Simon reiterated that only very rarely could provocation be applied in cases where there was *an intention to kill*. His Lordship then underlined the court's judgment with reference to the Bard: "Even if Iago's insinuations against Desdemona's virtue had been true, Othello's crime was murder and nothing else." So the final appeal was lost; words alone were not, by and large, sufficient to reduce a crime. (However, the discovery of a partner *in the act of adultery* was deemed sufficient provocation to reduce murder to manslaughter.)

The legal battle for Leonard Holmes's life was over, and on 28 May 1945 he was hanged.

UNITED STATES
PERSON OR PERSONS UNKNOWN

Hearing that there was oil beneath the farmland worked by black minister Rev'd Isaac Simmons, a white mob rounded up Simmons and his son and drove them to a remote spot where the clergyman was tortured and shot, and young Eldridge Simmons was savagely beaten up and run out of the county. Although Eldridge Simmons later identified his father's killers, the local coroner's inquest returned a verdict of death at the hands of "a person or persons unknown."

1945

UNITED KINGDOM
KARL GUSTAV HULTEN AND ELIZABETH MARINA JONES

The Wartime Bonnie and Clyde. *An American army deserter and a London prostitute join forces to live out their Hollywood gangster fantasies.*

It was a late afternoon in the October of 1944, towards the end of the Second World War, when the man who liked to call himself Second Lieutenant Richard Allen, of the 501 Parachute Infantry Regiment, US Army, walked into a small café in Queen Caroline Street on London's Hammersmith Broadway. Coincidence was about to cross his path with that of a young woman; between them they would commit one of the most cold-blooded, senseless killings of the twentieth century.

Karl Gustav Hulten, who for no honest reason was masquerading under the sobriquet "Ricky Allen," recalled the meeting at his subsequent trial, "I saw Len Bexley [an acquaintance] sitting there with a young lady. I took another seat, but he asked me to come over and join them, which I did." Bexley introduced "Ricky" to Elizabeth ("Betty") Jones, an eighteen-year-old stripper who worked under the name Georgina Grayson; under this latter name she rented a room at 311 King Street, not far from where they now sat. Born and brought up in South Wales, Betty had been married when she was only sixteen to a soldier, a man ten years her senior with a quick temper and a brutish manner. When he punched her on their wedding day it was for the last time; she walked out on him then and there, making her way up to London and a succession of seedy, unfulfilling jobs—waitress, barmaid, cinema usherette, and striptease dancer at the Blue Lagoon Club, an occupation from which she had recently emerged unemployed.

Hulten further remembered, "We were there a while in the cafeteria, and afterwards we all got up and left together. Mrs. Jones and I walked towards the Broadway. I asked her if she would care to come out later on."

At 11:30 that same evening—Friday, 13 October 1944— Betty Jones was just about to give up her wait outside the Broadway Cinema, when a two-and-a-half-ton ten-wheeled US Army truck pulled up in front of her with Hulten in the driver's seat. Betty was soon sitting up beside him in an appropriately bizarre start to an affair which was to destroy them both.

In a sense they were still children, still locked in the world of celluloid fantasy that comprised wartime entertainment. We know from subsequent statements that the conversation on that first date was not the normal run of boy-girl talk. "Ricky" opened by telling his new friend that the truck was stolen, and that he was a lieutenant in the US paratroops (in fact Private Hulten was a deserter). This obviously appealed to Betty's sense of the romantic, and she responded that she had always wanted to do something exciting "like becoming a gun moll like they do in the States." Hulten then boasted, quite untruthfully, that he had "carried a gun for the Mob" in Chicago, and started to brandish a stolen pistol.

Perhaps the point of no return had already been reached, with both now committed to act out the roles they had chosen for themselves, and admired in each other. At any rate, a sequence of events that would not stop short of murder had been put into motion.

Past midnight on the road outside Reading, Berkshire, the truck overtook a lone girl on a bicycle. Stopping the vehicle, Hulten stepped down and waited for the girl to pass and as she did, pushed her off her machine and grabbed the handbag which had been slung over the handlebars. Before their startled victim could regain her feet, these modern highwaymen were speeding back to London, the proceeds of their crime just a couple of shillings and some clothing coupons. At 5 a.m. Betty Jones was tucked up in bed at King Street, Hulten in a nearby car-park in the truck.

On Thursday, 5 October the wartime Bonnie and Clyde climbed once more into the cab of the ten-wheeler. Robbery was once more on their minds. Their first decision, to "do" a pub, was abandoned. Betty suggested robbing a taxi-cab; Ricky forced one to stop, and with a gun at the driver's head, ordered him to "Let me have all your money." Luckily—as future events would show—the cabbie had a passenger, whose evident alarm panicked Hulten, and this robbery too was abandoned in an undignified scramble to escape. Driving back into London's blackout along the Edgware Road, at Jones's suggestion the pair picked up a young woman making her way to Bristol via Paddington station; Hulten offered to drive her out as far as Reading (which seemed to have some magnetic attraction for him), and the girl climbed gratefully into the truck between them. Hulten later recollected, "When we were almost through Runnymede Park going towards Windsor I stopped the truck off the road. I told the girl we had a flat tyre. We all got out . . . I hit the girl over the head with an iron bar." While Hulten held her face down on the ground, Jones rifled the girl's pockets. "By this time the girl had ceased struggling. I picked up her shoulders and Georgina [Jones] picked up her feet. We carried her over and dumped her about three feet from the edge of a stream." Proceeds of this crime? Less than five shillings. The victim, thankfully, survived.

The next day, Friday, Hulten once again called for Jones at King Street, and in the early hours of the following morning they decided to try another taxi robbery.

By 2 a.m. they were approaching the Chiswick Roundabout in the back of George Heath's hired car, a grey Ford V-8 saloon, registration number RD 8955.

"We'll get out here."

Heath pulled into the kerb. According to Betty Jones. "As Heath was leaning over [to open the door for Jones] I saw a flash and heard a bang . . . Heath moaned slightly and turned a little towards the front. Ricky said, "Move over or I'll give you another dose of the same." I heard [Heath] breathing very heavily and his head was slumped on his chest.''

Hulten now replaced Heath behind the wheel of the saloon, and while he drove off towards Staines his companion systematically emptied the dying man's pockets. Heath struggled to keep hold of his life for just fifteen more minutes before succumbing to a massive internal haemorrhage. His corpse was unceremoniously cast into a ditch by Knowle Green, just outside Staines. The couple arrived back in home territory at 4 a.m., and after wiping the car of fingerprints, dumped it in the cinema carpark behind Hammersmith Broadway. After a quick snack in the Black and White café, they went back to Jones's room to look over the loot.

Six hours after it had been discarded, George Heath's body was discovered in its resting place by auxiliary fireman Robert Balding. Heath's less immediately useful possessions, such as his chequebook and driver's licence, lay where they had been thrown out on to the Great Southwest Road by Betty Jones the night before; they were found by John Jones, an apprentice electrician. This gave a possible identity to the recently found corpse, and a description of George Heath and his car was circulated to all police units.

In the meantime the gunman and his moll had been disposing of their victim's marketable possessions: his fountain pen and propelling pencil were snapped up by Len Bexley; a wristwatch went to Hulten's hairdresser, Morris Levene. They passed the afternoon spending the proceeds at the White City greyhound track, and in the evening they watched Deanna Durbin in the film *Christmas Holiday*. But bravado had become the new name of their dangerous game, and on the night of Sunday, 8 October the couple were openly driving around in George Heath's V-8. After spending the next morning in bed at King Street, Hulten again climbed behind the wheel and took a trip to Newbury, to his old army camp; in the evening he returned to London and the arms of another girlfriend, Joyce Cook.

Patrolling his customary beat on this Monday night, PC William Walters spotted a Ford saloon parked in Lurgan Avenue, off the Fulham Road. The car's number was RD 8955.

In response to his call, Walters was soon joined by Inspector Read and a sergeant, who set watch on the car. At about 9 p.m. Hulten left Joyce's house and got into the stolen V-8.

"Is this your car, sir?" inquired PC Walters.

Back at Hammersmith police station, Hulten introduced himself as Second Lieutenant Richard Allen, 501 Parachute Regiment. In his hip pocket had been found a Remington automatic and a handful of ammunition. "Allen" claimed that he had found the car abandoned out at Newbury. In the early hours of Tuesday morning Lt. Robert Earl de Mott of the American CID took Hulten to their headquarters in Piccadilly. This was in perfect accord with wartime protocol, which recognized the "sovereignty" of American servicemen while stationed in Britain, and did not permit them to be tried in a British court. The Americans, however, in an almost unprecedented act of disdain for Hulten, waived this right and returned him to the ministrations of British law and justice.

Meanwhile Hulten had given the police Jones's address at King Street, and she had been interviewed at Hammersmith police station, where she made a statement and was released. Clearly haunted by her part in what had become known as "The Cleft-Chin Murder" (descriptive of George Heath), and prompted by a chance meeting with an old friend, Henry Kimbelly (who, coincidentally, was a War Reserve police constable), Elizabeth Jones made a full confession of her part in the crime, albeit laying much emphasis on Hulten's dominant role. She later enlarged the point by claiming that she was afraid of Hulten and terrified by his threats of violence. Karl Hulten gave as good as he got, and blamed Betty for egging him on to the final deed: "If it hadn't been for her, I would never have shot Heath."

Six months before VE day, Hulten and Jones appeared at the Old Bailey before Mr. Justice Charles. Six days later, on 21 January 1945, sentence of death was pronounced on them both. Appeals were dismissed in February.

For Karl Hulten, the last reel of the third-rate gangster movie he had made of his life came to an end on 8 March 1945, a week after his 23rd birthday, at the end of a rope. His co-star, too, had made her last appearance. Reprieved just two days before her execution date, Betty Jones spent the next ten years in gaol, and was released on licence in 1954.

UNITED STATES
THE MAN WHO KILLED REDHEADS

Joe Medley was a professional criminal whose previous convictions included armed robbery, for which, had he not escaped, he would have served a sentence of from 30 to 60 years. When he did escape, for no discernible reason he took exception to redheaded women and built a new career on killing them. After prison, Medley went to New Orleans where he met Laura Fischer, a 28-year-old redhead. On Christmas Eve 1944, Laura's body was found drowned in the hotel bathtub, though the subsequent autopsy could find no marks of violence that might have indicated foul play. By this time Medley was headed for Chicago, where he registered at a hotel with another redhead, Blanche Zimmerman. Blanche was found on 17 February 1945, dead, as Laura Fischer had been, in a tub of water in the hotel bathroom. The fact that her body contained no small quantity of alcohol and drugs at the time contributed to a coroner's jury returning a verdict of accidental death. In Washington, Medley next became acquainted with 50-year-old redhead Nancy Boyer. No baths this time; Nancy was found shot dead on the floor of the kitchen in her apartment. It was March 1945, and Joe Medley would soon be no further threat to redheads. The FBI had traced Medley to St. Louis where he was arrested in possession of some of Mrs. Boyer's belongings. Extradited back to Washington, he was charged with her first-degree murder, and on 7 June 1945, he was sentenced to death. On the morning of 3 April 1946, still waiting on Death Row at Washington State Prison, Medley and a fellow prisoner, Earl McFarland, escaped. Medley was recaptured eight hours later still close to the prison; McFarland was picked up a week later in time to meet his execution date. Joe Medley died in the electric chair on 20 December 1946.

1946

UNITED STATES
OTTO STEVEN WILSON

An Unnatural Urge. *For no better reason than "an urge to kill and destroy women," Otto Wilson destroyed two lives before being taken into custody.*

In the early afternoon of 15 November the body of Virginia Lee Griffin, the 25-year-old wife of a truck driver, had been found by a chambermaid, stuffed into the closet of a run-down Skid Row hotel room; she had been choked to death and mutilated with a knife. Almost immediately after, the body of Mrs. Lilian Johnson was discovered in a hotel room only a few blocks away; she too had been choked to death and hideously mutilated.

Before nightfall, a manhunt was under way, centering on the bars and hotels of Skid Row. Police patrolmen were issued with the description of a man who had booked into the rooms where the victims had been found.

Patrolman Harold Donlan of the city police recalled that he had seen a man answering this description drinking around the local bars, and made a particular point of diverting his route around the liquor dives. At 5:30 p.m. he found Otto Wilson, just about to buy a drink for a new girl he had met. "I walked over and put the handcuffs on him," Donlan said later. And in doing so he probably saved Wilson's companion from being his third victim.

By 7:30 p.m., Wilson had confessed to both murders, pleading that he was searching for love, but had always been mentally unstable and had lost control of himself. The psychiatrists were not quite so benevolent in their assessment of Otto Wilson: "He has an urge to kill and destroy women. He may be considered a sexual psychopath and degenerate. His hatred of womankind has unquestionably been built up for years and increased by alcoholic stimulation. If he had not been apprehended, there is no telling how many other victims of his lust and passion there might have been."

Wilson's trial commenced on 18 June 1945, and he pleaded not guilty by reason of insanity; on 28 June, a jury found him sane and guilty of murder. Otto Wilson was given a capital sentence, and died in the gas chamber on 20 September 1946.

FRANCE
THE WARTIME ENTERPRISE OF DR. PETIOT

A practising physician and one-time mayor of the town of Villeneuve, Dr. Marcel Petiot had a long history of criminal involvement (notably drug trafficking) before the Second World War broke on Europe's doorstep, providing him with the lucrative diversion of robbing and then killing wealthy Jews whom he had promised to help escape from the excesses of the Germans. Death in most cases was by lethal injection. The authorities finally caught up with the deadly doctor when the chimney of his Paris surgery caught fire during a mass corpse-burning session, and Petiot confessed to a total of sixty-three murders. He also claimed, in mitigation, that he was a member of the French Resistance and was simply executing Nazi collaborators. Dr. Petiot was eventually charged with the murders of the 27 people whose remains were found in the basement incinerator at his surgery; he was put to the guillotine on 26 May 1946.

UNITED KINGDOM
THE SADIST

Neville George Clevely Heath was a sexual sadist who indulged in extreme forms of flagellation and bondage. On 20 June 1946, these practices developed into murder when staff at the Pembridge Court Hotel, where Heath had booked in with Miss Margery Gardner, found her mutilated body:

Margery Gardner's naked body lay on its back, the feet tied together with a handkerchief; her wrists, judging by the marks, had also been bound, though the ligature had been removed. Her face had been severely bruised consistent with having been punched repeatedly. There were no fewer than seventeen vicious slash marks on various parts of her body—marks with a distinctive criss-cross pattern. In addition the breasts had been bitten, the nipples almost bitten off. Finally some rough object had been forced into her vagina causing excessive bleeding. The unspeakable savagery of the injuries were compounded by the fact that Margery Gardner had been alive when they were inflicted; death came later, from suffocation.

Heath killed once more before his arrest, this time in Bournemouth where he murdered and mutilated Doreen Marshall. It is characteristic of his cynical attitude that before succumbing to the hangman, Heath is said to have asked the prison governor for a whisky, adding: "You might as well make that a double."

1947

UNITED STATES
THE "BLACK DAHLIA" CASE

A tarnished tale of Tinsel Town, the "Black Dahlia" was found dead on a Los Angeles vacant lot, the letters BD hacked into her thigh with a knife. Despite a huge investigation, the case remains one of America's unsolved classics.

Over the decades since it became the world's movie Mecca, Hollywood has acquired a reputation for ruining thousands of young lives—mostly those of country and small-town girls attracted by the razzle-dazzle and the promise of fame and fortune as a "star." Few ever made it. Some got as far as occasional extra-work, fewer still made "starlet" grade; most went home disillusioned and penniless. Those that hung around drifted into the less glamorous worlds of waitressing, barmaiding and prostitution.

Elizabeth Short *might* have been one of those girls, but she wasn't. The truth is, Beth was into all kinds of trouble long before she hit the streets of Tinsel Town, and in many ways her end was as predictable as if it had been etched in stone. Elizabeth was born in Medford, Massachusetts. In 1942 she left home for Miami where she worked as a waitress. With America's involvement in the Second World War, the country was beginning to fill up with handsome young men in uniform, which was fine by Beth—and they seemed to enjoy her company too. 1943 found Beth in California where she continued waitressing, "modelling," and entertaining the troops. She was doing just that in a Santa Monica bar on an evening in

September; and while the bunch of sailors getting merry on booze and Beth's company were entitled to be there, at nineteen Beth wasn't. She was picked up in a police raid and sent back to her mother in Medford. Within days Beth was back in Santa Monica with a new job working in the stores at Camp Cooke, the local army base. Never happier than when she was among servicemen, it didn't take Beth long to make "Camp Cutie of the Week," and soon afterwards she moved in with a sergeant. Not exclusively of course—after all, Miss Short had a lot of charms to spread around.

One of the other "friends" was a young Air Force Major, Matthew Gordon, to whom Beth became engaged. It may even have been true love—we will never know—because not long after they met, Gordon was posted, and in the summer of 1946 he was killed in an air crash. It would be convenient to think that it was this tragedy that pushed Elizabeth Short on to a one-way track of self-destruction, but she had already climbed on to that roller-coaster years before.

Beth had by now decided to swop "Camp Cutie" for a more promising future as "Screen Cutie," and had hit the road to Hollywood. Here she set about reinventing herself as the enigmatic "Black Dahlia," emphasising her naturally black hair by never wearing any other colour clothes, from her underwear outwards. She was much more successful, by most accounts, at getting into producers' beds than into their films, and while she was waiting to be plucked off the sidewalk and turned into a star the Black Dahlia could always use her natural charms to make ends meet. At this time she was staying with a friend named Dot French, a cinema usherette with a home out at Pacific Beach. Beth Short stayed here over the December of 1946, and on 8 January she called a manfriend named "Red" to pick her up from the house and drive her to the Biltmore Hotel in Los Angeles; she said she was going to meet her sister. Over the next few days Beth was seen around town but no significant information ever came out of these vague sightings.

On the morning of 15 January 1947 the body of a young woman was discovered on waste ground in a suburb of Los Angeles. She had been crudely cut in two at the waist, and the remains had been horribly mutilated; on one of her thighs the letters BD had been carved with a knife. Subsequent post-mortem examination revealed that the victim had died not long before her corpse had been found, and a fingerprint check proved the woman's name was Elizabeth Ann Short—the Black Dahlia. As days passed during which detectives pieced together the tawdry life and loves of the failed starlet, the wackos queued up for the privilege of confessing to her murder. All major homicides attract their share of cranks eager for the limelight, but the death of the Black Dahlia seemed to bring them crawling out of the woodwork; some were women claiming that they had killed Beth for stealing their man. Ten days after the discovery of the murder the *Los Angeles Examiner* received an envelope on which was pasted a message in cut-out letters promising: ''Here is Dahlia's belongings. Letter to follow.'' The belongings turned out to be Elizabeth Short's birth certificate, social security card and other oddments such as snapshots and newspaper clippings; there was also an address book with one page torn out—presumably the page on which the name of the sender was written. Fingerprints on the envelope were too smudged for matching with FBI records. The promised letter proved to be an anti-climax. Like the previous communication the words were collaged letters cut from newspapers; it read simply: ''Have changed my mind. You would not give me a square deal. Dahlia killing was justified.''

Elizabeth Short, the Black Dahlia, was quietly buried on Saturday, 25 January 1947 in the Mountain View Cemetery at Oakland, California. To date, nothing more has emerged to help close the file on her murder.

ABOARD SHIP
THE TRIAL WITHOUT A BODY

In October 1947 ship's steward James Camb raped and murdered actress Gay Gibson aboard the *Durban Castle* out of South Africa. Although Camb disposed of his luckless victim out of one of the liner's portholes and the body was never found, fresh scratches on the suspect's arms and back indicated his involvement in a fierce struggle. Blood-flecked saliva on the pillow cover of Miss Gibson's bed was consistent with manual strangulation, and in situations of abject fear such as that Gay Gibson must have felt at the hands of her attacker, it is common for the bladder to empty—which accounted for the extensive urine staining on the bed. In March 1948, after the ship had docked in Southampton, Camb was tried, convicted and sentenced to death; however, he did have one stroke of luck. At the time his execution was scheduled to take place, Parliament was debating the abolition of capital punishment, and the Home Secretary thought it only fair to suspend executions until the matter was resolved. As it turned out James Camb was especially fortunate, because the clause was finally deleted from the Bill and hanging recommenced.

1948

UNITED KINGDOM
PETER GRIFFITHS

Marks of Cain. *In the search for the brutal killer of three-year-old June Devaney, the head of Lancashire's Fingerprint Bureau masterminded the country's first exercise in mass-fingerprinting.*

At twenty minutes past midnight on 15 May 1948 staff nurse Gwendoline Humphreys was making her routine round of CH3, a children's ward in the Queen's Park Hospital outside Blackburn. Of the twelve cots only six had occupants, and the oldest of these small sleeping figures was June Anne Devaney, not yet four. June had been admitted to the ward ten days before with mild pneumonia, had made a good recovery and had been looking forward to being collected by her parents later in the day.

Ten minutes later Nurse Humphreys heard a sound like a child's voice calling and looked out of the window on to the grounds, then put her head round the door of CH3; finding everything as it should be, she returned to the kitchen. At 1:20 a.m. she felt the draught from an open porch door giving access to the hospital grounds; the catch of the door had been faulty for some time so she closed it and thought no more of it.

While she was on her feet, Nurse Humphreys put her head round the door of the children's ward to make sure all her charges were tucked up safely. As she looked down into the empty cot where June Devaney had been sleeping an hour before, the nurse's heart skipped a beat. The drop side of the cot was still in place, which could only mean the girl had been bodily lifted and taken out. With the help of the night sister, Gwen Humphreys made a search of the immediate area, noticing as she did a large "Winchester" bottle beneath June's bed. The last time the nurse had seen it it had been on her 12:20 round, when it was in its proper place on an instrument trolley at the end of the ward. She also noticed some footprints on the highly waxed floor.

Having failed to locate the child, the hospital authorities alerted the local police, and officers began to carry out a systematic search of the extensive hospital grounds. At 3:17 a.m. the body of June Anne Devaney was found by a police constable close to the boundary wall; she had suffered terrible injuries to the head, and first indications suggested sexual interference.

Mr. C. G. Looms, Blackburn's Chief Constable, Detective Superintendent Woodmansey, and a police surgeon arrived within the hour. Detective Chief Inspector John Capstick and Detective Sergeant John Stoneman from Scotland Yard were met off the morning Preston train by a police car which sped them to Blackburn.

On that bleak afternoon of Saturday 15 May, the Yard officers waited in the drizzling rain as the waterproof sheeting was peeled back revealing the tragic body of June Devaney. Jack Capstick recalled that first glimpse later: "I am not ashamed to say that I saw it through a mist of tears. Years of detective service had hardened me to many terrible things; but this tiny pathetic body, in its nightdress soaked in blood and mud, was something no man could see unmoved, and it haunts me to this day."

Detective Chief Inspector Colin Campbell, head of the Lancashire Fingerprint Bureau, had been at the hospital since 5 a.m. and had already assembled a catalogue of potentially vital clues. These included a vast number of fingerprints, among them those on the Winchester bottle. There were also the footprints which had been seen by Nurse Humphreys. Colin Campbell ordered photographs to be taken of the prints, and then the wax beneath the prints was carefully scraped off for further forensic tests for microscopic fibres and particles.

It became the task of a team of detectives to trace and fingerprint every person who in the past two years could have had a legitimate reason to have been in the children's ward; there were 642 of them. When all the prints but one set on the Winchester bottle had been eliminated, DCI Campbell could state with confidence that these were the marks of June Devaney's killer. However, fingerprints are of use only if there is a suspect whose prints can be compared with them, or if a matching set can be found in one of the police fingerprint bureaux. In this case there was no suspect, and there were no matching prints on file—the person who killed June Anne Devaney had no criminal record.

Knowing their killer was just a fingerprint away the Yard men, in consultation with local forces, decided to take the unprecedented step of fingerprinting every male over the age of sixteen who was in Blackburn on 14 and 15 May. Using twenty officers and the electoral register, Inspector William Barton began a two-month trawl of more than 35,000 homes, and Chief Inspector Campbell designed a special compact card for the convenience of the "mobile" fingerprint squad. Towards the end of July the fingerprinting had been all but completed, but without success. It began to look as though June Devaney's killer had slipped through the net. Then a procedure was tried that would not be possible today. In the immediate post-war years, rationing persisted, and records were kept of the issue of ration books and the Registration Number by which they and their owners were identified. It was a simple, if time-consuming, operation to check the local registration officer's file against the National Registration numbers on the fingerprint cards to see who had been missed. One of those numbers belonged to Peter Griffiths, a 22-year-old former soldier then living in Blackburn. At 3 p.m. on Thursday, 12 August, Chief Inspector Colin Campbell confirmed that Griffiths was the owner of the prints on the Winchester bottle.

When Griffiths left home for work on the night shift at a local flour mill he was intercepted and arrested. After a half-hearted attempt at denial, Griffiths made a full confession, adding by way of defence that he was drunk at the time: "I picked the girl up out of the cot and took her outside by the same door. I carried her in my right arm and she put her arms round my neck and I walked with her down the hospital field. I put her down on the grass. She started crying again and I tried to stop her from crying, but she wouldn't do, like, she wouldn't stop crying. I just lost my temper then and you know what happened then.''

On Friday, 15 October 1948, Griffiths' trial opened before Mr. Justice Oliver at the Lancaster Assizes; by now the prosecution had considerably more than a confession and a fingerprint to offer the jury. After retrieving the prisoner's suit from a pawn shop the police forensic laboratory had uncovered two further damning pieces of evidence: fibres taken from Griffiths' clothing proved a perfect match for the fibres adhering to the victim's body and those found on the window ledge where the killer had entered the hospital. Human bloodstains were found in several places on both the suit jacket and trousers—blood group A, the same group as June Devaney's.

Such was the solid weight of indisputable scientific evidence that Griffiths' defence of insanity stood little chance of influencing the decision of the jury; they retired for a bare 23 minutes before returning to empower Mr. Justice Oliver to pass the only sentence that the law then allowed in the case of murder: death. On Friday morning 19 November, the sentence was carried out at Liverpool Prison.

On 3 November the police had honoured their pledge to the citizens of Blackburn; about 500 people took up the option of having their fingerprint record returned to them, while the remaining 46,500 were ceremoniously pulped at a local paper mill observed by the Mayor and a coterie of journalists, photographers and newsreel cameramen.

JAPAN
MASS MURDER IN TOKYO

Japan's most famous murderer and its longest serving prisoner, Sadamichi Hirasawa, was convicted of the killing of twelve bank employees. On 26 January 1948 Hirasawa entered the Imperial Bank of Tokyo building posing as an

(continued)

official from the Health Department and announced that due
to an outbreak of dysentery all employees must be given a
dose of preventive medicine. Within seconds of drinking
the cyanide liquid, bank staff began to drop dead on the
spot; Hirasawa fled with 180,000 yen. After nearly 40
years' incarceration, Sadamichi Hirasawa died in prison in
1987.

1949

UNITED KINGDOM
JOHN GEORGE HAIGH

The Acid-Bath Murders. *Haigh's misunderstanding of the term* corpus delicti *led to his over-confident confession to the killing of Mrs. Olive Durand-Deacon, and his arrest. Haigh's trial was enlivened by his ludicrous attempt to establish a defence of insanity by claiming to have drunk his victims' blood!*

John George Haigh first saw the light of day on 24 July 1909; less than 24 hours later Louis Bleriot made history by crossing the English Channel for the first time in an aeroplane. John Haigh would also make history one day—history of a very different kind.

Among his schoolfellows Haigh, who was known as "Ching" because of his almond-shaped, almost oriental eyes, presented something of an enigma. The carefully scrubbed and slickly groomed exterior belied a lazy brain and a dishonest temperament incapable of telling the truth. While Ching's problem undoubtedly arose in part from his parents' refusal to allow him any social intercourse with his peers outside school, a heavy burden of responsibility must rest within Haigh's own personality, and his uncontrollable urge towards spitefulness, malice and dishonesty. He particularly delighted in punching and tweaking little girls and anybody else younger and weaker than himself; and if there were no human playmates to torment, then little Ching was content to torture insects and small animals.

Academically, Haigh was perceived as a dullard as well as an idler, and to nobody's surprise he left school at seventeen quite without distinction or qualification—unless one counts a certain *savoir-faire*, a sort of affable cunning. The pattern of John Haigh's personality was summed up in an uncannily perceptive description given by his first employer: "He was lazy; he was always late. But he had charm. I had to like him."

By the age of 22, Haigh had started his own estate, insurance and advertising agency, though this must have seemed too much like hard work, because he later became a car salesman. Not that there is anything intrinsically dishonourable about that calling—the problem in Haigh's case was that the cars were just not his to sell. Through the simple deception of using fictitious letter-headings to obtain money on hire-purchase agreements, John Haigh became prosperous. On 6 July 1934, at Bridlington, Haigh married Miss Beatrice Hamer. Four months later he was imprisoned and Mrs. Haigh left, never to communicate with him again. On his release fifteen months later, Haigh transferred his dishonesties to Glasgow, where he earned himself a four-year stretch for fraud.

Released once more on to the streets, and clearly undismayed by recent setbacks, Haigh's prospects went from strength to strength as he drifted from fraud to fraud. In the summer of 1944 he renewed the acquaintance of a man he had first met in 1936. The man's name was William Donald McSwan, and their meeting proved to be the turning point in Haigh's life of crime—the point at which Haigh the swindler, Haigh the blackguard, became Haigh the Acid-Bath Murderer.

In his later confession, Haigh recalled:

We met at the Goat public house in Kensington High Street, and from there we went to number 79 Gloucester Road, where in the basement I had rented I hit him on the head with a cosh, withdrew a glass of blood from his throat and drank it. He was dead within five minutes or so. I put him in a 40-gallon tank and disposed of him with acid, washing the sludge down a manhole in the basement. I had known this McSwan and his mother and father for some time, and on seeing the mother and father I explained that he had gone off to avoid his "Call up." I wrote a number of letters in due course to his parents purporting to come from him and posted, I think, in Glasgow and Edinburgh, explaining various details of the disposition of properties, which were to follow. In the following year I took separately to the same basement the father Donald and the mother Amy, disposing of them in exactly the same way as the son . . .

. . . I met the Hendersons by answering an advertisement offering for sale their property at 22 Ladbroke Square. I did not purchase. They sold it and moved to 16 Dawes Road, Fulham. This runs in a period from November 1947 to February 1948. In February 1948, the Hendersons were staying at Kingsgate Castle, Kent. I visited them there and went with them to Brighton, where they stayed at the Metropole. From here I took Dr. Henderson to Crawley and disposed of him in a store room at Leopold Road by shooting him in the head with his own revolver. I put him in a tank of acid as in the other cases. This was in the morning and I went back to Brighton and brought up Mrs. Henderson on the pretext that her husband was ill. I shot her in the store room and put her in another tank and disposed of her with acid. In each of the last four cases I had my glass of blood as before.

In February 1949, Haigh was living at the Onslow Court Hotel, west London, and had become friendly with fellow resident Mrs. Olive Durand-Deacon, a widow of independent means whose modest fortune Haigh had already earmarked for his own use. On the pretence of assisting Mrs. Durand-Deacon in a scheme for marketing false fingernails, Haigh lured her down to his ''workshop'' outside Crawley, Sussex. Here he shot the unsuspecting woman through the neck, and having stripped it of any valuables, steeped her body in a 40-gallon oil drum of sulphuric acid.

In the course of the subsequent inquiry into the disappearance of Mrs. Durand-Deacon, police interviewed Haigh on several occasions and formed a very poor opinion of his oily, ingratiating manner. A visit to his Crawley workshop revealed significant enough clues—not least a recently fired .38 Webley revolver and traces of blood—to place Haigh under arrest. Under questioning, Haigh made this startling announcement:

"Mrs. Durand-Deacon no longer exists. I've destroyed her with acid. You can't prove murder without a body." Of course Haigh was quite wrong; a number of significant cases *have* been proved without a corpse. But he was also wrong about Mrs. Durand-Deacon no longer existing. It was true that the acid had succeeded in its grisly task of reducing Mrs. Durand-Deacon's flesh and bones to a greasy sludge—but what Haigh had not taken account of was the longer time needed to destroy plastics. A set of acrylic dentures, custom-made for Mrs. Durand-Deacon, were positively identified by her dentist, and her red plastic handbag, with many of its contents, was positively identified by her friends.

Haigh's extravagant claim that he was a vampire who drank the blood of his victims was seen for what it was—a rather unsophisticated ruse to establish a defence of insanity and exchange Broadmoor for the noose. As it was, John George Haigh kept his appointment with the hangman at Wandsworth Prison on 10 August 1949.

CANADA
DEATH IN THE AIR

With two other people, Albert Guay blew up a Quebec Airways DC-3, killing all 23 passengers and crew. While they were checking the passenger lists the police came to the name of Rita Guay, whose husband was a known crook and at the time involved in a romantic liaison with a woman named Pitre; Pitre was identified as having delivered a package to be transported aboard the fatal flight. Albert Guay was arrested and made a confession implicating his accomplices; all three were tried, found guilty of murder and, in 1951, hanged.

UNITED STATES
"I'D HAVE KILLED A THOUSAND . . ."

In the space of just twelve minutes, Howard Unruh shot thirteen people dead on the streets of Camden, New Jersey. He would certainly have claimed many more lives and provided a lot more work for the local medical services if he had not simply run out of ammunition; "I'd have killed a thousand," he told a psychiatrist, "if I'd had bullets enough." The shootings took place on 5 September 1949, but the problem had started years before that. A withdrawn, almost hermetic man, Unruh just hated his neighbours. Of course, they were really no worse than anybody else's neighbours—it was Howard that had the problems. The folks in the next street wouldn't dream of persecuting him—Howard just thought they did, and had begun to keep a careful note in his diary of all these imagined grievances, and at the same time set about perfecting the marksmanship skills he had acquired on army service. Unruh was 28 years old at the time he made the headlines, and the inevitable crack might not have appeared for some time if the security gate he had fitted to the house to keep the neighbours out had not been stolen. Perhaps Howard Unruh found the seclusion he so desired in the Trenton State Hospital for the insane.

1950

UNITED STATES
ERNEST INGENITO

A Family at War. *A criminal since his youth, Ingenito married Theresa Mazzoli and the couple went to live with her family, where Theresa's mother nagged Ernie mercilessly. The marriage began to disintegrate and before long Ingenito had been thrown out of the family home for infidelity. He returned armed, and in one night of terror left seven people dead.*

Ernie was born in 1924 into a poor rural Pennsylvanian family, and did not benefit overly from an early education—save that kind of *ad hoc* training in cunning absorbed through running with the local street gangs. At fifteen the boy was arrested during the course of a burglary—not his first crime, just the first he was arrested for—and put away in the Pennsylvania State Reformatory. In 1941 Ernie's much-loved mother died, and with her passing the last restraint on his criminous career was severed. Like so many of his kind Ingenito drifted into the US Army having failed to appreciate that the services necessarily run on discipline; after a brief undistinguished career, he served two years in the stockade for assaulting an officer before being dishonourably discharged.

In 1947 Ernest Ingenito married Theresa Mazzoli and went to live with the Mazzoli family in Gloucester County where, over the course of the next few years, he fathered two sons. The domestic arrangements were not ideal—for a start Theresa's mother, Pearl, took against Ernie, and had a tendency to nag him. And Mike Mazzoli didn't seem to understand his

47

son-in-law's fondness for drink and other women. It was this that finally led Mazzoli to throw Ernie out on his ear and forbid him to see his daughter again; Theresa in her turn forbade him to see the children again. On 17 November 1950 Ernie Ingenito was told by his lawyer that he would only get access to his sons through a court order; it was the final straw. Ernie returned to the lodging-house where he had taken a room and selected a .32 carbine and two pistols from his collection of guns. Then he went visiting.

When he knocked on the front door of the Mazzoli house Ernie came face to face with Mike Mazzoli, who told him in plain language to push off. They were the last words he uttered before his son-in-law gunned him down. Next on the hit-list was Theresa, though mercifully she later recovered from her wounds in hospital. When the shooting had started, Pearl Mazzoli fled to her parents' home nearby, but nothing was going to stop Ernie now—he was going to track down every last damn member of the Mazzoli family. After shooting Pearl, he rampaged through the house slaughtering Pearl's mother Theresa Pioppi, her sister-in-law Marion, brother Gino and Gino's nine-year-old daughter, and finally brother John. Ernie had just one more murderous trip to make—out to Mineola where Michael Mazzoli's parents lived; there he massacred Frank and Hilda Mazzoli. By midnight it was all over, and Ernie Ingenito had wreaked his insane revenge. He had also, not surprisingly, attracted the attention of the police.

Before armed officers took him into custody, Ernie made a half-hearted attempt to take his own life, but he was patched up in time for his trial in January 1951. He was indicted on a sample charge of murdering Mrs. Pearl Mazzoli and sentenced to life imprisonment, and as Ernie was clearly as mad as a hatter his sentence was ordered to be served in the New Jersey State Hospital for the Insane at Trenton. It was, to be sure, a rather more benign punishment than the one suggested by Ernie's wife from her hospital bed: "I wish they would hang Ernie," she said. But for good measure Ernest Ingenito was put on trial again in 1956; charged with a further four counts of murder, he was convicted and handed down a life sentence for each.

1951

UNITED KINGDOM
HERBERT LEONARD MILLS

Ode to Death. *Mills telephoned the News of the World claiming to have found the body of a woman in a wood; he then attempted to sell the newspaper his confession to her murder. It transpired that Mills, like others before him, was trying to commit the perfect murder. Like others before him, he failed.*

It is not often that a national newspaper gets the chance of a scoop, of a totally exclusive murder story, so it must have seemed as though Christmas had come in August when a voice came through on the *News of the World*'s newsroom telephone: "I've just found a woman's body. It looks like murder."

Of course it was more than the fragile cooperation between police and journalist could have withstood to have kept the law in ignorance of such a dramatic revelation; so, having ascertained the location of the public booth from which the informant had telephoned, and its number, the reporter asked the young man to wait by the box for a return call. In the meantime the Nottingham police force were alerted that there was a possible murder in their area. The *News of the World* had barely time to resume telephone contact before the police had arrived at the call box.

The caller, it was discovered at the police station, was nineteen-year-old Herbert Leonard Mills, of Mansfield Street, Nottingham. The youth had certainly not been lying about finding a woman's body; it was there in a secluded part of the woods near Sherwood Vale, and judging by the marks of strangulation and bludgeoning, he had been right about murder. The victim was later identified as Mrs. Mabel Tattershaw, aged 48, who had lived at Longmead Drive.

Mills also had possession of a broken bead necklace which he claimed to have picked up at the scene of the crime, and he gave a rather hazy description of a man with a limp whom he had seen in the neighbourhood of the body.

After giving blood samples and fingernail parings, Leonard Mills was released to the eagerly waiting *News of the World* where he seemed in his element. He expounded to crime reporter Norman Rae how he had had this idea for a sonnet—Mills had great, though as yet unfulfilled, literary ambitions—and sought romantic inspiration in the leafy glades of Sherwood. Then he found the woman's body, ''very white and pale,'' and had taken up Shelley's *Ode to Death* to read; he had then telephoned the newspaper. There was an obvious feyness to the story, but it seemed at least credible. In return for cash, Mills was to make several more increasingly elaborate statements to Rae.

Meanwhile the police had been probing into the background of Mabel Tattershaw, trying to find a motive for what on the face of it seemed to be a senseless murder. Mrs. Tattershaw was married to a man who worked away from home more often than not, and by him she had two daughters, one living in Nottingham and a fourteen-year-old still at home with her mother. To make her meagre ends meet, Mrs. Tattershaw took in lodgers. Poverty had been unkind to Mabel; it had aged her beyond her middle years and had taken its toll of what physical attraction she may once have claimed. Like a shabby spectre on life's periphery, she came and went, unremarked, about her humdrum existence. Who, detectives wondered, even *noticed* poor Mabel Tattershaw, let alone felt compelled to kill her?

Norman Rae, a detective of a different kind, was finding it difficult to stop Leonard Mills making statements to his newspaper, each a little more explicit than the last, and each accompanied by a similar exaggerated demand for payment. On 24 August they met again at a hotel in Nottingham, where in an episode that must be unique in British criminal history, Mills was to write for a newspaper journalist (on hotel notepaper) his complete confession to the killing of Mrs. Mabel Tattershaw. With the scrupulous correctness that dignified the best of his profession, Norman Rae cautioned Mills that he must acknowledge that he made the statement of his own volition, and that "I have warned you, if it contains information material to the murder, I will take your statement and yourself to City police headquarters." For the next hour Mills wrote in silence; on the following morning Rae accompanied him to Nottingham and handed over the document to Superintendent Ellington.

At the beginning the statement contained Mill's motive—"I have always considered the possibility of a perfect murder"—and at the end, his confession: "I now confess I murdered Mrs. Tattershaw"; between the two was the story of a cold-blooded, pointless killing.

On 2 August 1951 Mabel Tattershaw had gone to the Roxy Cinema in Nottingham; seated next to her was Herbert Leonard Mills. We do not know what he used as an opening gambit, but before long they were whispering together in the dark like old friends. We do know what was in the young man's mind: "Seeing the possibility of putting my theory into practice, I consented to meeting her on the morrow." To be noticed, and by a young man at that, must have thrilled Mabel for the first time in many dull years. Little surprise, then, that she kept the assignation; little surprise that she was willing to follow wherever her escort might lead. He led her into the seclusion of the woods, and then "She took off her coat and laid down . . . she said she was cold, I covered her with her own coat, and then my coat . . . I put on a pair of gloves . . ."

That he was happy with the result of his "experiment" is clear from Mills's statement: "I was rather pleased. I think I did rather well. The strangling itself was quite easily accomplished.

But this formed only part of the evidence carefully collected and assessed by police officers in preparation for Leonard Mills's trial; there was also the medical testimony. Professor Webster, pathologist with the Home Office Laboratory in Birmingham, detailed the many other bludgeoning injuries committed on Mrs. Tattershaw's body, both before and after strangulation. Further forensic evidence linked Mills with the murder by identifying hairs from his head on the victim's clothing, while fibres from under Mabel's fingernails came from the blue suit that he had worn on the afternoon of the murder.

All this made it very difficult for Mr. Elwes KC to construct any kind of adequate defence at the Nottingham Assizes in November 1951. It was Mr. Elwes's contention—on behalf of his client, for it is difficult to see how so able a counsel could have taken his brief with anything approaching optimism— that Mills had come across the woman's body in the wood and, in an attempt to gain notoriety and money, had *invented* a sequence of stories which he told to the Press.

But for the jury Mills's story was just too good to be false; they concluded that it was he who had killed Mabel Tattershaw, leaving it to Mr. Justice Byrne to condemn him to death. And so in December the brief moment of fame ended for Leonard Mills on the drop at Winson Green Prison.

FRANCE
UN CRIME PASSIONNEL

Yvonne Chevallier was the wife of Dr. Pierre Chevallier, member of the French Cabinet and former mayor of the town of Orléans, where the couple lived with their four-year-old son Matthieu. In 1951 Madame Chevallier fired five bullets into her husband's body in what she claimed was a fit of jealous rage over his affair with Madame Jeanette Perreau. Although public disapprobation had been so strong as to have necessitated the removal of the trial from Orléans to Rheims in the hope of finding an impartial jury, no sooner did the court find out that it had a mistress to hiss at than Madame Chevallier was restored to popularity and, amid tumultuous cheers in court, she was acquitted.

1952

FRANCE
GASTON DOMINICI

A Very French Affair. *The Drummond family were on a camping holiday in France when they were shot dead. The finger of suspicion pointed at the Dominicis who owned a farm close by—and in particular old Gaston Dominici. Gaston confessed several times, and retracted his confessions; he attempted suicide during the police reconstruction of the crime. Finally he was tried, convicted, sentenced to death and then reprieved.*

In the summer of 1952, 61-year-old Sir Jack Drummond, a distinguished English biochemist, took his wife, Ann, and eleven-year-old daughter on a camping holiday to southern France. On the night of 4 August, Sir Jack brought the Hillman station wagon to a halt at a picturesque spot by the river just outside the Provencal village of Lurs.

Early the following morning local police were alerted by Gustave Dominici, a 33-year-old farmer who had come across the dead bodies of the Drummond family at their campsite. Sir Jack and his wife had been shot, Elizabeth had been bludgeoned to death.

The nearest habitation to the scene of the murders was a farm named Grand 'Terre, some 150 yards away, owned by 75-year-old Gaston Dominici and worked by his sons, one of whom was Gustave. Despite their deep suspicion that the Dominici family were involved in the killings, a search of Grand 'Terre revealed nothing incriminating. It was not until several weeks had passed that investigating officers received their first promising lead. A railway worker told detectives that Gustave Dominici had admitted to him that young Elizabeth Drummond had still been alive when he found her. It wasn't much, but sufficient to have Gustave charged with the offence of failing to help a person in danger of dying. But still the police could not penetrate the smoke-screen of lies and deceits thrown up by the machinations of the unscrupulous Dominicis. Eventually the seriousness of the crime and the eminence of the victims resulted in no less an official than Commissaire Edmond Sebeille, Superintendent of the Marseilles police, being given charge of the inquiry.

For almost a year Commissaire Sebeille and his team worked away trying to undermine the resistance of the Dominicis, until finally Gustave and his 49-year-old brother Clovis admitted that they knew the identity of the killer: it was their father Gaston. Despite his loud accusations of treachery, old Gaston eventually made a confession. He had been on a nocturnal prowl around the area of the farm, carrying his rifle as always, when he stumbled upon the Drummonds' camp. As it was obvious that Sir Jack and his wife were undressing for bed the old farmer decided to hang around and watch. Unfortunately for them all, Jack Drummond caught Dominici at it, and during the ensuing struggle was shot dead. Fearing identification, Dominici then shot Ann Drummond and, as she tried to run away, bludgeoned Elizabeth about the head with the butt of his gun. Or so he said then. Because over the course of the next several weeks Gaston Dominici retracted and confessed again with monotonous regularity. At one point he accused Gustave of the murders, which resulted in Gustave retracting his accusation of Gaston in favour of another assassin. The whole bizarre situation was crowned when, during one of those reconstructions of the crime so beloved of the French authorities, Gaston broke free from the police and tried to kill himself by jumping off a railway bridge.

Gaston Dominici was put on trial at the Digne Assizes in November 1954; after an eleven-day hearing he was found guilty of murder. His advancing years saved Dominici from the guillotine, and he served only a brief period in prison before being released in 1960; he died in 1965 at the age of 83.

1953

UNITED KINGDOM
CHRISTOPHER CRAIG AND DEREK BENTLEY

For the Sake of Example. *One of Britain's most infamous cases, and one of its most celebrated miscarriages of justice. The execution of Bentley for the murder of PC Miles led to increased pressure for the abolition of capital punishment. In 1991 the case was referred back to the Court of Appeal and it is to be hoped that at last Derek Bentley will receive a long-overdue posthumous pardon.*

The early 1950s witnessed the emergence of the Teddy Boys, Britain's first modern youth cult. They were popularly caricatured with their drape coats and drainpipe trousers, their crepesoled blue-suede shoes; and with flick-knife, bicycle chain and knuckle-duster as accessories an otherwise harmless cult of adolescent fashion was manipulated into the bogey and scapegoat of post-war apprehension. "Teenagers" were discovered, and their "delinquency" came to be seen as a social problem. The authorities, notably the police, were quite unprepared for this development. It was in any case difficult enough to comprehend or control, but Press and public were demanding action. The police were determined to use the heaviest of heavy-handed tactics in order to combat disruptive behaviour, and in those cases that came before a court the judges were equally enthusiastic in handing out exemplary sentences to all young tearaways. This background—which has become more familiar over successive decades and successive cults—is essential to an understanding of the controversial trial of Christopher Craig and Derek Bentley.

THE ACCUSED

Christopher Craig came from a "good" home. His father was chief cashier at a bank, and had been a captain in the London Scottish Regiment during the First World War. The family lived in a comfortable house, 9 Norbury Court Road, Norbury, in southwest London; Chris was born on 19 May 1936 and attended Norbury Secondary School until the age of fifteen. He suffered from dyslexia—a condition which was little understood at that time—and left school barely able to read or write. To counteract this potential embarrassment, young Chris Craig affected the outward image of the hard man, using as his role model the American gangsters of the 1930s. This included acquiring guns, which were then, so soon after a war, easy to get hold of; the final collection numbered 40, which he used to take to school to impress his friends and enhance his playground credibility. The second unfortunate influence on Craig was his brother Niven, ten years his senior and already embarked on a serious criminal career. He had been involved in an unsuccessful armed robbery at Waltham Abbey with four other men, and when arrested at a flat in Kensington was in possession of a loaded revolver. On Thursday, 30 October 1952, Niven Craig was convicted at the Old Bailey of robbery with violence and resisting arrest, and was sentenced to two concurrent terms of twelve years' imprisonment. Christopher Craig, sixteen years of age, was an admiring onlooker at the trial.

Derek Bentley had been born on 30 June 1933, and lived at 1 Fairview Road, Norbury, not far from Craig. His father owned an electrical business and the family had been bombed out twice during the Blitz. Young Derek had received head injuries on one of these occasions and to this was attributed his below-average intelligence. When he left school he was for most practical purposes illiterate, and took occasional jobs as a dustman and a removal man; but his ruling passion in life was bodybuilding. He was soon convicted of shop-breaking and sent to Approved School. On returning to Norbury he took up with Christopher Craig, whom he hero-worshipped. Together they carried out a number of small-scale burglaries, but on at least one occasion Bentley refused to accompany Craig because he was carrying a gun. In November 1952 Bentley was nineteen years old.

THE CRIME

In the late afternoon of Sunday, 2 November 1952, Chris Craig went to the pictures with his girlfriend. He saw *My Death Is a Mockery,* a B-picture in which a policeman is shot and the hero hanged after being captured in a shootout. Craig then went home for tea and was out on the streets again by 8:30 p.m. He called round to the Bentleys' house, where Mrs. Bentley said Derek was out. Actually Derek was in—watching television—but his parents had an instinctive mistrust of Craig and worried about his influence on their son. A little later two other friends, Norman Parsley and Frank Fazey, came round for Bentley and he followed them out, where they found Craig, hanging about on the street. After a bit of chatting the other two went off and Craig and Bentley decided to catch a 109 bus into Croydon. Craig was armed with a revolver with a sawn-off barrel, a knuckle-duster and a sheath-knife; Bentley had a smaller knife. On the bus, Craig passed the knuckle-duster over to Bentley.

The two young men got off the bus at West Croydon Station and walked down the length of Tamworth Road to Reeves Corner; then they walked back up the other side of the street, stopping about twenty yards up to look in the window of a sweet shop. Craig then shinned over the six-foot iron gate of Barlow and Parker, wholesale confectioners, to be followed a few moments later by Bentley.

Across the road a woman, putting her child to bed, saw all of this activity out of the window and telephoned the police. It was 9:15 p.m. Immediately a police van and a police car from Z division set out to investigate the call. In the van were DC Frederick Fairfax, PC Norman Harrison, PC Budgen and PC Pain. The car contained PC Sidney Miles and PC James McDonald, in all a very formidable show of strength for a suspected break-in. They arrived at Tamworth Road at 9:25 p.m.

Meanwhile Craig and Bentley had climbed a drainpipe on to the flat roof of the building. Thinking they had seen a light in the garden below, they hid for some minutes behind the winding-shed of a lift, from where they heard the arrival of the police. DC Fairfax climbed the iron gate and, seeing a footprint on the window sill beyond, climbed on to the roof by way of the drainpipe. Vaguely aware of the figures behind the lift housing, he approached across the roof.

Fairfax: I'm a police officer! Come out from behind that stack!

Craig: If you want us, fucking well come and get us!

Fairfax: Alright.

With this the officer rushed forward and grabbed Bentley. Still holding him, Fairfax then tried to approach Craig, but Bentley broke free.

Bentley: Let him have it, Chris!

Craig then shot at the policeman from a distance of six feet, grazing him on the shoulder. Fairfax stumbled, got up and chased the nearest figure, who happened to be Bentley, and floored him with a punch. Using Bentley as a shield, he then ducked behind a roof light and began to frisk the lad, relieving him of the knuckle-duster and his small knife.

Bentley: That's all I've got, guv'nor. I haven't got a gun.

DC Fairfax next manoeuvred Bentley behind the head of a staircase on one side of the roof, while Craig retreated to behind the lift housing at the opposite end. Fairfax then let go of Bentley in order to help PC McDonald on to the roof beside him.

Fairfax: He got me in the shoulder.

Bentley: I told the silly bugger not to use it.

As PC Harrison also tried to climb on to the roof to the right, two shots rang out and Harrison ducked behind a chimney stack.

Harrison (To Fairfax): What sort of gun has he got, Fairy?

Bentley: He's got a .45 Colt and plenty of bloody ammunition, too.

By this time more police had arrived outside the building, along with at least six officially issued .32 calibre police guns.

PC Miles had originally gone off in search of the confectioners' manager and now returned with the keys to the building. He and PC Harrison entered the building and went up the internal staircase. As the two policemen emerged through the roof door a shot was fired and PC Miles fell dead, shot through the forehead, just above the left eyebrow. As another shot rang out in the direction of DC Fairfax and PC McDonald, the latter dragged the body of PC Miles behind the stairhead, leaving Bentley temporarily unattended. At the same time PC Robert Jaggs was climbing the drainpipe to join his colleagues and further shots rang out.

Craig: Come on, you brave coppers! Think of your wives!

Bentley (to Jaggs): You want to look out. He'll blow your head off.

PC Harrison then proceeded to throw his truncheon, an empty milk bottle and a piece of wood at Craig.

Craig: I'm Craig! You've just given my brother twelve years! Come on, you coppers! I'm only sixteen!

Harrison next dashed out of the stairhead door to join the other policemen on the roof. PC Lowe Stewart also climbed the drainpipe, but, seeing the body of PC Miles, he climbed down again and positioned himself in a small yard to the west of the building, immediately beneath where Craig was hiding.

Craig: It's a Colt .45—Are you hiding behind a shield? Is it bullet-proof? Are we going to have a shooting match? It's just what I like . . . Have they hurt you, Derek?

Fairfax, McDonald and Jaggs then began to push Bentley round the stairhead and down the stairs.

Bentley: Look out, Chris! They're taking me down!

When Bentley was safely down the stairs DC Fairfax then returned to the roof, armed with a .32 automatic.

Fairfax: Drop your gun—I also have a gun!

Craig: Come on, copper—let's have it out!

Fairfax then ran out of the stairhead and, as a shot came in his direction, returned it with two of his own. He then manoeuvred around the roof lights towards Craig. Four times an empty click came from Craig's gun.

Craig: See—it's empty.

Craig climbed over the railings at the side of the roof and stood poised on the edge.

Craig: Well, here we go. Give my love to Pam.

With this he hurled himself from the roof, a drop of 25 feet, hitting on the way (according to the police) the edge of an old greenhouse. PC Lowe Stewart, waiting below, came up to him as he lay on the ground.

Craig: I wish I was fucking dead! I hope I've killed the fucking lot.

In fact he had almost killed himself; he had fractured his spine and broken his breastbone and forearm. At 10:45 p.m. Craig was taken to Croydon General Hospital in the same ambulance as DC Fairfax.

THE TRIAL

At 11:45 p.m., Christopher Craig was charged with the murder of PC Sidney Miles by Detective Chief Inspector John Smith, while lying in the cubicle next to Fairfax in hospital. At 1:15 a.m., DCI Smith and DS Shepherd visited Craig's home, where they discovered a .45 bullet in his bed-clothing and a box containing 137 rounds of ammunition in the attic.

Meanwhile Derek Bentley had been taken by police car to Croydon police station. He was claimed to have said, "I knew he had a gun, but I didn't think he'd use it. He's done one of your blokes in." At the station, however, he made a statement which denied this, "I did not have a gun and I did not know that Chris had one until he shot." He was then also charged with the murder of PC Miles.

The trial of Christopher Craig and Derek Bentley opened at the Old Bailey on Tuesday, 9 December 1952. The judge was the Lord Chief Justice, Lord Goddard. Mr. Christmas Humphreys prosecuted, Mr. John Parris, a Leeds lawyer, represented Craig, and Mr. F. H. Cassels undertook Bentley's defence. The whole atmosphere was highly prejudicial to the defendants; even Cassels openly stated his belief that "both the little bastards ought to swing." It was realised early on that Craig, on account of his age, could not be sentenced to death, and much attention was paid to the question whether Bentley could have been an accomplice in the murder, as well as the attempted robbery, when he was already in police custody?

Craig appeared in the dock on crutches; his lawyer had received the brief only three days before the trial opened. Several of the police witnesses contradicted each other as to the sequence of events on the roof, how many shots were fired and what exactly was said. The bullet which shot PC Miles was never produced in court, and evidence was brought of callous and boastful remarks made by Craig in hospital, which seemed highly dubious in view of his seriously injured and often comatose state. The prosecution's case as to Bentley's culpability in the crime was strongly supported by the judge, who seemed to take great pleasure in wielding Bentley's knuckle-duster during his summing up. The trial lasted three days and it took the jury only 75 minutes to find both defendants guilty, though they added a recommendation for mercy on Bentley's behalf.

Craig, because of his age, was ordered to be detained during Her Majesty's pleasure. Bentley was sentenced to death.

THE ANGER AND THE DOUBTS

On 6 January 1953 Detective Sergeant Fairfax, as he now was, was awarded the George Cross, PCs Harrison and McDonald received the George Medal, and PC Jaggs the British Empire Medal. This was all before Derek Bentley's appeal had been heard on 13 January and could hardly have created a calm and unbiased atmosphere in which to consider Bentley's fate. The appeal was quickly dismissed.

The Press was largely in support of the verdict, liberally airing their prejudices about teenage delinquency; nevertheless, there was an audible volume of protest from the growing lobby of citizens opposed to capital punishment. There was a justifiable feeling that Bentley was to hang simply because they couldn't hang Craig. He had been largely convicted on the famous phrase ''Let him have it, Chris,'' yet at the trial no mention had been made of the possible opposite meaning to that phrase: ''Let him have the gun.'' Even from the police version of events, his subsequent words seemed to support this interpretation. In any case, the phrase referred to the injuring of DC Fairfax and not the shooting of PC Miles which occurred some time later. Yet beyond all of this lay the undeniable fact that it seemed to defy natural justice that a man, already in police custody, should hang when the actual perpetrator of the crime did not.

Derek Bentley was hanged in Wandsworth Gaol at 9 a.m. on Wednesday, 28 January 1953, by the official executioner, Albert Pierrepoint. Before he died Bentley asked his parents, "I didn't kill anyone. So why are they killing me?" Outside the prison gates a crowd of some 5,000 people shouted "Murder!" and sang *Abide with Me* as nine o'clock arrived. The notice of Bentley's execution was ripped from the prison gates and angrily destroyed.

The ultimate sanction, death by hanging, was not revoked for another twelve years, but the case of Derek Bentley, along with those of Timothy Evans, Ruth Ellis and James Hanratty, provided the most eloquent evidence in the campaign to change the law.

It should be remembered, though, that Christopher Craig did not hang. He served just ten and a half years in prison and was released in May 1963. He moved to Buckinghamshire, where he was not known, became an engineer and married in 1965.

CANADA
TOO HONEST FOR HIS OWN GOOD

In June 1953 the shot bodies of three American hunters were found in a remote area of Quebec province. Wilbert Coffin, a gold prospector, told police he had met the men and helped them fix their broken-down car. For his honesty Coffin was arrested and charged with the hunters' murders. During his confinement Coffin remembered that he had seen another jeep at the same time, carrying two Americans, but vital information was ignored. Instead, Wilbert Coffin was convicted of the killings and sentenced to death. In 1955 he escaped from jail using a fake gun carved out of soap, but on the advice of a lawyer gave himself up; he
(continued)

was executed in February 1956. In 1958 a man confessed to the murder of the three hunters and implicated a second man—theirs, he said, was the other jeep that had been seen by the late Wilbert Coffin.

1954

UNITED KINGDOM
JOHN DONALD MERRETT

"Mother has shot herself..." *Acquitted in 1926 of murdering his mother, Merrett changed his name to Chesney and married Vera Bonner. In 1954 he drowned his wife and strangled his mother-in-law, and then before the police could catch up with him, committed suicide. Fibre traces on Chesney's clothing confirmed his guilt.*

It didn't take young Merrett long to get into serious trouble—eighteen years to be exact. In 1927 he stood before judge and jury at Edinburgh's High Court of Justiciary charged with the murder of his own mother.

Donald was born in New Zealand in 1908, the only child of John and Bertha Merrett. In 1924 Mr. Merrett abandoned Mrs. Merrett and went his own way, leaving Bertha to return to her native England with the boy, then sixteen years of age and with the promise of a fine future. He attended the prestigious Malvern College for a year before passing on to Edinburgh University in 1926. Sadly, for all his academic promise, Donald was not comfortable soaking up the wisdom of academe, and it was barely a month before he took to walking out of the house in the morning with the pretence of going to study, and then getting up to whoever knows what illicit pastimes. Mrs. Merrett was deceived at the other end of the day as well. In the evenings, when Donald took to his room "to pursue his studies" she fretted that he might be overdoing things in his quest for knowledge. Not a bit of it;

64

he had slipped out of the house by the back way and was pursuing the knowledge of such things as his worthy mother would never have imagined—mostly at the Palais de Danse in Dunedin's Picardy Place. Nor did poor innocent Bertha Merrett realise that her treasured "Donnie" was also plundering her bank account by the simple means of forging her signature on cheques. It was a state of affairs that could not go unnoticed for long; sooner or later Mrs. Merrett would receive a bank statement . . .

On the morning of 17 March 1926, Mrs. Merrett and her son were in the drawing room, she writing a letter, he reading a book. A little after 9:30 the maid, who was at her duties in the kitchen, heard a shot; moments later "Donnie" rushed in, crying, "Rita, Rita, my mother has shot herself." When they got back to the drawing room, there was Mrs. Merrett lying on the floor, barely alive, and with blood draining from a bullet wound through her right ear.

Bertha Merrett was rushed to the Edinburgh Royal Infirmary where she was treated as a suicide case. When she had recovered sufficiently Mrs. Merrett told the doctor: "I was sitting down writing letters; my son Donald was standing beside me and I said "go away, Donnie, don't annoy me," and then I heard a kind of explosion. I do not remember anything after that." On 27 March Bertha Merrett drifted into a coma and four days later she died. Donald, meanwhile, had continued to lead a life filled with pleasure, and continued to finance it with his mother's money—in fact by the time she passed beyond caring, her Donnie had reduced the bank balance to just four pounds and a couple of shillings. But in the face of such success, Donald seems to have become careless, and soon both the Midland Bank and the local police were taking an interest in his activities.

In November 1926 John Donald Merrett was arrested and charged with the murder of his mother, and on the first day of February the following year he was arraigned before the Lord Justice Clerk, Lord Alness, at the High Court of Justiciary in Edinburgh. In one of his rare appearances for the defence Sir Bernard Spilsbury gave his expert medical opinion that the trajectory and distance from which the bullet had been fired was entirely consistent with Mrs. Merrett having shot herself. The jury was clearly swayed by this evidence, and although Merrett was convicted on several counts of forgery the jury, by a majority, found the charge of matricide against Donald Merrett "not proven." Merrett served eight of a twelve-month sentence and on his release re-entered the world he knew best—the criminal underworld. And for this purpose he became John Ronald Chesney.

As Chesney, he married Vera Bonner the following year, and towards the end of 1929 inherited £50,000—a great fortune in those days. Generous with his new-found wealth, Chesney put £8,400 of the windfall in trust for his wife; she was to enjoy the interest on this capital until her death, when it reverted to Chesney. The next twenty-odd years were busy ones for Ronald Chesney—busy spending his inheritance, busy making more money (mainly as an ocean-going smuggler), busy spending that . . . By 1953 he had separated from his wife and was penniless. How he wished he had not been quite so generous to Vera all those years ago; how he wished he could get his hands on that £8,400 again! There was only one thing for it.

At the time Chesney was living in Germany, though we know that he visited England on 3 February 1954, and during that time he and his estranged wife went to the cinema together. He also made a second trip, this time on a passport in the name of "Leslie Chown." Vera was now living with her mother, a rather eccentric woman who insisted on calling herself "Lady" Menzies; between them they managed a small home for the elderly at Montpelier Road, Ealing. It was at this address that Chesney arrived at about 10:30 p.m. on 10 February bearing two bottles of gin. Having rendered his wife unconscious through drink, Chesney lifted her into the bath, part-filled it with water, and pushed her under until the unfortunate woman drowned. It was, in many ways, a perfect plan: he had slipped unobserved into the house, had fabricated a terrible but believable accident, and was about to slip out again and travel back to Germany as Leslie Chown.

But few plans are entirely perfect, and this one reckoned without an unexpected encounter with "Lady" Menzies in the hallway. Having battered and strangled his mother-in-law to death, Chesney tried to hide her body under some cushions in an unused back room. But by this time events were quite beyond his control—a tragic death caused by falling drunkenly into a tub was one thing, but the hastily concealed, bloody corpse of an elderly woman was bound to arouse suspicion.

Chesney got back to Germany, but he knew it was only a matter of time before the police caught up with him. And so it was. Ronald Chesney had already got away with murder once, and he knew there would be no "not proven" verdict this time. When the British police arrived on 16 February, Chesney's body had already been found in a wood outside Cologne. He had shot himself through the head.

FRANCE
THE PRICE OF LOVE

When Denise Labbé's two-and-a-half-year-old bastard child drowned in a wash-basin at Blois in November 1954 people couldn't help recalling the two previous occasions on which the unfortunate infant had almost met a similiarly watery end while in its mother's care. The result of the combined wagging of tongues was that 28-year-old Denise was taken in for questioning at the gendarmerie and thence before the examining magistrate; here she confessed to what she enigmatically described as "a ritual murder" of her daughter. She had, it transpired, fallen under the spell of Second Lieutenant Jacques Algarron of the St. Cyr military school; he in turn had fallen under the spell of Friedrich Nietzsche and arrogantly supposed himself to be a representative of that philosopher's breed of "Supermen." At any rate, he exerted an unhealthy and total control over Denise Labbé, who was informed on 1 May 1954 that "The price of our love must be the death of your daughter . . . an innocent victim must be sacrificed." The idea seemed to be that only through suffering could their union become strong. Exactly one year after the "monstrous act," Labbé and Algarron stood their trial, she receiving a lifetime of penal servitude, he collecting twenty years' hard labour.

1955

UNITED KINGDOM
RUTH ELLIS

The Last Woman to Hang. *Convicted of shooting her unfaithful lover, Ruth Ellis was the last woman to be hanged in Britain; her controversial execution led in great part to the eventual abolition of the death penalty.*

Ruth was the unremarkable, rather brassy night-club hostess-turned-manageress of The Little Club, a tawdry late-night drinking establishment in London's West End. Her life so far had not been entirely a bed of roses, having been born in 1926 into a large impoverished family, been made pregnant by a married French-Canadian soldier at the age of sixteen, and then left to bring up her son alone. To pay the bills, Ruth took up modelling for a camera club until, at nineteen, she was taken on as a Mayfair club hostess by one Morris Conley, a man much involved in the leisure industries of drinking, gambling and prostitution. Then Ruth married a violent alcoholic named George Ellis, a Southampton dentist. She gave birth to his daughter, Georgina, just before Ellis filed for divorce—it was almost a year to the day after their wedding. Ruth returned to London and willingly into the clutches of Morris Conley again. She briefly hopped back up on her bar stool at Conley's Carroll's club, before being offered the job as his manageress at The Little Club in 1953. Not a bed of roses by any means—so if Ruth drank just a bit too much and enjoyed the loud company that gravitated to the club, who could deny her these modest pleasures?

David Blakely was a member of The Little Club, and Ruth was later to claim that he was the first customer she served there. However that may be, there was instant sexual attraction; a good-looking, if somewhat degenerate youth, with a generous manner, a romantic occupation—he was a racing driver—and an above average appetite for drink, Blakely was probably just what Ruth needed at the time.

The romance lasted for about a year, during which time Ruth became pregnant and had an abortion, and seemed to be going about as well as such a match might reasonably be expected to go. And then things began, some said inevitably, to sour. Blakely had started seeing other women, Ruth had started to object, Blakely began to make his escape.

Nevertheless, he and Ruth still saw each other, and despite the fact that she had started living with a man named Desmond Cussen, seemed to be getting on well together. They arranged to meet on Good Friday, 8 April 1955, and David was to pick Ruth up and take her back for drinks at Tanza Road, Hampstead, where his friends Anthony and Carole Linklater lived. In the end, Blakely decided not to collect Ruth, and went back to Tanza Road with Linklater alone. At about 9:30 p.m. Ruth telephoned and was told by Anthony Linklater that David wasn't there. At midnight she presented herself on the doorstep, ringing furiously on the bell; nobody answered. So Ruth attacked Blakely's van parked outside. It wasn't long before the police were advising Mrs. Ellis to go home and stop making a nuisance of herself. She did go, but not before pushing in a couple more of the van's windows.

Early the following morning, 9 April, Ruth telephoned the Tanza Road number and whoever answered just hung up. On the 10th, Easter Sunday, she made an early morning telephone call which was answered by "Ant" Linklater. Ruth just had enough time to blurt out "I hope you're having an enjoyable holiday . . ." before he put the receiver down. She was going to add "because you've ruined mine." That evening, after a day spent with the Linklaters and their new baby on Hampstead Heath, David Blakely, his hosts and friend named Clive Gunnell were having an impromptu party back at Tanza Road when they ran out of beer. David and Clive Gunnell obligingly drove down to the local, a pub called the Magdala, to stock

up, and while they were there took the opportunity to have a
quick one for the road back. When they came out of the pub
at around 9:20 p.m., they saw Ruth standing there. Ignoring
her, Blakely walked to the driver's door of his car. As Ruth
followed him she pulled a revolver from her handbag and shot
at him. Blakely ran, then fell, and Ruth stood over him and
emptied the chamber into his back.

Ruth made no attempt to escape, and by an irony an off-
duty policeman had witnessed the whole scene. Later at the
police station, Ruth admitted that "I intended to find David
and shoot him." She was just as co-operative at her Old Bailey
trial, though in deference to her legal advisers Ruth formally
entered a plea of not guilty. In reality, there was not much in
legal terms that could be said in Ruth Ellis's defence; she had
been clearly seen by witnesses to shoot Blakely, she had admitted to the police that she killed him, and any plea of provocation would have been futile because of Ruth's
premeditation and planning.

It is almost certain that if Ruth Ellis were to be put on trial
today, charged with the same offence, she would advance a
plea of "diminished responsibility." This defence was made
possible by the Homicide Act of 1957, which states that
"Where a person kills or is a party to the killing of another,
he shall not be convicted of murder if he was suffering from
such abnormality of mind (whether arising from a condition
of arrested or retarded development of mind or any inherent
causes or induced by disease or injury) as substantially impaired his mental responsibility for his acts or omissions in
doing or being party to the killing."

In practical terms this converts the murder charge into one
of manslaughter, a considerable advantage in the barbarous
days when a capital sentence was mandatory for murder. The
plea of diminished responsibility puts the burden of proof on
the defence and, as in the case of Insanity pleas, the proof
need not be "beyond reasonable doubt" but "on a balance of
probabilities." Medical evidence must obviously be presented
on the defendant's behalf as to their state of mind, but it is
for the *jury* and not expert witnesses to decide, on the basis
of the evidence offered, whether the "abnormality" amounts
to diminished responsibility.

As it was, Ruth Ellis was predictably found guilty of murder and, according to the law of the time, sentenced to death. Ruth rejected all attempts to persuade her to appeal, and despite petitions galore calling for commutation of the sentence she was hanged at Holloway Prison in London at 9 a.m. on Wednesday, 13 July 1955. Among her last words, on being told of the people petitioning on her behalf, were: ''I am very grateful to them. But I am quite happy to die.''

For what consolation it may have been to her, Ruth's execution had finally sickened politicians and public alike of the capital sentence. Ruth Ellis was the last woman to be hanged in Britain, and a decade later, with the double execution of Peter Allen and Gwynne Evans in 1965, hanging effectively ceased.

UNITED STATES
THE DEATH OF FLIGHT 629

Jack Gilbert Graham insured his mother's life for $37,000 and then planted a bomb on United Airlines Flight 629 which she boarded at Denver. The device exploded just ten minutes after take-off, killing all 44 passengers and crew. Graham, who had nurtured a hatred of his mother ever since she placed him in an orphanage for the first eight years of his life, readily confessed and was sent to the Colorado Penitentiary gas chamber in January 1957 (see also 1949).

1956

UNITED KINGDOM
THE FATAL TRIANGLE

One of history's most curious examples of the fatal love triangle, solved to the satisfaction of a jury by a recreation of the murder by forensic serologists.

The Albert Goozee story, at least in as far as it concerns the criminologist, began in January 1955, when the ex-merchant seaman took lodgings with the Leakey family at their home in Poole, Dorset. The family comprised Thomas Leakey, a World War I veteran who had lost a leg in the service of his country and now operated a wood-lathe in a local factory, his 53-year-old wife Lydia Margaret and their twelve-year-old daughter Norma. The Leakeys had two more children, but they had grown up and left home. Goozee, somewhere in his early thirties, was, in the parlance of the day, a "ladies man." During his stay with the Leakeys he ran through a number of mundane service jobs—bus conductor, roundsman, that sort of thing—and was usually dismissed for over-familiarity with female customers. He was also becoming decidedly familiar with Margaret Leakey, though it is fair to say that she never complained.

Norma Leakey's thirteenth birthday fell on 4 February 1955, and "Uncle" Albert was the life and soul—he even managed to win a kiss in the dark from Mrs. Leakey during the game of Postman's Knock. That night, according to Goozee, Margaret Leakey crept uninvited into his bed, followed shortly afterwards by Norma; Albert Goozee must have thought all his Christmases had come at once. However, it was not a situation guaranteed to result in marital harmony, and after some months the long-suffering Thomas Leakey took himself off to Andover.

Leakey obviously thought better of his move, because at the beginning of June 1956 he returned to Poole and threw Goozee out instead. And while Albert Goozee might then have been happy to leave well alone, he was pestered by notes from Margaret Leakey asking him to "come back home, and I will be a mother to you," or words to that effect. He continued to see the matronly Mrs. Leakey, but by no means exclusively. On 15 June, a Friday, Albert Goozee and two friends visited the theatre in Bournemouth. Outside they encountered a woman and her teenaged daughter trying to get in to see the show. Generously, or so the woman thought, Goozee offered a spare ticket to the fourteen-year-old while her mother was found a place at the rear of the stalls. However, Albert's motives proved far from altruistic, and before the entertainment had reached the first interval he was hauled into the manager's office and thence to the police station where he was charged with indecently assaulting the girl. Two days later, on Sunday afternoon, Albert Goozee collected Margaret and Norma Leakey from their home and ferried them in his car to a picnic at Bignell Wood, in the New Forest.

What followed we have only Albert Goozee's word for; his companions never lived to tell the tale. According to Goozee, then, it was Mrs. Leakey's intention to make a wood fire on which to boil the picnic kettle, and accordingly she went equipped with an axe! "Mrs. Leakey suggested we take one of the smaller paths into the forest, which we did. We started to get a fire going. She then told Norma to go for a walk while the kettle was boiling to see if she could find some bluebells. I had an idea that this was only a blind. Norma walked away and left us . . . Next thing I knew Norma was standing over her mother, screaming "You beast, why don't you leave Albert alone?" I did not realise she had the axe in her hand . . . She struck her mother across the head with the axe; she hit her once and went into hysterics. I hit Norma a couple of times in the face with my fist and she stopped screaming."

As Goozee pushed Norma into the back of the car Mrs.

Leakey was struggling to get into the front passenger seat, ending up slumped half in and half out of the vehicle with a knife in her hand. Goozee, according to his own narrative, tried to take the knife, but accidentally slipped and fell, and in doing so became impaled on the blade: "I thought my life was finished, so I jabbed the knife in her. Norma came out of the car and came at me screaming "What have you done to my mother; why don't you do the same to me?" After that my mind must have gone blank. I don't remember stabbing Norma. I passed out. I came to about an hour later and they were both lying there. They were both dead so I got in the car and drove down in the direction I could hear the traffic."

The strain of driving became too much for Albert, and he stopped at some point along the Cadnam-Brook Road where a passing motorist found him staggering about, bleeding and rambling that "There has been a murder in the forest"; adding, "I did it; I've got a knife in me; get the police." And so Albert Goozee came to the attention of the police for the second time in a weekend.

When his bloodstained car was searched, detectives found a letter addressed to the Chief Constable of Bournemouth, and a knife with a six-and-a-half-inch blade which proved to be the weapon which had stabbed Mrs. Leakey, her daughter, and Goozee himself. The distinctly odd letter read, in part: "I was told to leave the house. I did, but Mrs. Leakey still comes after me so I have come to the only possible way out before I go after another young girl. Please do not put too much trouble on my brother because he knows how Mrs. Leakey and Norma went after me. I went into the Army to get away from it all [in fact his service lasted just two weeks before he bought himself out]; but once you have messed about with a young girl there is not much you can do for yourself..."

"The only possible way out." Was that the truth of it? Did Albert Goozee deliberately set out to kill his lover and her daughter? Was it Goozee who had packed the axe, with a far more sinister plan in mind than chopping wood? Was it Goozee who finished the job off with a vicious blade, and then stabbed himself for effect?

As it turned out, the forensic serologists were able to cast light on the sequence of events. Albert Goozee had claimed that, despite his mind having "gone blank," he stabbed his two victims *after* he had fallen on the knife himself. If this were true, then the blood of the Leakeys should have been predominant on the blade. Laboratory tests showed, however, that most of the blood was Group O—Goozee's group—while the only Group A blood, which the two women shared, was found around the hilt. The inevitable conclusion was that "the knife had first been used on the women, and only then plunged into Goozee."

It certainly convinced the jury at Winchester Assizes, and Albert William Goozee was convicted and sentenced to death, though this was later commuted to life imprisonment. The ironic thing was that despite all Goozee's self-recrimination about having sexual relations with Norma Leakey, it was just a fantasy—the post-mortem examination revealed that Norma was still a virgin when she died.

1957

UNITED KINGDOM
THE CASE OF DR. ADAMS

One of the most disgraceful examples of "trial by newspaper" in modern criminal history. From the time he was charged, Adams was pilloried by the Press, with the exception of veteran crime reporter Percy Hoskins—whose faith was rewarded when Dr. Adams was acquitted of murder.

John Bodkin Adams was born on 21 January 1899 at Randalstown, County Antrim, the son of a prosperous watchmaker. He first attended school at Coleraine, where the family had moved, and later studied medicine at Queen's University, Belfast. In 1921 Adams graduated with a fairly good degree and, after a year on the wards of a general hospital in Bristol, went into general practice in Eastbourne. It was his first acquaintance with a town in which he would spend the rest of his life. The early years were good to Dr. Adams, and if he was not a brilliant doctor, he was an attentive one who quickly made a secure reputation for himself, his portly figure atop a motorcycle becoming a familiar sight in the resort. The doctor made a particular point of cultivating patients among the wealthier "county" set and minor gentry, and within a decade had enlarged his practice and become the most fashionable medic in Eastbourne. Adams's particular joy was his collection of motor cars, among which he numbered two Rolls-Royces. There was also another side to Dr. Adams—the man who worshipped regularly with the Plymouth Brethren and taught Bible class on Sundays. In short, he was nobody's idea of a serial killer.

In July 1956 Mrs. Gertrude Hullett, widow of a Lloyd's underwriter and a patient of Adams's, fell seriously ill. Adams had already been treating her for nervous collapse, and as a result of regular prescriptions of barbiturate drugs the unfortunate woman had become addicted to them. Although his patient was still alive, if unconscious, Dr. Adams felt for some reason that he should alert the coroner to this "peculiar" case and advise a post-mortem. On 23 July Mrs. Hullett died, and Adams certified the cause as cerebral haemhorrage. However, the autopsy revealed this to be a *very* "peculiar" case, because when Dr. Francis Camps performed the autopsy he declared cause of death as barbiturate poisoning. At the inquest on Mrs. Hullett the coroner, Dr. Sommerville, found that she had committed suicide; he also added in summing up that Dr. Adams had been guilty of "an extraordinary degree of careless treatment."

It was also discovered that Mrs. Hullett had left her Rolls-Royce to Adams in her will. Now the tongues began to wag; now the memories began to be jogged. And by the time Scotland Yard had completed their report it was known that over the previous ten years Dr. Adams had been a beneficiary in the wills of more than 100 patients, and had received numerous expensive gifts, including another Rolls-Royce. Some were constrained to joke blackly that Adams made his rounds with a bottle of morphine in one hand and a blank will in the other.

It was the case of Mrs. Edith Alice Morrell that the police decided to prosecute. Mrs. Morrell, the widow of a wealthy businessman, had arrived in Eastbourne from Liverpool in 1949, where Dr. Adams had treated her for severe arthritis and partial paralysis. Adams's treatment consisted, as it often did, mainly of heroin and morphine. As might be excused in a person of her age and infirmity (as well as her intake of heroin and morphine), Mrs. Morrell tended to be a little eccentric and unpredictable. She made half a dozen or more wills, one of which bequeathed *everything* to her dear, understanding doctor; then she made another in which he received not a brass farthing. Next she promised him a car and a chest of silver—then she denied it. Greedy as he certainly was, Adams even went to the sick woman's solicitor and asked him to add a codicil mentioning the gift; the solicitor, quite rightly, refused to do any such thing. In August 1950 Mrs. Morrell made her last will, this time relenting and leaving the silver and the car to Adams; but capricious to the last, Edith Morrell made a codicil just two months before her death on 13 November 1950, withdrawing the gift. In fact it was Mrs. Morrell's son Arthur who gave Dr. Adams not only the box of silver and the Rolls-Royce, but also an antique cupboard he had long admired. Dr. Adams was treating his patient right up to her last breath, and when that had been taken he certified death as being due to cerebral thrombosis.

During the trial of Dr. Adams for the murder of Mrs. Morrell, the Old Bailey jury heard a great deal of evidence from the nurses attending the deceased as to the medication administered by Adams—barbiturates, secomid, morphine, heroin . . . all in increasing quantities. The implication was clear: the doctor had been slowly killing his patient. Unfortunately it was quite impossible to verify the amounts of drugs in the body at death because Dr. Adams had given immediate authorisation for cremation, making exhumation for autopsy impossible. The court also heard from Detective Superintendent Hannam, who had interviewed Dr. Adams and recalled that in response to questions about Mrs. Morrell's death, the doctor claimed: "Easing the passing of a dying person is not all that wicked. She wanted to die—that cannot be murder. It is impossible to accuse a doctor." He was wrong.

Unsurprisingly a scandal such as this—a doctor killing off his elderly patients for a share of the estate—attracted the world's Press like vultures to carrion; and whether they believed Adams's guilt or not, most journalists *hoped* it was true. It had been said, quite fairly in retrospect, that John Bodkin Adams was tried and almost convicted by the newspapers. As always there are distinguished exceptions, in this case the redoubtable crime reporter Percy Hoskins who, against the odds, persuaded his newspaper, the *Daily Express*, to follow his own belief that Adams was innocent.* In fact, all that Percy Hoskins had done was the same as Geoffrey Lawrence QC, Adams's defence counsel—he had carefully looked at the case, and realised that for all their braggadocio the Crown had a very weak case. For a start the supposedly damaging testimony of the nurses who gave evidence of apparently reckless drug administrations was quite at variance with the written records contained in the medical log books. Furthermore, Adams had absolutely no personal motive for terminating Mrs. Morrell's life—he stood to gain nothing from the will, and he knew it. However, it was perhaps fortuitous that the doctor was charged only with the one murder—it ensured that suspicious-looking details of other patients' deaths could not be introduced as evidence.

On 10 April 1957 Dr. Adams was declared not guilty. Although he resigned from the National Health Service, he courageously returned to Eastbourne where he took on a few loyal private patients. Adams was subsequently struck off the Medical Register, but reinstated in 1961 when he resumed general practice. He died in 1983 at the age of 84.

Controversy still surrounds the Adams case; some remain convinced he was a murderer, others that he practised euthanasia. The truth of the matter is probably that Dr. Adams was simply a sloppy doctor with an ingratiating manner and an eye to personal advancement.

*When Adams was found not guilty, Lord Beaverbrook, proprietor of the *Express*, who had always been sceptical of his stance telephoned Percy Hoskins in Eastbourne with the message: ''Two men have been acquitted today—Adams and Hoskins.''

1958

KILLING OF JOHNNY STOMPANATO

Celebrated Hollywood "murder," in which Cheryl Crane, the fourteen-year-old daughter of star Lana Turner, stabbed to death her mother's gangster lover. In the end a sympathetic jury returned a verdict of justifiable homicide.

Ranking high among the tawdry scandals of Hollywood was the killing of actress Lana Turner's gangster boyfriend Johnny Stompanato. Johnny had his finger in so many crooked pies that his assassination did not come as much of a surprise; what caused the sensation was that his killer should be the screen star's fourteen-year-old daughter Cheryl Crane.

Lana (born Julia) Turner's life had already been touched by similar tragedy when she was barely a teenager and her stevedore father was murdered by robbers in a San Francisco alleyway. Her introduction to the silver screen has become one of Tinsel Town's most enduring legends. It is said that at the age of just fifteen, Julia Turner was strutting down Sunset Avenue wearing the skintight sweater and stiletto heels so beloved of aspiring starlets when she was seen by journalist Billy Wilkerson. In true Hollywood style he asked her if she'd like to be in the movies—really! And for a change somebody meant what they said. With Wilkerson's encouragement Julia got herself an agent, and, through him, a small part in the very unmemorable *They Won't Forget* and a new name—Lana.

At the age of nineteen, Lana Turner entered into the first of what would be a long succession of less than ideal marriages. Within two months of the ceremony she had parted from band-leader Artie Shaw and later they divorced. Lana's second hus-band was businessman Stephen Crane; they met at a nightclub, danced together, and were married the following week. Un-fortunately, Crane was not yet divorced from his previous wife and the marriage to Lana was temporarily annulled; by this time she was pregnant. Lana and Crane finally married and baby Cheryl was born five months later. When this marriage also collapsed Lana Turner became Mrs. Henry "Bob" Top-ping, and millionaire Topping was succeeded by one of the screen's most famous Tarzans, Lex Barker. The relationship with Barker came to an acrimonious end provoked, it is said, by Cheryl's jealousy, and Lana married in fairly quick suc-cession Fred May, Robert Eaton and Ronald Danse. Cheryl was now a confused and insecure ten-year-old with no very high opinion of her mother or her mother's morals. Just how seriously the relationship had deteriorated was illustrated by an incident at one of her many expensive boarding schools. Told by a teacher that if she did not write a letter to her mother she would go to bed without supper, Cheryl wrote: "Dear Mother, this is not a letter, it is a meal ticket . . ."

Lana, meanwhile, had fallen for the smooth patter of part-time gigolo, part-time crook Johnny Stompanato. Johnny, some say, had telephoned the star for a bet, and invited her out on a blind date. Lana, more impulsive than discriminating, became obsessively fond of her new lover and, it has to be said, he of her. In fact this was what fuelled the fires of tragedy that would end in his untimely and brutal death. Johnny be-came violently and irrationally jealous, and when Lana was obliged to travel to England to film *Another Time, Another Place*, he followed her out of jealousy of her co-star Sean Connery. It is recalled that Stompanato once burst on to the film set and threatened Connery with a gun—an ill-considered move that ended with the actor laying out the gangster with one swift blow to the chin. The quarrels between Lana and Johnny became so aggressive that the English police were fi-nally forced to deport Stompanato after he had tried to strangle Lana. Still they clung desperately to each other, and surpris-ingly the relationship actually brought young Cheryl closer to her mother than she had been for a long time; of all her mother's husbands and lovers Johnny was the one Cheryl seemed to take to.

By now Cheryl's enforced independence had given her a maturity and approach to life far in advance of her fourteen years. During the school holidays at Easter 1958, Cheryl joined her mother and Johnny Stompanato at their home in North Bedford Drive, where there was certainly no hint of the horror that was to come. On the evening of 4 April, Good Friday, Cheryl, Lana and Johnny were at home when one of the frequent quarrels erupted, during which Stompanato became his usual threatening, bullying self and Cheryl slipped into the kitchen and picked up a carving knife; she said later that she was afraid Johnny would hurt her mother. The row between Lana and Johnny was escalating, and according to Lana's later testimony, "I would have to do everything he told me or he'd cut my face or cripple me . . . he would kill me, and my daughter, and my mother . . ."

Events were beginning to take on a menacing physical threat, with Stompanato flailing his fists around . . . but before he or Lana realised what was happening, Cheryl rushed up to Johnny and drove the nine-inch blade of the carving knife into his stomach. Although he was still alive when the doctor arrived, by the time the police got to the scene Johnny Stompanato was dead.

In the days between the killing and the inquest the sensation was kept burning by the publication of Lana Turner's letters to her lover which had inexplicably found their way from the dead man's apartment to the offices of the Los Angeles *Herald Examiner*. The coroner's inquest opened on 11 April and was broadcast live on national television. Lana Turner gave the performance of her life as the abused and terrified mother fearful for her own and her child's safety from a man insane with violent jealousy, and told how, in the end, that innocent child was forced by circumstance to commit an unspeakable act in defence of her mother's life. There was scarcely a dry eye in the court, and after a token retirement the jury returned a verdict of justifiable homicide; Cheryl Crane was released to the joy of all.

Johnny's remains were flown back to his native Illinois

where he was given an extravagant funeral. One of his former employers, the gambler and gangster Micky Cohen, said of Johnny: "Look, this was a great guy." When the fuss had died down a little Johnny Stompanato's brother sued Lana and Stephen Crane for $800,000 damages, alleging parental negligence; in the end he accepted an out-of-court settlement of just $20,000.

Unlike many stars whose careers were shattered by personal scandals, Lana Turner survived the Johnny Stompanato incident and many have observed that the sensation had actually revived a flagging career. Cheryl Crane became a successful businesswoman in the field of real estate, and later published her autobiography in which she restated her court testimony on the Stompanato case.

AUSTRALIA
JUST SIGN HERE

Aborigine Rupert Max Stuart was picked up in 1958 in connection with the murder of nine-year-old Mary Hattam at Ceduna, South Australia, and according to the police made a full confession. Max Stuart later retracted the confession, claiming that police officers had written the document and forced him to sign his name. There was considerable support for this accusation in view of Stuart's poor grasp of the English language. Following a controversial trial and a long sequence of appeals against his death sentence, Max Stuart was imprisoned for life.

1959

UNITED KINGDOM
GUENTHER FRITZ PODOLA

Murdered on Duty. *Podola shot a police officer while resisting arrest for burglary. In the scuffle to recapture him, Podola hit his head and later claimed memory loss as a defence at his trial.*

By the middle of July 1959 the Metropolitan police had begun to close in on yet another of the capital's seedier villains; this time it was a man calling himself Fisher, who had been engaged in the unpleasant pursuit of blackmailing a 30-year-old model named June Schiffman whom he had previously burgled. On the afternoon of the 13th the telephone rang in Mrs. Schiffman's South Kensington apartment; she lifted the receiver and managed to keep the conversation going long enough for the call to be traced to a nearby telephone box. Waiting for just such a break Detective Sergeants John Sandford and Raymond Purdy sped to the call box on South Kensington underground station, dragged its inhabitant out and hustled him up the wide flight of steps to the exit. In the ensuing scuffle the blackmailer broke away and fled into a block of flats in Onslow Square; at the entrance the policemen separated, DS Sandford trying to rouse the block's caretaker. Suddenly the fugitive leapt out of hiding and shot Raymond Purdy through the heart before fleeing along Sydney Place.

Over the next two days the police mounted a massive manhunt for a man described as tall, slim, and speaking with an American accent. Although identifiable fingerprints had been left on a marble ledge at the flats, there was no matching set in the Fingerprint Department's records. On 16 July the manager of the Claremont House Hotel, Kensington, called to tell the police that one of his guests, a Mr. Paul Camay, bad been acting oddly ever since the fatal shooting. By now police had traced the killer's fingerprints to a 30-year-old German immigrant named Guenther Podola; he had been deported from Canada the previous year following sentences for robbery. Podola, Fisher and Camay were evidently one and the same man. On the afternoon of 16 July a team of detectives arrested Podola in his hotel room where they also found the weapon which had robbed their colleague of his life. During the encounter it was said that Podola struck his head on a door, and when he arrived at the police station he was dazed and suffering a number of superficial injuries. It was felt expedient to transfer Podola to St Stephen's Hospital, where he was put under observation while handcuffed to the bed. On 20 July he was charged with murder and remanded to Brixton Prison.

By the time his case reached the Old Bailey in September, Podola had taken advantage of the opportunity to elaborate his "dazed" sensations into a defence plea of total memory loss. Thus, before the trial could even begin, a jury had to be empanelled to decide whether Podola was fit to stand trial. Based on observations made in St. Stephen's and at Brixton, four doctors supported the prisoner's claim that he was suffering amnesia, and two reported that in their view he was malingering. The jury also decided that Podola's memory loss was not genuine and he was put on trial on 24 September. The bulk of the Crown's case rested on the eye-witness account of the shooting and the events leading up to it by Detective Sergeant Sandford. Speaking from the dock in his own defence Podola stubbornly repeated that he had no recollection of the incident at all. After a retirement of just half an hour, the jury returned with a verdict of guilty and Podola was sentenced to death. Through his attorney, Podola applied to the Court of Criminal Appeal, but the application was turned down, their Lordships deciding that "Even if the loss of memory had been a genuine loss of memory, that did not of itself render the appellant insane."

Guenther Podola was hanged at Wandsworth Prison on 5

November 1959, the last person in Britain to be executed for killing a policeman.

BERMUDA
"I GET NASTY..."

In March 1959 a 72-year-old woman was found dead in her home at Southlands beach, Bermuda; she had been raped and bludgeoned. A month later a second elderly woman was found in identical circumstances, and on 28 September a 29-year-old woman's body was found floating near a coral reef, mutilated by sharks but showing sufficient evidence of having been murdered. Wendell Willis Lightbourne first came to the attention of the police because he had been on the beach on the day of the last murder looking very agitated. Eventually the nineteen-year-old golf caddy broke down under questioning and confessed to the murder, concluding: "I get nasty." Lightbourne was convicted and sent to Britain to serve his sentence.

1960

UNITED KINGDOM
MICHAEL COPELAND

The Carbon-Copy Murders. *Copeland committed two murders—identical in every way—because he hated homosexuals. A third killing, in Germany, was committed for no reason at all.*

On Sunday, 12 June 1960 the body of 60-year-old William Arthur Elliott was found in isolated Clod Hill Lane, which crosses the moors near Baslow; he had been wearing no shoes. This was of great interest to the Chesterfield police who, on the previous day, had been called to Park Road where an Isetta "bubble" car had been found crashed and stained with blood; inside was a pair of men's shoes. While police began a search of the desolate moorland for the weapon used to bludgeon Mr. Elliott to death, detectives were making inquiries around his home at 9 Haddon Road, Bakewell, in an attempt to piece together the last hours of his life. In particular they wanted to talk to anybody who saw Elliott's ivory-coloured bubble car, registration number KLU 488, either before or after its accident.

As the search widened, the inquiry team, led by Detective Superintendent Leonard Stretton, learned of a bizarre incident that occurred about a week before William Elliott was killed. Fifty-one-year-old bus cleaner William Atkinson, of North Wingfield, claimed that he had been attacked in Boythorpe Road, which runs close to Park Road, in the same area the bubble car had been found. Mr. Atkinson bore a remarkable

physical likeness to the moors victim, and police had to allow
the possibility that he may have been assaulted in mistake for
Mr. Elliott. What's more, the two men were known to each
other, both being habitués of the Spread Eagle public house
in Chesterfield.

Another much-needed clue was provided by Gladys Vickers
of Sutton Spring Wood. Mrs. Vickers told police that she
thought she may have seen Mr. Elliott attacked the night before his body was found; she knew Mr. Elliott and said: "I
saw him being chased along an alley outside the Royal Oak
public house. The man chasing him was dark-haired, swarthy,
and with thin features, and he caught up with him. Then I
heard someone say 'Oh' and groan." The possibility now
arose that Elliott's bubble car had been used by his killer to
transport the body up to the moor, and had then been abandoned back in Chesterfield.

Despite an investigation during the course of which more
than 10,000 statements were taken, Superintendent Stretton's
murder squad were reluctantly forced to concede that, for the
time being anyway, the killer had slipped through their net.
At the inquest into his death, the coroner declared that William
Elliott had been murdered by "person or persons unknown."

Almost a year later, on Wednesday, 29 March 1961, an
unidentified man was found dead from severe injuries in Clod
Hill Lane, at almost the exact spot where William Elliott had
been found murdered. The victim of the so-called "Carbon-
Copy Murder" was named as 40-year-old Chesterfield industrial chemist George Gerald Stobbs. The police were now
working on the assumption that this was a "carbon-copy"
killing, and Detective Superintendent Stretton was given
charge of the new investigation. Later it was revealed that an
abandoned car had been found in exactly the same spot in
Park Road that Elliott's blood-stained bubble car had been left.

What happened next would tax the imagination of a crime-
fiction writer. Police issued a statement on 1 April which revealed another dramatic similarity to the original "bubble-car
murder." It appeared that a man named Gillespie, living near
Stubbing Court, and bearing a great resemblance to the victim
Gerald Stobbs, was attacked shortly before the latest killing.
As in the case of the assault on William Atkinson before the

Elliott murder, it was entirely reasonable that Dr. Gillespie was mistaken for Stobbs. But already a firm link was being established between the two murders. An unbelievably coy local newspaper reported on 3 April 1961:

PROBE INTO DOUBLE LIVES OF VICTIMS
Undercover Man in Hunt for Killer

It was announced by officers investigating the "Carbon-Copy Murders" that they are to give an "undercover" man the task of infiltrating the circles in which both of the victims moved. Police now believe that both Mr. Elliott and Mr. Stobbs led double lives of which even their closest relatives were unaware. Both men had acquaintances in common and drank in the same public house—the Three Horseshoes at Chesterfield.

For "double lives" read "closet homosexuals."

Despite this new revelation and the continued investigations by the Derbyshire constabulary, the case remained unsolved over the succeeding months. The only further dramatic incident was the death of 63-year-old Arthur Jenkinson shortly after he had been interviewed by the police. Although the coroner's jury returned a verdict of suicide, there was some persistent rumour that Mr. Jenkinson had been murdered—had been overcome and had his head forced into the gas oven.

As month followed month the likelihood of getting to the bottom of the Carbon-Copy Mystery grew more remote. And so it might have remained but for the determination of the Chesterfield detectives.

During the investigation of the Elliott murder one of the suspects questioned was 21-year-old Michael Copeland. Copeland was on National Service in Germany, but at the time had been on leave and living at home in Chesterfield. He already had a police record, but it was not this that drew Copeland to the attention of the police. He had apparently boasted to his girlfriend that he was the killer and she, honest girl, had gone to the police. Apart from this piece of bravado there was nothing tangible to link Copeland with the crime, and he was released after questioning and resumed his tour of duty in

Germany. But now Michael Copeland was back in Chesterfield; in fact he arrived back just a short time before the murder of George Stobbs. He was again taken into custody for questioning, and although he could not account for his whereabouts on the night of the murder there was no reason to suspect Copeland more than anybody else without an alibi. Or was there?

It was Chief Inspector Thomas Peat who first made the connection. Both Elliott and Stobbs were homosexual. Suppose their killer was a homophobe—suppose Copeland was homophobic? And so, slowly, Peat began to cultivate the confidence of his suspect. As it turned out it was a short-lived exercise, because Copeland got into a drunken brawl and earned himself four months inside. However, on his release there was another policeman waiting to keep up the pressure. It took Inspector Bradshaw two years, but he managed to build up a strong relationship with Copeland, who began by revealing small confidences and ended confessing not only to the killing of Elliott and Stobbs because they were homosexuals ("It was something I really hated"), but also the quite inexplicable murder of a German boy while he was on service. In November 1960, Gunther Helmbrecht, sixteen years old, was stabbed to death while walking with a girl in the forest near the town of Verden in Germany. That same night Copeland staggered into the guard room at his barracks with a knife wound in his leg and explained that he had been attacked by two German civilians. An obvious suspect, Copeland was intensively questioned, but nothing concrete could be found to link him with the death of Helmbrecht. Until now.

At his trial in March 1965, Michael Copeland claimed that he had made the confessions only in order to force a trial so that he could establish his innocence and get the police off his back. The court did not believe a word of it, and Copeland was found guilty and sentenced to death. At the time the whole issue of capital punishment was under review in England, and his sentence was commuted to one of life imprisonment.

AUSTRALIA
A FIRST FOR FORENSIC BOTANY

On 7 July 1960 eight-year-old Graeme Thorne—whose parents had recently won a large sum of money on the Sydney lottery—was abducted on his way to school; the kidnapper later demanded a ransom of A £25,000. On 16 August Graeme's body was found on a stretch of wasteland ten miles from his home. Stephen Leslie Bradley was trapped by the ingenuity of forensic botanists who proved that fungus spores found in the victim's lungs came from a rare combination of trees found only in Bradley's garden.

1961

UNITED KINGDOM
EDWIN ALBERT BUSH

A Question of Identity. *This was the first successful use of the newly introduced Identikit system in identifying a killer. Bush stabbed Mrs. Elsie Batten to death and was recognised by a patrolling policeman three days later.*

The Identikit system of identification was the culmination of research and development carried out by the Los Angeles Police Department, notably by Hugh McDonald. At its inception the "kit" comprised a set of interchangeable transparencies of drawings. These depicted the variations on facial features—eyes, noses, ears, et cetera—which in a collaboration between the police operator and a witness could be assembled to give a composite picture of the wanted person. In theory it was possible to combine the components into thousands of millions of likenesses; in practice the system proved rudimentary and inaccurate—even, as in the case of the "A6 Murder," a possible hindrance to the course of justice.

In 1959 the concept of Identikit was introduced to the investigating officers of Scotland Yard, but it was not until 1961 that the system was put to practical use. Britain's first Identikit Face was that of 21-year-old Edwin Albert Bush, author of a senseless and lacklustre crime in the heart of London's theatreland. Bush, obligingly enough for the launch of Identikit, was a fairly distinctive half-caste Indian who had walked into Louis Meier's antiquities shop in Cecil Court on 2 March 1961—the day before the murder—and made inquiries as to the cost of a dress sword. He had been told £15, and then he went across the pedestrian court to the shop of a gunsmith named Roberts who replied to his question that, yes, he did occasionally buy swords, but would need to see it before agreeing a price.

On the following morning Edwin Bush returned to Louis Meier's shop, where he stabbed to death Meier's assistant, Mrs. Elsie Batten, wife of Mark Batten, President of the Royal Society of Sculptors, and helped himself to a dress sword. At 10 a.m. he re-opened his transaction with the gunsmith, leaving the ill-gotten blade in the care of his son Paul Roberts, suggesting a price of, say, £10. He never returned to hear the gunsmith's verdict, but Bush (as prime suspect in the murder) could now be reliably identified by three people. This enabled a fairly accurate Identikit portrait to be made; accurate enough, anyway, for Police Constable John Cole to identify and arrest the subject while on patrol in Old Compton Street, Soho, on 8 March.

At Bow Street police station where he was interviewed by Detective Chief Superintendent John Bliss, Bush expressed the opinion that the Identikit looked like him, but denied any connection with the killing of Elsie Batten. However, it was not long before Edwin Bush was making his statement: "I went to the back of the shop and started looking through the daggers, telling her I might want to buy one, but I picked one up and hit her in the back . . . I then lost my nerve and picked up a stone vase and hit her with it. I grabbed a knife and hit her once in the stomach and once in the neck."

But aside from his confession, Edwin Bush's catalogue of carelessness had not ended at regularly showing his face in the area where he had committed murder; he had also left behind in the shop an identifiable footprint. There was blood on his clothing, and two fingerprints and a palm print on the sheet of paper he had used to wrap the sword.

Edwin Bush stood trial at the Old Bailey on 12 and 13 May. In his evidence he admitted going into Mr. Meier's shop with the intention of stealing a ceremonial sword; he was then, he said, going to sell the sword to Mr. Roberts in order to buy an engagement ring for his girlfriend. Bush then began to haggle over the price and: "She let off about my colour and said,

'You niggers are all the same. You come in and never buy anything,' I lost my head . . .'' He then repeated his previous account of the killing.

Bush had the benefit of Mr. Christmas Humphreys QC as his defender, but at the end of the trial he was convicted, sentenced to death by Mr. Justice Stevenson, and hanged. Of PC Cole's part in the apprehension of Mrs. Batten's killer, the judge commented: ''You deserve the congratulations and gratitude of the community for the great efficiency you displayed in recognising Bush. You have been the direct instrument of his being brought to justice. Your vigilance deserves the highest praise, and I hope it will be clearly recognised by the highest authority.''

SOUTH AFRICA
KILLER BY NAME . . .

With much the greater part of his wealth deriving from the uncertain and dangerous illegal diamond trade, South African playboy Baron Dieter von Shauroth wisely took out substantial life insurance, and unwisely retained a young crook named Marthinus Rossouw as a bodyguard. When von Shauroth's corpse was found on 25 March 1961 it had two gunshot wounds in the head; he had clearly been robbed, and in his haste the assassin had spilled diamonds on the floor. When Rossouw—who affected the unfortunate *nom de guerre* ''Killer''—was interviewed he told police the extraordinary story that his employer had paid him 2300 Rand to kill him. Not surprisingly, the jury at his trial did not swallow this preposterous defence and convicted Rossouw of murder, for which he was later hanged. The insurance companies, however, eager as always for a loophole to avoid paying out, refused to honour the policies because of the suggestion of a ''murder-by-request'' which would have nullified the insurance. It was only after lengthy legal negotiations that Mrs. von Shauroth was awarded a compromise *ex gratia* payment.

1962

UNITED KINGDOM
THE A6 MURDER

The hanging of James Hanratty for what became known as the A6 murder has been the source of endless controversy. Hanratty was accused of killing Michael Gregsten and the attempted murder of Valerie Storie; however, many informed commentators have laid the blame on another suspect in the case, Peter Louis Alphon.

At approximately 9:30 p.m. on the late summer evening of 22 August 1961, Michael Gregsten, a young married research scientist, and his girlfriend, Valerie Storie, were relaxing in his car at a lay-by outside the village of Dornley on the A6 road through Bedfordshire. It was an unlikely prelude to the five-and-a-half-hour nightmare that was to leave 36-year-old Gregsten dead and Valerie Storie crippled for the rest of her life. There in the quiet of the cornfield a man stepped from the darkness and tapped on the driver's side window; when Mike Gregsten wound the window down he found himself face to face with the barrel of a revolver. "This is a hold-up."

For two hours the gunman sat nervously in the back seat of the grey Morris Minor covering his prisoners with the weapon while relating a rambling and improbable story about his recent flight from the police. At 11:30 p.m. Gregsten was ordered to start his car for the first leg of a terrifying journey along the A6, traversing three counties and finally coming to an end at the prophetically named Deadman's Hill, where he was shot twice through the head at point-blank range. After compounding his savage attack with the rape of Valerie Storie, the killer bundled her from the car and fired five bullets in quick succession into her body, causing injuries that robbed her for ever of the use of her legs, and almost of her life.

On 11 September, the manager of the Vienna Hotel in London Maida Vale found two spent cartridge cases in a basement bedroom which had last been occupied three weeks before. These proved to match a gun which had recently been recovered from its hiding place beneath a seat cushion on the top deck of a number 36A bus; ballistics experts identified the weapon as that which killed Michael Gregsten. Checking the hotel's guest register for the time around the date of the murder, police discovered that Peter Louis Alphon, a 30-year-old drifter and petty crook, had booked in under a false name on the day after the shooting on Deadman's Hill. Although he resembled the description given by Valerie Storie of her attacker, when Alphon was paraded before her at Stoke Mandeville Hospital, Miss Storie failed to identify him; indeed she identified another man quite unconnected with the inquiry. Peter Alphon was released from custody.

By now the police had a second suspect, 24-year-old James Hanratty. Like Alphon he was a petty crook, and like Alphon he had booked into the Vienna Hotel under an alias. Hanratty had been the last occupant of the basement bedroom in which the cartridge cases had been found. The hunt was now on for James Hanratty who, on account of a number of outstanding burglaries, had gone to ground. However, it is significant that as soon as he became aware of police interest in him, Hanratty telephoned Chief Superintendent Bob Acott, then in charge of the enquiry, in order to protest his innocence and to tell Acott where his clothing could be found for forensic examination. On 11 October, Hanratty was traced to a café in Blackpool and arrested. Like Alphon before him, James Hanratty was put into an identification parade and this time Valerie Storie picked him out—though according to one witness it was not without difficulty. Hanratty was taken from the hospital and charged with murder, attempted murder and rape, and so began what was to become one of crime detection's most controversial decisions. It was Hanratty whose fate was to be the bewildering ordeal of the due process of law—the police stations and the magistrates' court, culminating in the trial at Bedford Assizes, and the then longest murder trial in British criminal history where, still protesting his innocence, James Hanratty was convicted and sentenced to hang.

The evidence against Hanratty was almost entirely based on identification—first by Valerie Storie, who was carried into the court on a stretcher, and then by witnesses who had seen the supposed killer driving Michael Gregsten's Morris Minor on the morning after the murder. In his defence Hanratty claimed that he left the Vienna Hotel on the evening of 22 August bound for Liverpool, where he anticipated selling some stolen jewellery. However, he could not remember either precisely where or with whom he had spent the night. This was clearly not satisfactory either to Hanratty's defence or to the Crown. And so Hanratty obligingly, if unwisely, changed his alibi and now maintained that he had not, after all, stayed in Liverpool but travelled west to the North Wales coastal resort of Rhyl. As it was, for all his protestations that this *was* the truth, Hanratty was not able to give an address or a name for the guest house in which he claimed to have spent the night. However, he could give a description, and was emphatic that there was a green bath in the attic room in which he stayed. While the trial progressed, the boarding houses in the town of Rhyl were searched for the green bath. The guest house called Ingledene, run by Mrs. Grace Jones, was as Hanratty had described it; furthermore Mrs. Jones recognised a photograph of Hanratty and agreed to come down to London to give evidence at his trial. Unfortunately, through a small lapse of protocol (Mrs. Jones inadvertently spoke to another witness in the case and then denied it) her credibility as a witness was seriously undermined. As part of the Rhyl alibi, Hanratty also recounted going to visit an old acquaintance named Terry Jones. When he saw that Jones's taxi-cab was not outside the house (a sure sign that he was away from home) Hanratty left.

After 22 arduous days, Mr. Justice Gorman sent the jury out to consider their verdict. They returned twice—once for further guidance from his Lordship, and a second time (much to his irritation) to ask for refreshments. After a retirement of ten hours, the jury finally delivered its verdict of guilty. On 3

April 1962, James Hanratty wrote a final letter to his parents:

> . . . I have always loved you and Dad and all of my family
> and I don't think there is a son anywhere in the world that
> loves his Mum and Dad as much as I do at this stage.
> Though I will never see you again, through the fault of
> others, I will know in my own mind, as my love for you is
> very strong, your love for me will be just as strong . . . I am
> sitting here Mum and you have been on my mind all eve-
> ning. But I will be glad when morning does come . . .

The following morning James Hanratty walked with dignity
on to the scaffold at Bedford Gaol.

But already serious doubts were beginning to be expressed
about the safety of Hanratty's conviction. In particular Jean
Justice had already begun a campaign on Hanratty's behalf
before the execution. On that November day in 1961, when
Hanratty had stood in the dock of the magistrate's court at
Ampthill, his unlikely champion sat just feet away in the public gallery. The 31-year-old son of a Belgian diplomat, Justice
was about to embark upon a crusade which would last 30 years
until his untimely death in July 1990. In particular, Jean Justice cultivated the acquaintance of the enigmatic Peter Alphon,
one-time police suspect in the A6 case, and over the course
of years encouraged Alphon to make various confessions. In
one of his books on the case, Jean Justice recalled a phantas-
magoric journey by car, in the company of barrister friend
Jeremy Fox and Alphon, to the fatal cornfield at Dornley
Reach:

> . . . I was riding through the night with the A6 murderer.
> This time he was sitting where Valerie Storie had sat. As I
> studied his dark head against the windscreen, a gust of fear
> swept over me and I began trembling convulsively. I had
> suddenly realised what Peter's next move would be, for he
> would have only one name for what I now had to do: Be-
> trayal . . .

In a dramatic and unexpected telephone call to Jean Justice in March 1964, Peter Alphon revealed not only the real motive for the A6 murder, but also named the man (referred to subsequently as "Mr. X" to avoid libel suits) who paid him to "separate" Michael Gregsten and Valerie Storie. In October of the same year Jean Justice's *Murder vs. Murder* was published in Paris by the Olympia Press. The book named Alphon as the A6 murderer and was produced abroad to evade Britain's prevailing libel laws.

Just under one year later, in December 1965, investigative journalist and veteran campaigner Paul Foot entered the arena with Justice and Fox, and six years later compiled his immensely persuasive summary of the case for Hanratty's innocence *Who Killed Hanratty?* (Jonathan Cape, London 1971). In the meantime the issue of *Queen* magazine for 14 September 1966 contained an article by Foot, naming Peter Alphon as the A6 killer for the first time in a British publication. Alphon countered with a denial on the BBC *Panorama* programme, and furthermore demanded that the Home Office compensate him over alleged persecution by Jean Justice. On the strength of evidence presented in the programme, Home Secretary Roy Jenkins decided that there was a case to answer in the matter of James Hanratty's alibi.

One of the most dramatic performances in the whole troubled case took place on 12 May 1967, when Peter Alphon called his "World Press Conference" in the bar of the Hôtel du Louvre, Paris, for the sole purpose of confessing publicly to the A6 crimes: "I shall also produce proof," he claimed. In fact the proof turned out to be that he had received £5,000 into his account at Lloyds Bank—payment, he insisted, for "breaking up" the relationship between Michael Gregsten and Valerie Storie.

Five days after this charade, Peter Alphon repeated his confession on the ITN programme *Dateline*, and then three days later, on 21 May, while he was in Dublin, retracted his confessions in an interview with *People* newspaper crime reporter Ken Gardner. Alphon later telephoned Paul Foot to announce that the *People* retraction was a lie concocted by Ken Gardner. On 26 May, Foot and Jean Justice telephoned Alphon in Dublin, this time recording the calls, during which Peter Alphon

once again confessed to murder, implicated "Mr. X" and confirmed this latest statement in a letter to Paul Foot. Alphon
confessed several more times to the A6 murder: to Home Secretary Roy Jenkins on 28 September 1967; to Home Secretary
James Callaghan on 15 December of the same year, and again
in October of the following year.

And so the evidence collected by the then well-organised
"A6 Committee" founded by Justice, Fox, Foot, and by 1968
including the late John Lennon and his wife Yoko Ono, was
painstakingly collated and woven into a powerful case which,
they hoped, would persuade the new Home Secretary, Reginald Maudling, to institute an official enquiry; this was later
undertaken by Lewis Hawser, a senior Queen's Counsel. Hawser reported, predictably, that in his opinion there was no reason to question the original verdict in the Hanratty case, and
so the campaign went on, and on.

Jean Justice died in 1990, but as if to prove that old prov-
erbs sometimes have a grain of truth, a silver lining appeared
in the person of Bob Woffinden, himself no stranger to the
crusade against miscarriages of justice. Woffinden was at the
time working on a new film analysis of the A6 case, imagi-
natively sponsored by Channel 4 television, called *Hanratty—
The Mystery of Deadman's Hill.*

As well as new evidence questioning the strength of Valerie
Storie's identification of Hanratty, and further information on
police interviews that cast shadows over Peter Alphon's evidence, the programme also introduced a most remarkable document in the form of a new, detailed, *written* confession by
Alphon to the shootings on Deadman's Hill. Sadly, this information has also met with the customary blank-wall response
from the British Home Office.

However, there is one possible solution, a solution never
even dreamt of at the time of the A6 murder. It has been
revealed that, because the crime involved sexual assault, there
exists as part of the tangible evidence in police possession
semen samples recovered from the victim's clothing. These
biological samples could, with no difficulty, be subjected to
DNA profiling in order to prove once and for all time whether
or not James Hanratty was the attacker. Clearly Hanratty him-

self is unavailable to provide a control sample for comparison, but it is in the nature of DNA to carry unique hereditary factors which would enable another member of the same family to provide the sample—James's brother and tireless champion, Michael, has offered complete co-operation in any scientific tests. Professor Alex Jeffreys, the scientist responsible for the discovery and development of DNA profiling, has expressed his willingness to conduct the tests himself. Nevertheless, for reasons known only to themselves, Scotland Yard and the Home Office have refused the Hanratty family's solicitor, Mr. Geoffrey Bindman, access to this vital evidence. It is difficult not to be deeply suspicious of this official refusal to pursue the truth. As Bob Woffinden observed, "it is a classic Catch 22 situation"—Scotland Yard will not release the samples until the Home Office reopens the case, and the Home Office will not reopen the case without strong new evidence, such as a DNA profile.

AUSTRALIA
THE MAN WHO "MURDERED" HIMSELF

Between June 1961 and November 1962 the savagely emasculated corpses of four vagrants were found in various parts of Sydney. In one of the most bizarre episodes in Australian homicide, one of the bodies was identified as Allan Brennan—which came as a great surprise to those who knew Allan Brennan and regularly saw him, apparently alive and well, going about his business around the city. Police investigations, however, revealed that Brennan's real name was William McDonald, and that far from being a victim, McDonald was "his own" murderer. What began as an entirely coincidental misidentification ultimately led to the arrest of a serial killer. The gross perversion of the killer's sexual mutilations was attributed by

(continued)

psychiatrists to an incident in McDonald's youth when he had been indecently assaulted by a corporal while serving in the Army.

1963

UNITED STATES
ASSASSINATION OF PRESIDENT JOHN F. KENNEDY

The most famous assassination in modern world history, the incident has inspired more theories and counter-theories than any other crime.

> All my dreams of love are dim.
> I kill myself in killing him.
> I am of Satan, the expression
> Of evil will through my aggression.
> (Richard Eberhart, *The Killer*)*

Saturday, 23 November 1963†

KENNEDY ASSASSINATED

President Kennedy is dead. He was assassinated today when a sniper's bullet felled him as he rode slowly in an open-top car through a cheering Dallas crowd, his wife Jacqueline beside him. With the Kennedys in their car were Governor John Connally of Texas and Mrs. Connally. The President was waving to the crowd lining the route. The crowd was cheering,

---

*From *On Poetry and Power*, a collection of verses and texts on the assassination of President Kennedy. Basic Books, New York, 1964.
†This text is a composite derived from contemporary newspaper accounts of the assassination.

even though Texas is an anti-Kennedy state. As the presidential convoy approached a huge underpass Mrs. Kennedy waved and smiled too, saying: "You can't say Dallas isn't friendly to you." That was the same moment the gunman chose to open fire. The first bullet, fired from above, from a nearby warehouse, hit President Kennedy in the right temple and passed down to his neck. The second and third struck Governor Connally in the chest and wrist. President Kennedy slumped over in the back seat, face down; blood poured from his head. Mrs. Kennedy cried out "Oh, no!" and fell to her knees to cradle his head in her lap. Governor Connally remained half-seated, slumped to the left, there was blood on his forehead and face and blood was spattered over the limousine and over Mrs. Kennedy's pink wool suit. At once everything was panic and turmoil.

President Kennedy's limp, unconscious form was still cradled in his wife's arms when, five minutes later, the limousine with an escort of police and Secret Service cars reached Dallas's Parklands Hospital. Then came the desperate half-hour while doctors struggled to do what they could. Surgeons, doctors and two priests were rushed to the hospital as the desperate battle for the President's life began. The White House physician Rear-Admiral George Burkley dashed to the hospital to set up the emergency operating theatre where the President was being given oxygen and transfusions of Type B blood. An operation was performed to relieve his breathing.

Father Oscar Hubert of Holy Trinity Church, Dallas, administered the Last Sacrament of the Roman Catholic Church to President Kennedy, and at 1 p.m. (7:30 p.m. British time) he was dead. Surgeons Dr. Kemp Clark and Dr. Malcolm Parry faced a stunned Press and described the 30-minute fight to save the President's life. Dr. Parry said: "We never had any hope of saving him. Immediate respiration methods were taken, but the President's condition did not allow complete resuscitation. He was critical and moribund . . . we inserted chest tubes, but the President lost his heart action."

"Flash—Dallas. Kennedy seriously wounded. Perhaps fatally." Now we know he has died in Jackie's arms. And the rest is silence. What is there to say? For Kennedy was of my generation. He fought my war. He endured our peace. All the songs he sang as he grew up, I sang too . . . And all his hopes for a better world, for his two young children, and mine, were my hopes.

(Bruce Rothwell, American columnist)

Once again an assassin's bullet had changed the course of American history.

SUSPECT

An hour after the President's death was announced from Parkland Hospital, as a vast manhunt for the killer got under way, there was a dramatic shootout in another part of Dallas. Police received a tip-off that a man suspected of being President Kennedy's killer was in the Texas Theatre, a cinema in the Oak Cliff area. Patrolmen John D. Tippit and M. N. Macdonald burst into the cinema, saw their quarry, and Officer Tippit opened fire. The man shot back and Tippit fell dead. Macdonald leaped on the gunman and in the struggle that followed the officer received a gash in his face. The fugitive was overpowered and arrested, and is reported to have said: "Well, it's all over now." A police statement issued later named the man as Lee Harvey Oswald, chief suspect in the killing of the President. Already the police had identified the window from which the fatal shot had been fired—on the fifth storey of a book depository. On the floor of the room detectives found a rifle—said to be a 7.65mm German Mauser—with one bullet in the chamber, and three empty cartridge cases on the floor. The gnawed remains of a fried chicken showed the killer had waited some time with his rifle beside him. Lee Harvey Oswald was employed as a stock clerk in the same building.

Something of Oswald's strange life history now began to emerge. He was an ex-US marine who had defected to Russia in 1959, but had defected back again, arriving in America with a Russian wife and baby daughter in May 1962. He turned up later in New Orleans where he became chairman of the pro-Castro committee "Fair Play for Cuba."

Monday, 25 November 1963

"I DID IT FOR HER"

The man accused of assassinating President Kennedy was himself shot dead today—in a Dallas police station. Fifty-year-old Jack Ruby, owner of the Carousel Lounge striptease club, was among a crowd surrounding armed police transferring Lee Harvey Oswald to a Texas jail when suddenly Ruby sprang forward and pushed a snub .38 revolver into Oswald's stomach and pulled the trigger. Oswald simply cried out "Oh!" and fell to the ground. There was pandemonium; a police lieutenant jumped on Ruby and disarmed him as officers drew their guns and surrounded Oswald, half-pulling half-carrying him to the lift. A few hours later Lee Harvey Oswald died in Emergency Ward Two of Parkland Hospital; President Kennedy had died in Ward One two days before.

Taking the arrest of Jack Ruby on a murder charge as an opportunity to issue a statement, Police Captain Will Fritz announced: "There's no doubt in my mind that Oswald was the man who killed the President. We have all the evidence. As far as I am concerned the case is closed." One thing is certain—the disgrace of the Dallas police is now complete. They have already been criticised for their lack of precaution in the Kennedy shooting; now they have let Suspect No. 1 be shot down before their very eyes. As for Jack Ruby, he was revelling in his newfound celebrity. He told the Press: "I did not want to be a hero, I did it for Mrs. Jacqueline Kennedy. I wanted to spare her the grief and the agony of having to return to Dallas and testify in this man's trial." His lawyer, Mr. Tom Howard, said: "Mr. Ruby is a very fine man and was a great admirer of President Kennedy . . . there are many people here pitching for him."

Meanwhile the Moscow morning newspapers were leading with the story "Murderers of President Kennedy are trying to cover their traces; the police give no answers to justified questions." In East Berlin similar reports were being fed to the people, claiming that Lee Harvey Oswald was "a scapegoat for a Right-wing plot."

And so before the late President's body had even been buried, the conspiracy stories were circulating. And in the thirty years

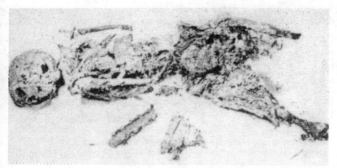

The decomposed and charred body of Mrs. Rachel Dobkin

Mrs. Dobkin's dental record as drawn by her dentist and matched with the skull of the body in the crypt

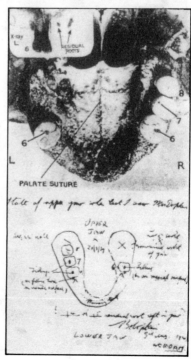

Contemporary newspaper photograph of Karl Hulten

Elizabeth Marina Jones

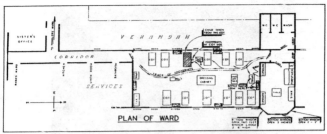

Track of the killer's footprints through the children's ward

The Winchester bottle

Peter Griffiths

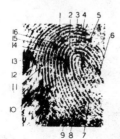

(Left) The print found on the Winchester bottle; (right) Peter Griffiths's fingerprint

The dapper Mr. Haigh

Haigh's Crawley "workshop"

Gaston Dominici, handcuffed and under heavy police guard (Popperfoto)

Christopher Craig (Syndication International)

Derek Bentley

(Left) *Mrs. Bonnar, alias "Lady Menzies," at her marriage to "Lord Menzies"* (Syndication International)

John Ronald Chesney— Lieutenant-Commander turned smuggler

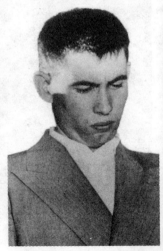

Jack Gilbert Graham (Topham)

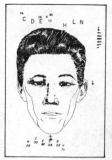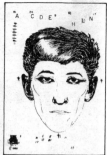

Edwin Bush, flanked by the two Identikit pictures which led to his arrest

Alphon
(Hulton
Deutsch)

Hanratty
(Syndication
International)

Interior of Louis Meier's antiquities shop showing (center right) the collection of swords

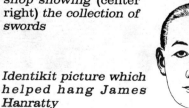

Identikit picture which helped hang James Hanratty

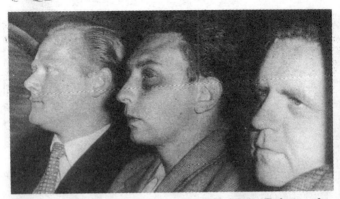

Podola on his way to remand in Brixton Prison; the controversial bruises still visible on his face (Syndication International)

Dr. Gilbert Bogle

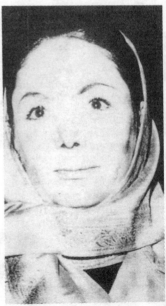

"Red-headed Gloria"

Hannah Tailford
(Hulton Deutsch)

Irene Lockwood
(Syndication
International)

Margaret McGowan

Helen Barthelemy

Mary Fleming

Bridie O'Hara

*Identikit picture of "Jack the
Stripper" circulated to pros-
titutes throughout London's
West End*

Graham Young as he saw himself; a photo-booth snap

Diagram showing the distribution of Speck's victims around their shared apartment

Richard Speck (Syndication International)

Two of the modern world's most notorious killers, Ian Brady and Myra Hindley (Syndication International)

The Hosein brothers, Arthur (left) *and Nizamodeen* (Syndication International)

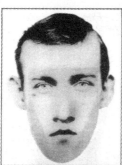

Identikit image of the killer of Mrs. Patience

John Brook, sentenced to life for the murder of Muriel Patience

The unfortunate George Ince

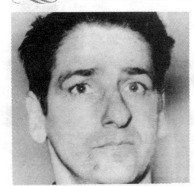

Albert DeSalvo under arrest (Topham)

"Butch" DeFeo in the care of the police (Topham)

Lesley Whittle (Popperfoto)

The "Black Panther" as his victims saw him

Police artist's impression of "Son of Sam"

"I'm Sam," the true face of the "Son of Sam" killer (Topham)

Map showing the distribution of the "Son of Sam's" attacks

The Reverend Jim Jones (Topham)

Early Identikit of the "Ripper"

Official police photograph of Nilsen (Metropolitan Police)

Sheila Caffel and her sons
(Anglia Press Agency)

The strain starts to show
as Jeremy Bamber is
taken to jail (Syndication
International)

Nevill and June Bamber
(Anglia Press Agency)

Newspaper headlines
declare Bamber's guilt
(Syndication Interna-
tional)

Robert Sartin arriving at court (Syndication International)

A remarkably accurate police artist's impression of the "Railway Killer"

John Francis Duffy (Syndication International)

Rachel McLean with John Tanner (Rex Features)

since the tragic and untimely death of John F. Kennedy the plots have escalated in number and absurdity. Few groups have escaped blame for the "plot" at one time or another. The Warren Commission was set up to investigate the evidence, and in 1964 submitted its report to President Johnson—in brief, it found that Lee Harvey Oswald was acting alone when he shot the President and they could find no evidence of a conspiracy. Inevitably, the Warren Commission was itself accused of perpetuating a conspiracy and of a cover-up. This accusation was formalised in the 1976 report of the House of Representatives Select Committee on Assassinations. This concluded that President Kennedy had "probably been assassinated as the result of a conspiracy," suggesting that two gunmen were involved and, not for the first time, the Mafia were suggested as the culprits. And so the conspiracy theories multiplied and continue to multiply. Buried somewhere is the needle of truth, but it has been surrounded by an impossibly huge haystack of rumour, myth and, above all, secrecy.

UNITED STATES
THE CASE OF THE BAD LOSER

It is quite extraordinary how little some people are prepared to kill for. We have all become familiar with the tragic stories of desperate attackers preying on innocent strangers for the small change in their pockets or purses; but consider the case of Mark Fein. At the age of 32, New York businessman Fein was at least a millionaire, and a small part of that hard-earned fortune was devoted to financing his less certain speculations on horse racing, through the intermediary of Mr. Rubin Markowitz, a bookmaker. In November 1963 Rubin, the betting man's friend, was dragged from the Harlem River, his bloated body the heavier for four .22 calibre slugs. As might be expected from a tale set against this backdrop of the twilight world of illegal gambling, there was the inevitable "moll"—in this case a redhead

(continued)

with a greedy nature and criminal inclinations named Gloria Kendall. Gloria confided to detectives investigating Rubin Markowitz's premature retirement from the turf that she had been in Mark Fein's apartment when the trunk containing Rubin's corpse had been collected for disposal; she also mentioned that Fein had owed him a gambling debt. With commendable impartiality, a jury preferred to believe Miss Kendall's version of the story to that concocted by the influential Mr. Fein—resulting in the latter being sentenced to a prison term of thirty years to life. The question remains: why should so wealthy a man commit murder to avoid paying what turned out to be a very modest gambling debt? Was he just a bad loser?

AUSTRALIA
THE BOGLE-CHANDLER MYSTERY

One of Australia's most enduring mysteries of true crime involved the strange deaths of physicist Dr. Gilbert Stanley Bogle and Mrs. Margaret Chandler after a New Year's Eve party in Sydney in 1963. The two bodies were found the following morning, and although Bogle appeared to be dressed, his clothes had just been draped over him. Mrs. Chandler's state of dress was rather more complete, but the position of her skirt indicated some sexual activity. Both bodies contained large quantities of alcohol, and it was assumed that this had some connection with their untimely departure from life. However, in spite of the most exhaustive forensic tests, no definite cause of death could be established. Dr. Bogle's sensitive position as a Government scientist led to much wild speculation centring on international conspiracies to undermine the Australian defence programme, and in particular that Bogle had been engaged
(continued)

in the development of a death-ray weapon. A more prosaic explanation was offered by the fact that, when he was in party mood, Dr. Bogle indulged in the hallucinogenic drug LSD, and, for what he supposed to be its aphrodisiac qualities, encouraged his paramours to do the same. One slightly sinister postscript is that although the case was considered closed in Australia, the United States Federal Bureau of Investigation kept an open file on the Bogle case for some years.

1964

UNITED KINGDOM
WILLIAM BRITTLE

The Bugs and Beetles Case. *Although William Brittle provided an alibi for the time his alleged victim was killed, Professor Keith Simpson, with his unique knowledge of the breeding cycles of the insects that infest dead bodies, was able to disprove it.*

It was maggots that they were looking for on that June day in 1964; the two thirteen-year-olds scouted through Bracknell woods in the hope of finding a dead pigeon or squirrel, any dead meat that might be home to the fat white maggots that they needed for fishing bait. Then they found them; thousands of the things. The excitement ended as soon as the boys saw what the maggots were feeding on; as soon as they saw the arm. Terry King and Paul Fay, bright lads, went to the police: "There's a dead body buried in the woods!"

For pathologist Keith Simpson the call-out was routine—a body discovered in suspicious circumstances. Beneath the covering of moss and leaves was the body of a man, lying on his back, his head wrapped in towelling. The corpse was too far decomposed for any normal time-of-death tests—in fact the police thought it might have been there for up to two months. But they had reckoned without a very special study that Keith Simpson had made his own. Simpson put the time of death as at least nine or ten *days*—"but probably not more than twelve; it's astonishing how quickly maggots will eat up flesh."

The pathologist had routinely collected samples of the insect infestation and identified the maggots as those of the common blue-bottle (*Calliphora erythrocephalus*): "The larvae I was looking at were mature, indeed elderly, fat, indolent, third-stage maggots, but they were not in pupa cases. Therefore I estimated that the eggs had been laid nine or ten days earlier. Adding a little more time to allow for the blue-bottles getting to the dead body, I reckoned death had occurred on 16 or 17 June."[*]

Post-mortem examination revealed that the bones of the larynx had been crushed, and death had resulted from blood seeping into the windpipe. Identifiable features indicated that the victim was Peter Thomas, reported missing from his home at Lyndney on 16 June. It was also learned that Thomas had lent the sum of £2,000 to a man named Brittle. Under questioning William Brittle admitted that he had met Thomas at Lyndney on 16 June—in fact he had gone there specifically to repay the loan, or so he claimed.

Now it came to light that Brittle had been trained in unarmed combat while serving in the Army—information which was not lost on Professor Simpson, whose report on Thomas's throat injuries were entirely consistent with a blow such as a karate-chop. It was the firm belief of the police that Brittle *had* visited Peter Thomas on 16 June, not to repay the £2,000, but to dispose of his debt rather more decisively; he had then transported Thomas's body in the boot of a car to Bracknell woods. Unfortunately, the police had an independent witness who adamantly insisted that he had seen Peter Thomas, alive and well, in Gloucester on 20 June.

In the end William Brittle was committed for trial and the main scientific evidence was offered by Professor Simpson. Simpson testified that he had found maggots of the common blue-bottle (*Calliphora erythrocephalus*) on the corpse, and that they had not yet pupated; this put the time since death at nine or ten days. Though he was appearing as an expert witness for the defence, the eminent entomologist Professor McKenny-Hughes corroborated Simpson's findings, and William Brittle was convicted of murder and sentenced to life imprisonment.

[*]*Forty Years of Murder,* Professor Keith Simpson, Harrap, London, 1978.

AUSTRALIA
THE BEAMISH
CONTROVERSY

During the first nine months of 1963 the inhabitants of Perth were put in fear by a spate of brutal and apparently pointless murders. Despite assistance from London's Scotland Yard and the United States Federal Bureau of Investigation, it was a piece of gratuitous luck that led to the apprehension of the assassin. A young couple had found a rifle hidden behind a rock, which forensic identification identified as the weapon used in the last of the killings. When Eric Cooke, a Perth truck-driver and burglar, went to retrieve his gun from its hiding place on 1 September he was arrested. Rejecting a defence plea of insanity, the jury found Cooke guilty of murder and he was sentenced to death. While awaiting execution, Cooke made a further confession and admitted to a murder for which a deaf mute named Beamish was already serving time. In one of the most controversial decisions in the history of Australian criminal law, the authorities decided not to accept Cooke's unsolicited admission of guilt, and Beamish remained in prison until he was paroled in 1971. Eric Edgar Cooke was hanged at Fremantle on 26 October 1964.

UNITED STATES
THE BOY WHO COULDN'T KEEP HIS MOUTH SHUT

An inadequate youth, Charles Schmid compensated by living in a world of make-believe and violent fantasy. In May 1964 he declared his intention to kill, and in company with two friends picked up fifteen-year-old Alleen Row, drove her out into the desert, and raped and killed her. He then began to boast of other murders—among them two girls who had recently been reported missing. In the end Schmid's friends became so terrified of him that they turned him in to the police. After a lengthy and complex trial, Charles Howard Schmid was sentenced to death, but narrowly escaped execution when the US Supreme Court temporarily suspended capital punishment. He died later in prison.

1965

UNITED KINGDOM "JACK THE STRIPPER"

The first modern British crime to be recognised as "serial murder." Although it is officially unsolved, one police suspect in the case committed suicide after questioning.

The first victim of the killer who became known as "Jack the Stripper" was Hannah Tailford, found strangled on the foreshore of the Thames near Hammersmith Bridge on 2 February 1964. She was naked but for a pair of stockings, and her underwear had been forced into her mouth. Nobody could have foretold that the death of one member of that vulnerable profession was the overture to one of London's most notorious cases of serial murder.

At first the death of Hannah Tailford could have been attributed to either murder or suicide. Dr. Donald Teare, the pathologist called in to prepare the post-mortem report, found bruising around the jaw, but this could as easily have been sustained from a fall as from a deliberate blow. In the end the coroner, Mr. Gavin Thurston, returned an open verdict.

Two months after the discovery of Hannah Tailford's body a second prostitute was found dead on the foreshore of the Thames at Duke's Meadows, Chiswick, about three hundred yards from where Hannah's remains had been found. The woman was later identified as Irene Lockwood, who also called herself Sandra Russell.

Investigating officers, then under Detective Superintendent Frank Davies, had entertained their share of the publicity seekers and lunatics who dog any such enquiry, including a believable 54-year-old bachelor caretaker who confessed to one of the murders while in custody on a theft charge; Kenneth Archibald was eventually found not guilty and set free after a trial lasting six days.

Twenty-two-year-old Helen Barthelemy was found sixteen days after the second victim, Irene Lockwood, on 24 March. Although she was naked, the pattern deviated in that the body had been dumped away from the river, in a driveway behind Swincombe Avenue, Brentford. Four of Mrs. Barthelemy's teeth were missing, though there was no bruising consistent with this being the result of a blow. Helen, or "Teddie" as she was called, had originally come from Scotland, reaching London via Liverpool and Blackpool's Golden Mile, where she had worked as a striptease dancer and prostitute. It was becoming clear now that a single killer was responsible for this series of murders, and a marked atmosphere of panic was spreading among the capital's vice girls. In the meantime, Commander George Hatherill, head of CID at Scotland Yard, made a personal appeal to the city's prostitutes to put aside their time-honoured mistrust of the police and to come forward in strictest confidence if they had information about men who "are odd or eccentric in their association with prostitutes, especially if they force them to strip naked." The appeal certainly had an effect, and although in the end it did not advance the inquiry much, dozens of street girls reported to Shepherd's Bush police station. A new team consisting of women officers was attached to the murder team to pose as prostitutes in the hope of flushing "Jack" from his lair. However, three months after his last attack, "Jack the Stripper" claimed another victim.

In the early morning of 14 July 1964, George Heard, a chauffeur, found the naked body of a woman in a seated position at the entrance to a garage in Berrymead Road, Chiswick. Mary Fleming had arrived in the capital from Scotland, stopping off at Barrow-in-Furness to get married. However, at the time of her death she was living alone with her two young children in a room in Lancaster Gardens; she supported herself and her family on the proceeds of prostitution.

By now forensic tests on the body of "Teddie" Barthelemy

had revealed particles adhering to the skin which were identified under the microscope as flakes of the kind of paint used
to spray cars; the laboratory also reported finding identical
traces on the body of Mary Fleming.

The fifth victim, another prostitute from the Notting Hill
district, went missing on 23 October. Margaret McGowan had
been working her beat with a fellow prostitute the night she
disappeared, but it was not until 25 November that her naked
and decomposing body was found in a makeshift grave at
Hornton Street, Kensington; she was identified by the tattoos
on her left arm.

Then, on 16 February the following year Bridie O'Hara, the
sixth of the ''Hammersmith Nudes'' was found on a patch of
waste land near the Thames at Acton. Dublin-born Bridie had
last been seen on 11 February at the Shepherd's Bush Hotel;
the cause of her death was asphyxiation after an unsuccessful
attempt had been made to strangle her. Her front teeth were
missing, and semen was found in the back of her throat.

Public concern over the apparent inability of the police to
solve this spate of brutal murders now resulted in Scotland
Yard's Assistant Commissioner summoning back from holiday
Detective Chief Superintendent John du Rose, one of the
Met's most experienced officers. Du Rose had already earned
the nickname ''Four Day Johnnie'' for the legendary speed
with which he solved his cases; he was going to need every
bit of that reputation now.

Du Rose immediately homed in on the most significant forensic clue—the paint traces—and organised a huge squad of
searchers who made a sweep through no less than 24 square
miles around the Thames at Hammersmith and Chiswick, min-
utely inspecting private and industrial buildings for evidence
of painting activity.

After exhaustive searching, officers located the paint-spray
shop where four of the bodies had been stored prior to disposal
in or beside the river; furthermore, it was located close to
where Bridie O'Hara's body had been found on the Heron
Trading Estate.

The fact that the women were all abducted between the
hours of 11 p.m. and 1 a.m., and dumped between 5 a.m. and
6 a.m., led police to make an educated guess that they were

looking for a night-shift worker. A list of suspects was drawn up, but despite anticipation that an arrest was imminent, no charge was ever brought in the case. Nevertheless, a 45-year-old-man whose name has never been revealed killed himself during the investigation; his suicide note read, in part, that he was "unable to stand it any longer." When Superintendent du Rose ordered an inquiry into the man's background it was discovered that he was a night security guard whose rounds included the paint shop on the Heron Trading Estate. Although there seemed to be no other evidence to incriminate the man, John du Rose wrote in his autobiography (*Murder Was My Business*): "I know the identity of Jack the Stripper—but he cheated me of an arrest by committing suicide."

1966

UNITED STATES
JACK HENRY ABBOTT

In the Belly of the Beast. *Having already spent a total of 21 years in prison, Abbott stabbed a fellow prisoner to death and earned another fourteen. At about this time his cause was taken up by prominent American author Norman Mailer who succeeded in engineering his early parole. Once out, Jack Abbott killed again. He has written two best-selling accounts of his time in prison.*

When Jack Abbott first came to the attention of American author Norman Mailer he was 37 years old. Of those 37 years, he had spent more than 21 in prison—fourteen in solitary confinement. In 1966 he stabbed a fellow prisoner to death and was sentenced to an additional fourteen years. During this time Abbott engrossed himself in an intensive programme of self-education, becoming familiar with most of the major branches of philosophy and in the end choosing Marxism for himself. Mailer was at this time engaged on writing *The Executioner's Song*, an analysis of the life and crimes of convicted double-murderer Mark Gary Gilmore. When Abbott learned of the Gilmore project through a newspaper article, he wrote a letter to Mailer offering the benefit of his own experience of violence in prisons; it was his contention that only a person who has endured a decade or more of incarceration can fully appreciate the principle and practice of institutional violence.

The result was an extraordinary series of letters in which

Mailer recognised "an intellectual, a radical, a potential leader, a man obsessed with a vision of more elevated human relations in a better world that revolution could forge." These letters were to constitute the basis of the best-selling autobiography *In the Belly of the Beast*. As a result of this success, and Mailer's conviction that he was "a powerful and important American writer," Abbott was released on parole. He worked for a brief period as Norman Mailer's researcher, and enjoyed the attentions of the New York literati; but the years of institutionalisation had ill-equipped Jack Abbott for a life outside prison.

In the early hours of the morning of 18 July 1981, Abbott became involved in an argument with 22-year-old Richard Adan, an actor and playwright then working as a waiter at the Bini Bon diner on Second Avenue, New York. Abbott had taken strong exception to being told that the men's lavatory was for staff use only, and reacted in the only way that seemed natural to him—he stabbed Adan to death. After two months on the run, Abbott was arrested in Louisiana and sentenced to be confined in the maximum-security prison, at Marion, Illinois.

In 1981, shortly after Adan's death, his wife Ricci had begun the proceedings to extract financial compensation for the "wrongful death" and "pain and suffering" caused to Richard Adan by his killer. In 1983, Abbott had been found liable for monetary damages, but the motion had been legally blocked by him for seven years until this present jury was empanelled to determine the amount of those damages.

On 5 June 1990, Jack Abbott was back in court again. Now aged 45, neat in a brown tweed sport jacket and jeans and wearing steel-rimmed spectacles, he declined the offer of legal aid and claimed instead his right to act as his own lawyer.

Under what has become known as the "Son of Sam"* law, criminals are unable to profit financially from stories about their crimes. In Jack Abbott's case, the considerable income

---

*During 1976-77 a wave of murders hit New York leaving six people dead and a further seven seriously wounded; the victims were all young couples sitting in parked cars. Ironically, the killer was traced through a traffic vio-

from *In the Belly of the Beast*, as well as a second book, *My Return*, and the subsequent film rights, was being held jointly by the New York County Sheriff and the New York State Crime Victims Board.

In *My Return*, Abbott discussed the Adan stabbing, and dismissed Mrs. Adan's claim that her husband endured "pain and suffering," commenting that far from it, he had benefited from a quick, painless death. Abbott also contended that because the whole argument only arose because of Richard Adan's apparent "lack of respect," he was at least in part responsible for his own death. The confrontation the court had been waiting for took place at the end of the fifth day, when Jack Abbott questioned Mrs. Ricci Adan.

"Are you under the impression I killed your husband?"
"You killed my husband. How could you do that?"
"What did I do?"
"I know you killed my husband with a knife. I know you thrust it into his chest and he died. He's dead."
"Does nothing else matter to you than that Richard Adan died at my hands?"
"Yes. Something has to be done. There has to be some kind of a balance, some retribution for what has happened to my husband. Some kind of payback. I don't know what."
"Did you attend my trial?"
"No I did not. I was in shock. I didn't want to see it all. I didn't want to see you."
"So you don't know what happened?"

---

lation ticket issued to him on the night of his last murder; when police traced the car they found on the back seat a loaded .44 Bulldog revolver which had been used in previous killings. Thus the murderer who had written an arrogant note to the police some months before claiming: "I am a monster. I am the Son of Sam," was identified as David Berkowitz.

Under arrest, Berkowitz claimed that mysterious voices had been ordering him to kill, and explained that his nickname had been taken from a neighbour, Sam Carr, whose black labrador dog kept him awake at night.

In August 1977, the Son of Sam was sentenced to 365 years' imprisonment, and his crimes attracted considerable media exploitation.

"I don't know."

"Do you care?"

"Objection!" yelled Mrs. Adan's lawyer. "You don't have to answer," responded Acting Justice Arber.

Such overtly provocative questioning, including the suggestion that her late husband's life was "not worth a dime," soon reduced Mrs. Adan to tears, a condition which Abbott berated with taunts like "Could you answer the question without using a Kleenex?" At the same time he sneered quite regularly at Mrs. Adan's continued attempts to secure financial compensation from Richard's untimely death.

On Friday, 15 June 1990, after six hours of deliberation and considerable use of an electronic calculator, the jury, to the apparent delight of everybody in court except Jack Abbott, awarded Mrs. Ricci Adan $7.575 million damages ($5.575 million for loss of her husband's potential earnings and $2 million for the pain he suffered). Before he was returned to continue his sentence at Auburn state prison, Jack Abbott commented: "It is a little excessive, your honour, I would say."

UNITED KINGDOM
THE MOORS MURDERS

On 6 May 1966 two killers stood in the courtroom of the Chester Assizes and listened to sentence being passed on them. During the fifteen days that the trial had lasted, the nation had been paralysed with disbelief as they heard recounted a succession of horrors too awful to take in. In the two years since 1964, Ian Brady and his lover Myra Hindley had abducted a number of children, subjected them to unspeakable sexual degradation, then brutally killed them and buried their small bodies on the deserted moors outside Manchester. The court listened in tears to a tape recording made by Hindley of ten-year-old Lesley Ann Downey pleading to be allowed to go home; she never saw home again, only a shallow grave on the bleak Saddleworth

(continued)

Moor. Sentenced to life imprisonment, Brady and Hindley are still confined to jail, still regarded as the epitome of evil. In 1987 new interest was awakened in the so-called ''Moors Murders'' when Myra Hindley confessed to a further two murders and both she and Brady assisted in a search for the bodies. That of Pauline Reade was uncovered on the moors, the remains of Keith Bennett, aged twelve at the time of his death, could not be found.

1967

UNITED KINGDOM
GORDON HAY

Murder at Biggar. *The first case of murder solved by bite-mark comparison, when Gordon Hay left his teeth imprints on the breast of his victim as he sexually assaulted and strangled her.*

What was to become a landmark case in forensic dentistry began on 7 August 1967 with the discovery of the battered and strangled corpse of fifteen-year-old Linda Peacock in a cemetery in Biggar, a small town between Edinburgh and Glasgow. The girl had not been raped, though the clothing on the upper part of her body had been disarranged. An observant police photographer whose job it was to record the scene of the crime and the victim's position drew the police surgeon's attention to an oval bruise-type mark on one of the girl's breasts, consistent, he suggested, with a bite mark. This was quickly confirmed by the pathologist, and Scotland's foremost forensic dentistry expert, Dr. Warren Harvey, was assigned to the team investigating Linda Peacock's murder.

Police officers had already eliminated the 3,000 people so far interviewed in the area. There remained a single group of 29 youths, all inmates of a local detention centre. Harvey suggested as a first step taking dental impressions of each of the men in an attempt to match a set of teeth to the distinctive bite mark on the victim's body. One mark in particular looked as though it might have come from an uncommonly sharp or jagged tooth.

Dr. Harvey was now able, on observation, to reduce to five the number of impressions that could not yet be eliminated from suspicion. At this stage he consulted with Professor Simpson, another pioneer of forensic dentistry, and the two experts concentrated their attention on the "jagged" tooth.

Of the five suspects, only one had a match. Investigations now centred on seventeen-year-old Gordon Hay, who was now known to have been missing from the Borstal dormitory at the time of Linda Peacock's murder; he had been seen returning just before 10:30 that night, dishevelled, breathless, and with mud on his clothes. Equally incriminating was the fact that Hay had met Linda at a local fair the previous day, and commented to a friend that he would like to have sex with her.

Hay willingly, almost eagerly, submitted to a further set of impressions being made of his teeth. From these the watertight evidence that would later convict him of murder was assembled. Closer examination by Warren Harvey revealed sharp-edged, clear-cut pits, like small craters on the tips of the upper and lower right canines—symptoms of a rare disorder called hypo-calcination. The upper pit was larger than the lower, and agreed with the bite mark on the victim's breast. Patient examination of no less than 342 sixteen-and seventeen-year-old boys produced only two with pits, one with a pit and hypo-calcination, and none with two pits.

In February 1968, Dr. Warren Harvey spoke for a whole day from the witness box at Edinburgh's High Court of Justiciary. It was the first time that a Scottish jury had been required to consider bite-mark evidence, and clearly they were impressed. Gordon Hay was eventually convicted of the murder with which he was charged and, on account of his youth, sentenced to be detained "during Her Majesty's pleasure."

UNITED STATES
MASSACRE IN CHICAGO

On the night of 14 July 1966 Corazon Amurao and five friends were at home in their Chicago nurses' residence. In response to a knock Corazon opened the front door and the
(continued)

six girls found themselves captives of Richard Speck who reeked of alcohol and waved a gun in one hand and a knife in the other. Speck then ordered the girls to lie on the floor and bound them with strips torn from a bed-sheet. It was at this point that he went on to assure himself of a place at the top of the list of the world's bloodiest mass murderers. At intervals of twenty minutes Speck dragged the girls one by one into another room and stabbed and strangled them. All, that is, except Corazon Amurao, who managed to wriggle under a bed and was miraculously overlooked by the killer. When Speck finally left, Miss Amurao raised the alarm and it was not long before the murderous Speck was identified by fingerprints left at the scene of his crime. After a brief trial Richard Speck was sentenced to die in the electric chair on 6 June 1967. However, the United States Supreme Court had suspended the death penalty and Speck was resentenced to a term of 400 years' imprisonment. He maintained his innocence until 1978 when he made a full confession. Richard Speck died in prison in 1991.

1968

UNITED STATES
ASSASSINATION OF DR. MARTIN LUTHER KING JR.

For an unbelievable second time in five years a major American politician is shot dead. Less than three months later this figure will increase when Senator Robert Kennedy is also felled by an assassin's bullet.

People have said that it was an assassination just waiting for the opportunity to happen. What is certain is that Dr. Martin Luther King Jr. was not enjoying the greatest of political popularity. On one side the great symbol of non-violent protest found himself assailed by a new wave of young black militants and, on the other, by the white authorities who had only recently witnessed the death of a teenager at a rally led by King.

Martin Luther King had arrived in Memphis, Tennessee, on 28 March 1968, to lead a march of striking dustmen; it had been a disaster, rioting erupted and a sixteen-year-old was shot and killed. Dr. King had already received a lot of death threats over the years but that, as they say, comes with the territory. On 3 April Dr. King was back in Memphis for meetings—prophetically, his flight was delayed by a bomb threat at the airport. During his stay King took room 306 at the Lorraine Motel. On the evening of 4 April, after a day of business appointments, he was in the motel room with Robert Abernathy, an aide, awaiting the arrival of their dinner host Revd. Samuel Kyles to collect them. Kyles arrived at 5:30 p.m., and while they were waiting for Abernathy to get ready, Dr. King stepped on to the small balcony looking out on the back of the motel. At just after six o'clock a shot rang out across the open ground and Dr. King was hurled backwards by the force of a bullet tearing into the right side of his face. Within seconds there was chaos—while Robert Abernathy went running on to the balcony to do what he could for his friend, Revd. Kyles was yelling down the telephone for an ambulance; bystanders were running around helplessly, seeking any kind of cover in case the shooting continued. It did not; a single bullet from the assassin's gun had robbed the civil rights movement of its most charismatic leader. Martin Luther King Jr. lived for less than an hour after being shot; he survived the ambulance journey to St. Joseph's Hospital but died at 7:05 p.m.

Back at the Lorraine Motel, police were already hunting the killer. Because of the tension of recent days in Memphis, and the previous threats to Dr. King's life, a low-key police surveillance was being kept by detectives in the near vicinity. It proved to be a little too low-key in the event, but despite what had been learned from the assassination of President Kennedy only five years earlier it was still all but impossible to protect controversial public figures from attack by a lone sniper with a powerful long-range weapon.

The whole area around the motel had been sealed off, and police had begun to question bystanders. Inside ten minutes they had pieced together a broad scenario of the murder; the shots had been fired from a window opposite the motel, from the direction of South Main Street. After the shooting, witnesses had seen a man run from a rooming house at 418/422 South Main, dump a bundle in a doorway and drive off at speed in a white Ford Mustang with red and white registration plates. The man was described as being between 26 and 36 years old, white, average build and wearing a white shirt under a black suit. It took officers no time to locate the hastily discarded bundle—it contained a high-power rifle and binoculars.

In spite of an all-cars alert, the white Mustang and its driver had, for the moment, got away. However, given the number of clues the fleeing gunman had left behind him, it did not take the police long to come up with a name—James Earl Ray. The puzzling part was that assassinating political leaders was not exactly in Ray's usual line of business. Sure, he was a crook, but a very petty one, and very inept. After a succession of small-time robberies followed by brief terms of imprisonment, Ray earned himself twenty years in the Missouri State Penitentiary for a supermarket robbery in 1959. In 1967 he escaped, and it was while he was on the run that he shot and killed Martin Luther King Jr.

What the police did not know was that after the murder, Ray had sped to Atlanta, Georgia, where he left the Mustang and hopped on a bus to Detroit. From there he travelled to Canada, the location of several of his earlier misdemeanours. In Toronto, Ray applied for a passport in the name of Ramon Sneyd and flew to London; from there he departed for Portugal where he tried to sign on as a mercenary to fight in Africa. Failing in this quest, as he had failed in most of life's quests, James Earl Ray returned to London. By now the FBI had begun to follow his trail—Atlanta, Detroit, Toronto—and it seemed that Ray was doubling back to meet them halfway. Or almost. The FBI had alerted Scotland Yard to the true identity of Mr. Sneyd, and when he tried to refill his rapidly emptying wallet by raiding a London bank, detectives found that the demand note was covered with Ray's fingerprints. Still trying to get a ringside seat for the fighting in Angola, Ray now booked a fare to Brussels where he heard they were recruiting mercenaries. It was another mistake. As he passed through airport security they found his unlicensed handgun; a quick check with Scotland Yard and Ray was arrested and flown, not to Brussels, but back to the welcoming arms of the FBI. The race was over and James Earl Ray, as usual, had lost.

As the result of a plea-bargain, Ray pleaded guilty in his trial in March 1969, and was sentenced to 99 years' imprisonment. He was confined to a secure unit in Nashville Prison, from whence he tried to escape in 1971, 1977 and 1979. As a result of the 1977 escape he actually managed to remain at large for three days before being recaptured. In 1978 Ray was given permission to marry Miss Anna Sandhu.

So, why did James Earl Ray, the undistinguished petty crook from nowhere, become a figure of international notoriety? It is true that he was always known to be neurotic, and around the time of his assassination of Dr. King was receiving therapy for severe depression—but he was no psychopath. He certainly did, though, display an almost desperate need for attention, but for attention of what he considered the right kind—he didn't want to be seen for the nobody that he was. In fact Ray was constantly threatening libel action against journalists and magazines who portrayed him as anything less than the heroic desperado of his own imagination. This was the secret. As one of his analysts later explained: "He yearns to feel he is somebody. The desire for recognition in him is superior to sex, superior to money, superior to self-preservation."

UNITED KINGDOM
THE PROFESSION OF VIOLENCE

Notorious for their Gangland activities in London during the 1950s and 1960s, Ronnie and Reggie Kray were eventually arrested on 8 May 1968. The Krays had made a very lucrative business out of "protection," which, due to their naturally psychopathic tendencies, was characterised by acts of extreme violence; but these were the minor indictments against them at their Old Bailey trial. Heading the charge sheet were the murders of George Cornell (a member of the rival Richardson gang) and Jack "The Hat" McVitie, and the alleged murder of escaped convict Frank Mitchell, known as "The Mad Axeman." Police had been hampered throughout their investigation into the gang's activities by the blanket of fear which the twins had cast over London's East End. For years nobody had dared open their mouth in accusation, but now, with the brothers and their heavies in custody, people began to come forward with information—even members of the Kray's own gang exchanged evidence for immunity from prosecution. After a trial lasting 39 days, during which the catalogue of crime and violence disclosed beggared imagination, Ronald Kray was sentenced to two life terms for murder, his brother

(continued)

Reginald to life for one murder and ten years as an accessory to the other; the recommendation was that they serve not less than 30 years. Other members of the Kray gang, including brother Charles, were sentenced to various terms of imprisonment. Ronald and Reginald Kray are still serving their sentences—Ronald, certified insane, serves his in Broadmoor.

1969

UNITED STATES
CHARLES MANSON *et al*

Family Business. *Manson, professional degenerate and self-styled Messiah, in company with members of his "Family," were responsible for a series of murders which were to become America's "crimes of the century." Despite his incarceration, Manson still has a huge following among young people on the fringe of today's society.*

Manson and his so-called "Family" created shock waves throughout California, a state not unused to bizarre murders and serial killers; shock waves which spread around the world.

An ex-convict, drug addict and all-round dropout, Manson dominated his equally unattractive disciples with a mish-mash of corrupted Biblical philosophy and mistaken interpretations of the lyrics of the Beatles' songs. This, combined with his magnetic sexual attraction to the female members of his Family, ensured Manson's complete physical and spiritual control of the group.

The first publicised murders took place in the summer of 1969. Just after midnight on Saturday 9 August four shadowy figures crept into the grounds of a secluded mansion at 10050 Cielo Drive, Beverly Hills. Manson was not on the raid himself; tonight it was the turn of "Tex" Watson, "Sadie" Atkins, Linda Kasabian and Patricia "Katie" Krenwinkel. The house on Cielo was occupied that night by actress Sharon Tate (her husband, the director Roman Polanski, was away on business) who was heavily pregnant, and four friends. In an orgy of overkill, the Family left all five victims literally butchered. Voytek Frykowski alone was stabbed more than fifty times, slashed, shot and so savagely bludgeoned with the butt of a gun that the weapon shattered. On the front door to the house the word "Pig" was painted in blood. Not one of the murderous gang had the slightest idea whom they had killed—they were just random targets.

Only one person was not pleased with the night's activities—Charlie Manson. When news of the bloodbath came through on the television it apparently offended Charlie's sensibilities that such a messy job had been made of it. He decided to show everybody how it should be done. Two nights later, Manson led Watson, Krenwinkel, van Houten, Atkins and Kasabian to the Silver Lake home of Leno and Rosemary LaBianca and butchered them both. Afterwards Manson and his disciples inscribed slogans in blood on the walls—"Death to the Pigs," "Rise," and "Healter [sic] Skelter" which, according to Manson, signified the time when the blacks of America would rise and wipe out the whites—with the exception of the Family, of course, who would survive and take control. In a final act of gratuitous violence, the word "War" was carved into Leno LaBianca's abdomen with a knife.

Following these utterly mindless killings, the Family went to ground. Susan Atkins was later arrested on a prostitution charge and while she was in custody admitted her part in the Tate murders. The Family were rounded up and charges of murder were laid against the principal members. Manson, Krenwinkel, Atkins and van Houten were tried together, and after one of the most extraordinary trials in California's history, they were convicted and sentenced to death. In view of the state's suspension of capital punishment, the sentences were subsequently reduced to life imprisonment. "Tex" Watson was tried separately with the result that he too was sentenced to life imprisonment.

Although no further charges were brought, there is reason to believe that many other murders, including several of their own members, could be laid at the door of the Family.

And if everybody thinks that Charlie's evil—and crazy, too—then Charlie is the first to agree with them. Since he became eligible for parole a dozen years ago, Manson has insisted on his right to a regular hearing. Not that he seems to take these occasions very seriously—certainly not seriously enough to stand a hope in hell of ever being released—but it is the one time every eighteen months or so when he can guarantee that a mass media committed to keeping the cult of Manson alive will be assembled *en masse* in an adjoining room listening to the proceedings and hanging on Charlie's every word. He rarely disappoints.

In an article on Stephen Kay, the Los Angeles County deputy district attorney whose mission it has been to oppose each and every one of the Manson Family's bids for parole, Martin Kasindorf* related how at the 1981 parole hearing Manson predicted that Stephen Kay would himself be murdered in the San Quentin car park as he left the meeting. Of course, Kay suffered no such dramatic fate, and was there facing Manson across the wooden table at his next parole board. But the point was that everybody *expects* something like this from mad Charlie—so who is he to disappoint them?

Then there was the time when Stephen Kay asked Manson why it was that he spent so much of his free time making scorpions out of the thread unravelled from his socks. By way of explanation, Manson rose in his seat and intoned: "From the world of darkness I did loose demons and devils in the power of scorpions to torment!" Needless to say this put the "Messiah's" parole chances back by a few years.

The year 1986 found Charlie reading his twenty-page handwritten statement, described as "bizarre and rambling" when parole was opposed by no less an authority than California's governor George Deukmejian; in 1989, Manson decided that he would not face the parole board with manacles on his wrists because: "They'll think I'm dangerous." They probably did anyway—but in his absence Charles Milles Manson was predictably denied the opportunity to join the world at large for a few years more.

Ironically, Manson made his latest appeal for freedom on 20 April 1992—it was within hours of the death sentence, the first in California for decades, being carried out on Robert Alton Harris. Manson's own death sentence could not be

The Independent Magazine, 12 August 1989, London.

reinstated, nor, it seemed, was he destined to win his freedom. According to the *Sun*'s correspondent in New York, Charlie surprised his new parole board by announcing: "There's no one as bad as me. I'm everywhere—I'm down in San Diego zoo; I'm in the trees; I'm in your children. Someone has to be insane, we can't all be good guys. They've tried to kill me thirty or forty times in prison; they've poured fire over me.* They haven't found anyone badder than me because there is no one as bad as me—and that's a fact." Charlie had blown his chance yet again.

UNITED STATES
THE ZODIAC KILLINGS

During a nine-month period in 1969 an unknown assassin killed five people and wounded two more in the state of California. The murders were each followed by letters to two San Francisco newspapers; they were so detailed that they could only have been written by the killer, and all of them were signed with a zodiac cross on a circle. Although there were no further killings, the San Francisco Police Department received another "Zodiac" letter in 1974 threatening "something nasty" and claiming a total of 37 murders. "Zodiac" has never been heard from again, and the crimes remain unsolved.

---

*This was a reference to an incident that occurred in September 1984, when Manson took exception to the chanting of a fellow prisoner who had adopted the Hare Krishna faith. In retaliation the man poured paint thinners over Manson and set fire to him.

1970

UNITED KINGDOM
ARTHUR AND
NIZAMODEEN HOSEIN

Murder at Rooks Farm. *A classic modern example of a trial conducted without the body of the victim being found. It has been suggested that Mrs. McKay's body may have been fed to the herd of pigs on the Hoseins' farm.*

In 1970, the headlines were proclaiming one of those rare, but by no means unique tragedies—the "Case of the Missing Body." In this instance the innocent victim was Mrs. Muriel McKay, wife of the deputy chairman of the *News of the World*. Mrs. McKay had been abducted from her home in Wimbledon on 2 December 1969, and ransom demands were made shortly afterwards. The whole kidnap had been bungled from the start: the intended victim had been the wife of millionaire businessman Rupert Murdoch. Then the demands were for a preposterously large amount of money: "We are from America—Mafia M.3. We have your wife . . . You will need a million pounds by Wednesday." It was later agreed that the amount could be paid in two instalments.

In all, eighteen telephone calls of an equally farcical nature were made to an increasingly anxious Alick McKay before, on 22 January, he received a ransom note accompanied by two letters written by his wife in which she admitted that the ordeal was causing her to "deteriorate in health and spirit." Having followed the bewilderingly complex instructions for delivering the money, during which a police officer posed as Mrs.

McKay's son, the kidnappers failed to collect the suitcase. "Mafia M.3" could hardly have failed to notice the extraordinary police presence of about 150 officers in various disguises, and some 50 unmarked cars.

A second attempt to deliver the money proved to be as burlesque; a young couple came across the suitcase full of money where it had been left on a garage forecourt. Good citizens that they were, the Abbotts called in the local force thinking that somebody had mislaid their luggage. But the police, under the experienced leadership of Detective Chief Superintendent Wilfred Smith, had laid their plans well, and when a dark blue Volvo saloon driven by two coloured men began cruising back and forth around the dropping point, they were sure they had their kidnappers.

The owner of the car, traced through its registration number XGO 994G, proved to be 34-year-old Trinidad-born Indian Arthur Hosein who, with his younger brother Nizamodeen, worked the ramshackle Rooks Farm at Stocking Pelham.

A painstaking search of the farmhouse provided sufficient clues for investigating officers to link the Hoseins with the kidnap, and by the time they reached the dock of the Central Criminal Court in September 1970, the scientific evidence against the brothers was overwhelming. Apart from indisputable fingerprint evidence that proved Arthur handled the ransom notes, a handwriting expert demonstrated to the court how the ransom note written in an exercise book found at the farmhouse perfectly matched the indentations on the following page.

Both the Hoseins were found guilty of murder and kidnap; on the former charge they were sentenced to life imprisonment and on the latter to additional lengthy terms of imprisonment.

Although every inch of Rooks Farm was meticulously covered by police searchers, not the smallest trace of Mrs. McKay was ever found. Among the suggestions made was that the victim had been cut up and fed to the Hoseins' herd of Wessex Saddleback pigs. Whatever the truth, an undiscovered body can only deepen the sense of loss felt by family and friends deprived of even a last resting place at which to mourn.

1971

UNITED KINGDOM
GRAHAM YOUNG

The Bovingdon Bug. *Having been released from Broadmoor whence he was sent for poisoning his own family, Young began work with a firm of photographic technicians where he used the readily available supplies of thallium to poison his work colleagues.*

Looking back, I can remember Graham sitting there, completely callous and totally detached, as though he were in no way connected with the suffering figure in the bed—just watching and studying him as though he were an insect or a small animal being experimented on by a scientist. Not a single sign of feeling or emotion. The word cold-blooded is rather a hackneyed one . . . but it is the only word to describe Graham.

The man lying in the hospital bed was Fred Young; Graham was the son who had just secretly poisoned him; the words were written by Graham's sister Winifred—he had tried to poison her too.

Graham Young had been born in Neasden in September 1947; a few weeks later his mother fell sick with pleurisy contracted while she was pregnant. She died when Graham was only three months old, and this must certainly have been a contributing factor in Graham's development into a solitary child and, as an adolescent, a loner among his peers. He was a highly intelligent youth, though in an off-beat and rather sinister way, and a great admirer of Adolf Hitler and the Victorian poisoner William Palmer. A school-teacher recalled how Graham had inscribed verses he had written in praise of poisons in his exercise books. He also took a precocious interest in chemistry, and at an early age was experimenting with explosives.

In 1961, when he was fourteen, Young expanded his interest to include the effects of poisons on the human body, a piece of academic research that required the administration of small doses of antimony tartrate to members of his immediate family and a school friend named Christopher John Williams. His sister Winifred suffered almost continual stomach upsets, vomiting frequently and occasionally publicly. In April 1962 Young's stepmother died. As he continued to lace his father's and sister's food and drink, they became increasingly ill. When Winifred began to suffer from dizzy spells after drinking some "bitter" tea, she was diagnosed as being the victim of belladonna poisoning; his father, by this time in a very weak condition, was admitted to hospital and diagnosed as suffering from arsenic poisoning. Young's response was disdainful: "How ridiculous not being able to tell the difference between arsenic and antimony poisoning!"

This, plus Graham's alarming obsession with toxic substances, aroused the family's suspicions and they lost no time in confiding them to the police—after all, one of them had already died, who might be next? When Graham Young arrived home from school on the afternoon of 2 May 1962 the police were already there waiting for him. His pockets were searched, but disclosed nothing more sinister than the normal contents of a schoolboy's pockets. Then Detective Inspector Coombe asked Graham to remove his shirt, and out dropped three tiny bottles.

"What is in these?" the officer asked him.

"I don't know," lied Graham.

It was antimony. The boy was taken into custody and later made a boastful confession before being transferred to Ashford Remand Centre to await trial.

The trial opened at the Old Bailey on 6 July 1962, when Young entered a plea of guilty to the charges of poisoning his father, his sister and Chris Williams. No charge was brought in the matter of his stepmother's death because her body had been cremated and it was impossible to determine whether she had died of natural causes, as stated on the death certificate, or as the result of one of Graham's experiments.

Despite a vigorous defence by Miss Jean Southworth, in which she spoke of Young as being "like a drug addict, to be pitied for his obsession," the most convincing evidence came from Dr. Christopher Fysh, a psychiatrist and senior medical officer at Ashworth. He was supported by consultant Dr. Donald Blair, who testified: "I would say he [Young] was prepared to take the risk of killing to gratify his interest in poisons. He is obsessed by the sense of power they give him. I fear he will do it again." It was the opinion of both specialists that Graham Young was a dangerous psychopath. Not surprisingly, he was found guilty but insane and removed to Broadmoor, where it was ordered that he be detained for at least fifteen years and then released only by order of the Home Secretary.

Nine years later, on 4 February 1971, Graham Young, now 23, walked free from Broadmoor certified as "cured." Presumably nobody had attached much importance to his alleged threat to "kill one person for every year I've spent in this place." Within a short time he found employment as a storekeeper with John Hadland's Ltd, a photographic-instruments firm located at Bovingdon, in Hertfordshire; he started work on 10 May 1971. In June—just weeks after Young had joined the company—Hadland's head storeman, 59-year-old Bob Egle, who supervised Graham, was taken ill at work suffering from diarrhoea, nausea, extreme backache, and numbness in the tips of his fingers. On 7 July, after eight days of intense pain, Egle died in St Albans hospital; death was attributed to broncho-pneumonia and polyneuritis. Among the mourners at Bob Egle's cremation was Graham Young. Meanwhile, Ronald Hewitt, another employee of Hadland's, had also been suffering diarrhoea, vomiting and stomach cramps—symptoms which continued until he left the firm two days after Egle's death.

In September 1971 another of the Hadland's workforce, 60-year-old Fred Biggs, fell ill. The symptoms were the familiar ones shared by Bob Egle and Ronald Hewitt. Later in the same month the firm's import-export manager, Peter Buck, fell similarly ill after drinking tea with Graham Young.

During the next month David Tilson, a clerk, and Jethro Batt, a storeman, also fell victim to what was now being called "the Bovingdon Bug." Both men grew worse; Tilson required hospitalisation and began to lose his hair. Mrs. Diana Smart developed stomach and leg cramps, nausea, and other symptoms. On 4 November Fred Biggs was admitted to hospital with severe pains in his chest; the following day he was joined by Jethro Batt. On 19 November Biggs died. Such was the alarm that several members of Hadland's staff handed in their notice.

Eventually the management were concerned enough to hold a medical enquiry into working conditions at the plant. In an attempt to defuse the mounting panic, and to assure workers that the chemicals they had been handling were safe and in no way responsible for the "bug," the medical team held a meeting with the entire workforce in the canteen. Dr. Arthur Anderson, who had headed the investigation, made himself available to answer questions, but was quite unprepared for the barrage shot at him by one particular member of Hadland's staff, and quite taken aback when Graham Young concluded his outburst with the question: "Do you not think, Doctor, that the symptoms of the mysterious illness are consistent with thallium poisoning?"

It was at this point that Hadland's management decided to check into the background of this young man who had continually evaded any discussion of his past. Within hours of them learning that he had only the year before been released from Broadmoor whence he had been committed for poisoning his family, Graham Young was under arrest. A search of his bedsit at Hemel Hempstead disclosed various types of poison and a diary pompously titled *A Student's and Officer's Case Book,* both of which would prove vital in convicting Young of murder—though, true to character, he finally admitted that he had poisoned six people, two of whom had died: "I could have killed them all if I wished, as I did Bob Egle and Fred Biggs, but I allowed them to live."

In June 1972 Graham Young was put on trial at St. Albans

Crown Court, charged with the murder of Egle and Biggs and several counts of attempted murder; he pleaded not guilty. Throughout the trial it was evident that he was having the time of his life. Incriminating extracts from his diary were read to the court: "October 30 [1971]. I have administered a fatal dose of the special compound to F[red Biggs], and anticipate a report on his progress on Monday 1st November. I gave him three separate doses." The court was also told that when arrested and searched, Young was found to have on his person a lethal dose of thallium—what he called his "exit" dose; for as he had written in his diary: "I must watch this situation very carefully. If it looks like I will be detected then I shall have to destroy myself."

Nevertheless, Young stubbornly and arrogantly continued to protest his innocence; the diary entries, he said, were simply working notes for a novel that he was writing. And he had no idea how the body of Fred Biggs and the ashes of Bob Egle came to carry lethal amounts of thallium. The jury, however, failed to be persuaded by the cool confident manner of the prisoner; they could see through the shell to the psychopath that lurked beneath, the man who had callously poisoned his colleagues like guinea-pigs in a laboratory experiment. Graham Young was sentenced to life imprisonment.

On Wednesday, 1 August 1990, warders making a routine visit to Graham Young's cell at Parkhurst prison on the Isle of Wight found him lying crumpled on the floor. Rushed to the prison hospital, Young was found to have died from a heart attack; he was 42 years old.

NETHERLANDS
THE DEADLY PEANUT BUTTER

Sjef Rijke was sentenced to life imprisonment in 1971 for the killing of three women in Utrecht—a rare example of a Dutch serial killer. The first murder was that of Rijke's fiancée, eighteen-year-old Willy Maas; the second, Mientje

(continued)

Manders, was also Rijke's fiancée. Three weeks after Manders' funeral Sjef Rijke married Maria Haas, who probably saved her own life by leaving him only six weeks after the wedding. However, his next lover was not so lucky, and suffered the most severe stomach pains as the result of eating the peanut butter which Rijke had liberally laced with rat poison. Sjef Rijke confessed to the killings and attempted killings, explaining that it gave him pleasure to see women suffer.

1972

UNITED KINGDOM
THE BARN MURDER

An alarming case of false identification in which George Ince was identified three times as a killer. Ince was tried twice for murder and only vindicated when, by chance, the real killers were arrested.

The Barn Restaurant was what one would call a "lively" place. And if the description "nightspot" endowed it with perhaps too great a glamour, still it was popular enough as a place to dine and dance; and the neon sign outside reading "Every Night Is Party Night" attracted the sort of clientele who liked to party. They were certainly partying on the night of 4 November 1972. The owner of the Barn, Bob Patience, was having a whale of a time doing what he liked best—giving his customers a good time while keeping his bank manager happy. At around 1:30 a.m. Bob's wife and faithful companion Muriel and her twenty-year-old daughter Beverley decided to call it a day and left the restaurant to walk the short distance to the family's luxury home behind the Barn. As they stepped into the house the two women came face to face with the barrel of a gun.

Shortly after 2 a.m. Bob Patience popped back and let himself into the house, pleased so far with the night's partying, and walked into the lounge to be confronted by two men, one menacing his wife and daughter with a gun. The demand was simple enough, the men wanted the key to the safe. Patience refused. "Don't be a bloody fool Bob, give me the keys."

There was a second's silence. "You mentioned my husband's name," said Muriel Patience in surprise. "This is a family affair," the gunman snapped back at her. Then he picked up a pink cushion from the sofa, held it in front of the gun and aimed it first at Muriel and then at Beverley: "Your wife or your daughter? Your wife, I think." And the room was filled with a muffled boom cut by Muriel's scream as she fell forward, a bullet in her head. "Give me the keys." Now Bob Patience moved; he picked the keys of the safe out of a bowl on the mantelshelf and the gunman made Beverley open the safe. Still aiming the gun directly at her, the man snatched up cash bags containing £900. When the raiders had tied up Bob and Beverley Patience, the man with the gun put a bullet into each of them before escaping in one of the family's cars.

So far an ordinary, if bloody, tale of East London gangsterdom from the period when a criminal's reliance on firearms was beginning to escalate. But for one man it would soon develop into a nightmare.

It was Bob Patience's son David who found the scene of carnage when he arrived home from the Barn at around 2:30 a.m. Bob had been lucky; the bullet meant to pierce his skull had just grazed him, Beverley was alive and recovered in hospital, but despite expert emergency treatment Muriel Patience died without regaining consciousness.

As soon as Beverley Patience had recovered sufficiently to give an interview the police were at her bedside taking a statement and, most important, a detailed description of the gunman. This was made into an Identikit picture and circulated. On 9 November the police had a tip-off: talk to George Ince.

Now Ince was certainly no angel; an East End gangster with a record of violence and theft, he had recently been suspected of involvement in a major silver bullion robbery. But that didn't necessarily make him a killer. Besides, Ince only fitted the descriptions given by Bob and Beverley Patience in the broadest outline. In fact when Bob Patience was shown a collection of photographs he picked out two possibles, neither of which was George Ince. Beverley, however, after careful consideration, chose the picture of Ince on two separate occasions. George was well and truly in the frame. On 27 November

1972 two men walked into the police station at Epping; one of them was George Ince, the other was his solicitor. Ince had heard of the manhunt for him and was there to protest his innocence.

At the identity parade Bob Patience failed to pick Ince out of the line-up as he had failed to identify his photograph. David Patience, who had the merest glimpse of the assassins as they drove his car away from the house, picked out Ince but was uncertain about his choice. Beverley positively identified George Ince as the man who had shot her. Still protesting his innocence, Ince was formally charged with the murder of Muriel Patience.

On 2 May 1973 George Ince stood trial before Mr. Justice Melford Stevenson at Chelmsford Crown Court. Predictably, perhaps, the trial was a noisy one, with opinions on the law and the judiciary freely and loudly expressed from the public gallery by friends and relatives of the participants; Ince himself was frequently abusive to the judge. Beverley Patience was the Crown's star witness, and she confirmed her identification of George Ince as the gunman who deprived her of a mother. On the fifth day of the trial Ince quarrelled with his attorney and sacked him, declaring that he would be offering no evidence in his own defence. Whether this was "unwise," as Mr. Justice Melford Stevenson commented, or not, it certainly had the jury confused. After almost seven hours they failed even to reach a majority verdict. George Ince, for better or worse, would have to face retrial.

The second trial opened on 14 May at the same court; on this occasion the judge was Mr. Justice Eveleigh. The evidence for the prosecution was much as before, but by now Ince had reinstated his counsel and was prepared to offer a defence: George Ince had spent the night of the murder in the company of a Mrs. Gray at her home, and had not left until the following morning. Mrs. Gray stepped into the witness box on 21 May, clearly apprehensive of the ordeal ahead, and well she might have been: in an unguarded moment Mr. John Leonard for the prosecution addressed Mrs. Gray by her real name. Now the whole world knew that George had spent the night of 4 November with Mrs. Dolly Kray, whose husband Charles had been imprisoned three years earlier along with his brothers

Ronald and Reginald. Ironically, it had been Mr. Justice Eveleigh who sentenced them. This time the jury had no difficulty in reaching a verdict—George Ince was innocent.

So if George hadn't killed Muriel Patience and wounded her husband and daughter, who had?

The police did not have long to wait to find out. On 15 June a man named Peter Hanson walked into a police station in the Lake District to turn himself in for a robbery. During the course of questioning Hanson mentioned that he had been working in a hotel alongside a man who had boasted that he had a gun and had murdered somebody with it. The somebody was Muriel Patience, and her killer's name was John Brook. Although at the time it seemed a bit far-fetched, the police made inquiries in London and finally Brook was taken into custody and his room searched. Sewn into the mattress on his bed was Brook's gun—the same gun, according to ballistics experts, which had been used to kill Muriel Patience. Now the police began to round up Brook's acquaintances for questioning. They struck lucky with Nicholas de Clare Johnson, at the time in prison but willing enough to put the finger on John Brook and to confess his own minor role in the Barn murder.

In January 1974 the third Barn trial opened at Chelmsford Crown Court, with John Brook facing the same charges with which the unfortunate George Ince had been indicted. But if Ince thought he was off the hook then he was wrong—Brook's defence was that it was Ince and Johnson who had been at the Barn that night. But by now Beverley Patience had seen a man even more like the gunman than George Ince, and he was standing in the dock in front of her. The trial lasted four weeks, but it took the jury less than two and a half hours to find John Brook guilty of murder and attempted murder, and Johnson guilty of manslaughter. They were sentenced respectively to life and ten years.

George Ince, meanwhile, had been banged up for his part in the silver bullion job back in 1972. In September 1977, he was allowed out of prison briefly to marry Dolly, now divorced from Charles Kray; in 1980 he was released on parole.

UNITED STATES
THE MAN WHO "SAVED CALIFORNIA"

Herbert Mullin began to establish his credentials as a multicide on instruction from the voices which he heard in his head—voices which he later recognised as Satan's, but which nevertheless convinced him that only by shedding blood could he save California from a devastating earthquake. What was more, the voices told him that the murder victims would be inexpressibly grateful for the opportunity to help out in this way. The first sacrifice was a vagrant, in October 1972; eleven days later he butchered a young female student. By the beginning of the following year Mullin had obtained a gun and was killing more randomly, and more frequently—as many as five murders during a single day in January—until he was arrested on 13 February 1973. Despite a history of in-patient treatment for paranoid schizophrenia and a long-established pattern of responding to "voices," Herbert Mullin's plea of insanity was rejected at his trial and he was convicted and sentenced to various terms of imprisonment for eleven murders.

1973

UNITED STATES
ALBERT DeSALVO, "THE BOSTON STRANGLER"

Between 1962 and 1964, the Strangler was responsible for the murders of thirteen women. Diagnosed schizophrenic and unfit to stand trial for murder, DeSalvo was instead sentenced to life imprisonment for sex offences and robberies committed before the crimes of the Strangler.

On 26 November 1973 one of America's most notorious serial killers was found dead in Walpole Prison hospital, Massachusetts; his body was discovered by a guard ten hours after the killing. Albert DeSalvo, the "Boston Strangler," who had been responsible for the deaths of thirteen women, had been stabbed no fewer than sixteen times, six times through the heart. Why he was murdered we may never know; the bitter hatreds and rivalries which grow behind prison walls flare up often for no very good reason at all. But if there was a motive behind the killing of DeSalvo then the conspiracy of silence among his fellow prisoners ensured that it, and the identity of the killer, remained secret.

The first victim's body, that of 55-year-old Anna Slesers, had been found by her son naked, raped and strangled with the belt of her own blue housecoat, on 14 June 1962. Over the next almost two years the killer's method would be unvarying. After targeting his victim, the "Strangler," as he became known, gained entry to the victims' homes by posing as a workman. All his victims were women, all were sexually assaulted and all were strangled—usually with an item of their own clothing, often a pair of stockings or tights which he tied with a bow under the chin. In some instances strangulation had been accompanied by biting, bludgeoning (as in the case of Mrs Slesers) and even stabbing. Despite the customary false confessions made by cranks and attention-seekers, and a blanket police response to the city's mounting panic, the Boston Strangler remained an enigmatic object of terror.

The murder of Anna Slesers was followed two weeks later by the death of 85-year-old Mary Mullen at Commonwealth Avenue. Mrs Mullen was the victim of heart failure, and it was not until DeSalvo confessed that he had been in her apartment and that she died of shock before he could rape her that she was added to the Strangler's list of victims. There was no doubt about the events of 30 June, two days after the Mullen incident. Nina Nichols, a 68-year-old widow, was found in identical circumstances to the first victim, in an apartment on Commonwealth Avenue, the same long street where Mary Mullen had lived. That same day the Strangler struck again, killing 65-year-old Helen Blake, a retired nurse, at Newhall Street, Lynn, a few miles north of Boston. Both victims had been sexually assaulted and strangled with an item of their clothing.

Following the murder of Helen Blake, police enlisted the help of forensic psychiatrists to help profile the killer they were hunting. In the opinion of experts he was a youngish man, eighteen to 40, suffering delusions of persecution, and with a hatred of his mother (so far only elderly women had been attacked). This "portrait" was run alongside records of known sex offenders, and although a number of suspects emerged from the files and were interviewed, the Strangler remained free to kill 75-year-old Mrs Ira Irga on 19 August, and 67-year-old Jane Sullivan the next day.

On 5 December 1962, the psychological profile of a "mother-hater" collapsed when student hospital technician Sophie Clark was murdered; she was twenty years old, just three years younger than two of the Strangler's next three victims.

Patricia Bissette, a pregnant 23-year-old from Black Bay,

was found strangled on 31 December, and in March and May the following year, 1963, 69-year-old Mary Brown and 23-year-old graduate Beverley Samans were added to the grim toll of the elusive Boston Strangler.

One of the interesting psychological aspects of DeSalvo's pattern of killing, which distinguishes him from most sexually-motivated serial murderers, is that his kill-rate was decelerating. From four deaths in the month of June 1962, to two in August and two in December of the same year, it was three months until the first murder of 1963, on 9 March, and two months before the next, on 6 May. Not until 8 September did the Strangler kill again, robbing 58-year-old Evelyn Corbin of her life, followed by 23-year-old Joann Graff on 23 November.

A reign of terror that had haunted the city of Boston since June 1962, leaving thirteen women dead, and the city with a modern legend, ended on 4 January 1964. He would strike once more, ineffectually; but at least the killing had stopped.

Nineteen-year-old Mary Sullivan was found, like all the other victims of the Boston Strangler, in her own apartment. She had been stripped and bound, raped and strangled; and in a final sadistic gesture, Mary's killer had left a New Year's greeting card wedged between the toes of her left foot.

After the death of Mary Sullivan, the ''father'' of American psychological profiling, Dr James Brussell, provided a new ''psychofit'' of a 30-year-old, man strongly built, of average height, clean-shaven with thick dark hair; possibly of Spanish or Italian origin—and a paranoid schizophrenic. The portrait was to prove remarkably accurate.

Meanwhile another specialist used to ''working in the dark,'' Dutch psychometrist and psychic detective Peter Hurkos, had entered the investigation. After some remarkable demonstrations of intuition, Hurkos revealed that the man the police were after was slightly built, weighing 130-140 pounds, five feet seven or eight, with a pointed sharp nose and a scar on his left arm. The psychic added: ''And he loves shoes.'' Unbelievably, there was just such a man on the suspect list, a perfect match down to his occupation as a ladies' shoe salesman. Unfortunately, he was not the Boston Strangler.

In the end it was for the Strangler to make himself known.

On 27 October 1964, posing as a detective, he entered, as he had done before, a young woman's apartment. The intruder tied his victim to the bed, sexually assaulted her, and then inexplicably left, saying as he went, ''I'm sorry.'' The woman's description led to the identification of Albert DeSalvo, and the publication of his photograph led to scores of women coming forward to identify him as the man who had sexually assaulted them. But DeSalvo was still not suspected of being the Boston Strangler. It was only in 1965, while he was being held on a rape charge and confined to the Boston State Hospital, that he confessed in detail to the Strangler's crimes. His knowledge of the murders was such that no doubt could be entertained as to the truth of his confession. Nevertheless, there was not one single piece of direct evidence to support these claims, and in a remarkable piece of plea-bargaining, DeSalvo's attorney agreed that his client should stand trial only for a number of earlier crimes unconnected with the stranglings. Albert DeSalvo never stood trial for the crimes of the Boston Strangler, but was instead convicted of robbery and sexual offences and sent to prison for life.

1974

UNITED STATES
RONALD DeFEO

The Amityville Horror. *A crime which attracted considerable notoriety by being turned into a film. DeFeo shot dead his whole family, telling police afterwards: "Once I got started I just couldn't stop."*

Greguski was the first officer on the scene. The call had come through to the Amityville Village police department at 6:35 p.m. that evening of 13 November 1974: "Hey, kid's just run into the bar. Says everyone in his family's been killed." So in the autumnal gloom patrolman Kenneth Greguski was despatched to Ocean Avenue where a small crowd was beginning to assemble. The centre of attraction seemed to be the young man crouched down sobbing that "they" had got his mom and his dad. It turned out that "they" had got a lot more than that. When Greguski worked his way through the house he made the body count six; later identified as Ronald DeFeo Sr. a wealthy motor trader; his wife Louise; their daughters Dawn and Allison, aged eighteen and thirteen respectively; and sons Mark, twelve years old, and John, seven. Still weeping on the porch was Ronald Junior, 23 years old and the only survivor of the DeFeo family massacre.

When he was finally settled in at the Amityville police station, Ronald "call me 'Butch'" DeFeo had a strange tale to tell. As the detectives listened, "Butch" told them that his father had been involved with the Mafia, and in particular he had crossed swords with one of the mob's hit-men, Louis Falini. A fortnight earlier there had been an armed hold-up when money was being transported from the DeFeo car showroom to the bank, during which Ronald Junior had been obliged to part with the company's takings. According to his present narrative, Butch's father had accused him of inventing the robbery story and stealing the money for himself.

On the morning of the murders Ronald Jr. had got up early and driven to the showrooms; several times during the morning he had tried to phone home but there was no reply. At noon Ronald returned to Amityville where he spent the afternoon drinking with friends. Early evening he left the bar for home, throwing over his shoulder the casual remark that he had forgotten his keys and would have to break in through a window.

While this interview was going on, and other officers checked out Butch's friends, and learned that he was a gun fanatic. What's more, the DeFeos had all been shot with a Marlin .35 calibre rifle—and in Butch's wardrobe there was a cardboard box which had contained a Marlin .35.

Not surprisingly Ronald DeFeo Junior found himself spending longer in police custody than he had bargained for. He whiled away the time inventing ever more preposterous accounts of the killings until at last he was detained on a holding charge of the second-degree murder of his brother Mark.

It was nearly a year later that DeFeo stood trial. He had made good use of the time feigning insanity, and had made a pretty good job of it—at least defence psychiatrist Dr. Daniel Schwartz was prepared to give expert testimony that at the time he killed his family Butch was suffering from mental disease—"paranoid delusions" the doctor said, a belief that if he did not kill them then they would kill him. As if to add weight to his insanity plea, when Ronald was shown a photograph of his mother lying dead on her bed he claimed: "I have never seen this person before." But Butch didn't have it all his own way. Dr. Harold Zola for the prosecution gave his opinion that the defendant was not a psychopath, but a sociopath who had so devalued human life that even his parents were expendable in his drive to assert his superiority. And the jury obviously agreed, because they found Ronald DeFeo Junior guilty on all six counts of murder. DeFeo was sentenced to 25 years to life on each count and confined to the Dannemora Correctional Facility, New York. As the six slayings are legally considered a single act, the sentences are being served concurrently.

And so a dreadful crime might have been forgotten. But that is to reckon without the power exerted when the supernatural meets Hollywood. The DeFeo home in Amityville, ironically called High Hopes, was subsequently sold to a family who, after only a year, fled following a series of disturbances by what they called "evil forces." This phenomenon was first re-created as a best-selling book and then not one but several films in the *Amityville Horror* sequence. It is just as well that the media cashed in when it did—the present owners of High Hopes find the place a very quiet and pleasant home.

UNITED KINGDOM
THE TIMELY DISAPPEARANCE OF LUCKY LUCAN

Richard John Bingham, Seventh Earl of Lucan—known to his friends as "Lucky" Lucan—disappeared on 7 November 1974, leaving behind in the London home of his estranged wife Veronica the brutally bludgeoned body of the Lucan children's nanny, Sandra Rivett. At the inquest in June 1975, the coroner's jury brought in a verdict of "murder by Lord Lucan" (the last time that a coroner's court was allowed to name a murder suspect). Although there have been reported sightings from every corner of the globe, Lord Lucan remains a fugitive—though it must be added that there has always been considerable speculation over his guilt. One recent theory is that Lucan hired an assassin to murder his wife in order to gain custody of the children, and that the killer bungled the job and killed San-

(continued)

dra Rivett instead. Another suggestion is that the victim disturbed a burglar who was attempting to steal Lady Lucan's jewellery, and forfeited her life.

1975

UNITED KINGDOM
DONALD NEILSON, "THE BLACK PANTHER"

A thief with a habit of murdering sub-postmasters, Neilson was already an accomplished killer before he committed the crime that was to launch one of Britain's biggest manhunts: the killing of seventeen-year-old Lesley Whittle.

The first of what were to be four brutal and unnecessary murders was committed on 15 February 1974 at Harrogate. Richard, the youngest son of sub-postmaster Donald Skepper, woke with a start to find himself looking down both barrels of the shotgun held by a man demanding keys to the safe. When the intruder failed to find them where the boy had indicated, he entered the parents' bedroom with the same demand. With more courage than forethought Donald Skepper shouted "Let's get him," and was immediately shot.

On 6 September of the same year, sub-postmaster Derek Astin tackled an intruder in his post office at Higher Baxenden, near Accrington; he was shot dead in front of his wife and two children.

Intense activity on the part of the Yorkshire constabulary forced the raider to transfer his activities to a different location, and mid-November found him in Langley, Worcestershire. Here he shot Sidney Grayland, bludgeoned his wife Margaret, fracturing her skull, and stole £800 from the cashbox.

By November 1974 the mystery man had notched up some

twenty robberies in seven years, with a combined haul of over £20,000. Worse still, the elusive thief had killed three times and left several other victims seriously wounded. The *modus operandi* was almost invariable: armed with a shotgun the intruder chose the early hours of the morning to drill through windowframes and release the catches, rouse the still-sleeping occupants, mainly of sub-post offices, and demand the keys to the safe. His working uniform was always the same: black plimsolls, army camouflage suit, white gloves, and the black hood which earned him his sobriquet of "The Black Panther."

Less than two months later, in the first month of the New Year, the Panther committed the crime that was to move the nation and make him Britain's most wanted man.

Beech Croft was the Whittle family home situated in the village of Highley in Shropshire. George Whittle, a successful businessman who had built up a prosperous coach business, died in 1970, leaving his widow Dorothy, son Ronald, who now ran the fleet of coaches, and seventeen-year-old daughter Lesley, a student. On the morning of Tuesday, 14 January 1975, Mrs. Whittle was alarmed to find her daughter missing from the house; Lesley seemed simply to have disappeared. However, it was not long before the family found three messages pressed out of red Dymo-tape in the lounge: there was now no doubt that Lesley had been kidnapped.

The first strip read: "No police / £50,000 ransom to be ready to deliver / wait for telephone call at Swan shopping centre telephone box 6pm to 1am / if no call return following evening / when you answer call give your name only and listen / you must follow instructions without argument / from the time you answer you are on a time limit / if police or tricks death." The second message gave details of the drop: "Swan shopping centre Kidderminster / deliver £50,000 in a white suitcase." The third listed the way the money was to be made up: "£50,000 all in old notes / £25,000 in £1 notes and £25,000 in £5 notes / there will be no exchange / only after £50,000 has been cleared will victim be released."

Despite the warnings, Ronald Whittle made immediate contact with the West Mercia police force, and although there was a quite obvious need for the police involvement to be kept secret, news of the kidnapping and of the ransom demand was leaked to a freelance journalist, who, with a callous disregard for Lesley Whittle's safety that characterised the worst elements of his profession, sold this information to a Birmingham newspaper and to the BBC, which went so far as to interrupt programmes to broadcast the newsflash.

On the following night, 15 January, an incident took place which provided the first major clues for the specialist Scotland Yard kidnap team which had been called in. Gerald Smith, a security officer at the Freightliner container depot at Dudley, was on a routine patrol when he observed a man loitering around the perimeter fence. So strange was the man's behaviour when Smith approached that he decided to call the police. Turning his back, the next thing he was aware of was the loud explosion of gunfire and a searing pain in his buttocks; the attacker then emptied the remaining five bullets into the unfortunate watchman and disappeared. Remarkably, Gerald Smith was able to crawl to a telephone and alert the police.

Subsequently, ballistics experts were able to confirm, by matching the telltale ejection marks left like "fingerprints" on the spent cartridges, that they came from the same gun that had been used in two earlier crimes—crimes known to have been the handiwork of the Black Panther. When investigating officers traced the green Morris 1300 saloon car that had been seen parked at the Freightliner depot they were rewarded with further vital pointers to the identity of the attacker. Among the items recovered from the car were a number of Dymo-tape messages, quite clearly pieces of a ransom trail and identical to those left at the Whittle home, and a cassette recorder containing a taped message from Lesley Whittle to her mother. Soon Gerald Smith's description of his assailant had been transformed into a portrait drawing that was to become one of the best-known faces in the country and was carried by the television networks as well as by the Press and cinemas.

Just before midnight on 16 January, Ronald Whittle received a telephone call from the man claiming to be Lesley's captor. Following a trail marked by further Dymo-tape messages, Ronald arrived at Bathpool Park near the town of Kidsgrove, Staffordshire. Here the kidnapper was supposed to respond with a torch to Ronald Whittle's flashing car headlights. In the event there was no contact and Lesley's brother and his "undercover" police escort were left once again help-less and frustrated.

For reasons best known to themselves, the police took more than a fortnight to get around to a detailed search of Bathpool Park, by which time the developments had received sufficient publicity to prompt a local headmaster to remember that one of his pupils had handed him a strip of Dymo-tape bearing the message "Drop Suitcase into Hole" which he found in the park a couple of days after the kidnapping. Another significant clue was a torch, found by another schoolboy, wedged in the grille of a ventilating shaft to the sewage system that runs beneath Bathpool Park.

Encouraged by these clues, police and tracker dogs began to search the underground culverts; it was during this operation that the naked body of Lesley Whittle was found at the bottom of one of the ventilating shafts. Around her neck was a noose of wire attached to the iron ladder. Still it was to be almost a year before the Black Panther was captured.

On the night of Thursday 11 December 1975, PCs Stuart Mackenzie and Tony White were on a routine Panda car patrol in the Nottinghamshire village of Mansfield Woodhouse. See-ing a small shambling man carrying a black holdall, the two officers decided to investigate; the suspect in his turn produced a sawn-off shotgun and forced White and Mackenzie back into the car. Taking the front passenger seat, and with his gun stuck in PC Mackenzie's ribs, the man issued only one instruction: "Drive!"

With a cool professionalism, the more remarkable given the circumstances, the two officers, using a combination of verbal and visual signals (via the rear-view mirror), conspired to dis-arm and capture the man holding them at gunpoint. Jamming his foot on the brake at a T-junction Mackenzie sufficiently surprised the gunman for White to lunge at the gun, which was now pointed away from his companion. In the struggle which followed the car became a riot of smoke and noise as the shotgun exploded into action, and despite injuries to White's hand from pellets, and the perforation of Mackenzie's eardrums by the explosion, they hung on to their former cap-tor. With assistance from Keith Wood, a member of the public who was queuing for fish and chips where the car had stopped and who had felled the gunman with a karate blow, the two officers were able to make an arrest. Although they did not know it yet, PCs White and Mackenzie—with a little public-spirited help from Mr. Wood—had just terminated the career of the Black Panther.

The Black Panther was born at Morley, near Bradford, on 1 August 1936. Christened Donald Nappey, he subsequently changed his name to Neilson to avoid repeats of the inevitable association with babies' underwear which had tormented him at school. It was a gesture characteristic of a man who, after being conscripted for National Service with the British forces in Kenya, Aden and Cyprus, became obsessed by the techniques of ''survival'' and of guerrilla warfare.

When the police searched his home at Grangefield Avenue, Thornaby, Bradford, they found all the evidence they needed to bring four charges of murder against Neilson. For each of these he was to receive a life sentence; for kidnapping he was condemned to 61 years' imprisonment.

Gerald Smith, the nightwatchman, died in March 1976 as a result of his confrontation with Neilson. However, the laws of England allow a charge of murder to be brought only if the victim dies within a year and a day of the assault.

GERMANY
THE ''PEOPLE'S WAR''

Among the most successful and most feared revolutionary terrorists in modern political history was the left-wing group under the leadership of Berndt Andreas Baader and Ulrike Marie Meinhof, who sought to undermine the federal German government and its economy, and engaged in robbery and murder as part of the so-called ''People's War.'' The leaders, including Baader and Meinhof, were put on trial in May 1975; almost one year later Ulrike Meinhof hanged herself in her prison cell. The rest of the defendants were eventually sentenced to life imprisonment.

UNITED STATES
THE JUDGE WHO DIDN'T AGREE

On Christmas Eve, 1975, William Thomas Zeigler Jr. telephoned the Orange County, Florida, chief of police and told him: "I think there's trouble . . . I'm at the store. I've been shot." The "store" was the furniture shop which Zeigler and his father ran at Winter Garden, and when the police arrived there had certainly been "trouble." As well as Zeigler Jr., who was bleeding heavily from a stomach wound, four other people lay dead on the floor of the showroom. Among the victims was a man named Charlie Mays who, according to Zeigler, had robbed the store, killed old Mr. Zeigler, his wife, and Zeigler Jr.'s wife Eunice before turning the gun on Zeigler Jr. himself, who had just had time to shoot Mays before collapsing from his own wound. As the result of one of those miracles of coincidence so beloved of crime novelists, a stray bullet had ricocheted off the walls and stopped the clock at 7:24 p.m.—more than an hour before William Zeigler called the police. This was suspicious in itself, but it took the skills of leading American forensic expert Herb MacDowell to analyse the scene of the crime and piece together indisputable proof that Zeigler had massacred his family before inflicting a gunshot wound on himself. Apparently his marriage to Eunice had taken a turn for the worse and she was about to leave him; he had responded by taking out a $520,000 insurance policy on her life and then shooting her. Convicting Zeigler Jr. of two first-degree and two second-degree murders, a remarkably lenient jury recommended a sentence of life imprisonment which was overruled by the judge, who handed down the death penalty.

1976

UNITED KINGDOM
MICHAEL GEORGE HART

"Give me some money..." *Hart shot bank clerk Angela Wooliscroft dead during a bank raid; although he protested that the gun had been discharged by mistake, forensic ballistics proved to the satisfaction of a court that the shooting was a deliberate act.*

On 10 November 1976, a heavily disguised man walked up to till number 3 at the Upper Ham Road branch of Barclays Bank at Richmond, Surrey. He levelled a sawn-off shotgun at the clerk behind the safety screen and, without raising his voice, simply said: "Give me some money."

As the terrified girl pushed money from the till across the counter the man's finger tightened on the gun's trigger, the safety glass shattered into a million fragments and Angela Wooliscroft was thrown from her stool by the impact of the burning shot ripping through her hand and chest. She died in the ambulance before reaching hospital.

An experienced team from Scotland Yard, led by Detective Chief Superintendent James Sewell, lost no time in issuing a description of the armed robber compiled from the recollections of shocked bank staff. Scene-of-crime officers painstakingly collected the glass and debris from the gun's discharge, and bagged for forensic examination a woman's yellow raincoat, in which the killer had concealed his weapon, and an empty plastic bag which had once contained chemical fertiliser. The pockets on the raincoat were found to contain two scraps of paper, one of which was to prove a vital clue in the hunt for Angela Wooliscroft's killer. Part of an entry form for a wine-making competition, it had been signed "Grahame," and its reverse side used as a shopping list. In response to police publicity Mr. Grahame James Marshall laid claim to the wine-club entry, and his sister to the shopping list. On the day of the shooting Miss Marshall had driven her car to Kingston and left it in the car-park at Bentall's department store. When she returned after shopping Miss Marshall noticed that the car was in a slightly different position and a pair of sunglasses and her yellow raincoat were missing from inside. The maroon Austin A40 had already been described by observers as the raider's escape car.

Meanwhile Home Office pathologist Professor Keith Mant had examined the body of the victim and drawn certain conclusions regarding the shooting that would prove vital in the case against the murderer. Material recovered from the body and the scene of the shooting were passed on to the ballistics team which immediately identified the weapon as a twelve-bore shotgun.

Chief Superintendent Sewell's next break came not from the police investigation, but from an informant who claimed to have seen a known criminal named Michael Hart putting a shotgun into the back of a car in Basingstoke. Although Hart initially provided a convincing alibi for his whereabouts at the time of the shooting, and a general search of his house revealed nothing incriminating, James Sewell felt that Hart's previous record was sufficient reason to keep him under supervision. It was the hunch that solved the crime, because on 22 November Hart's car, which had been involved in an accident, was picked up by the crew of a police patrol car; a search of the vehicle turned up a Hendal .22 automatic pistol with ammunition. During a more intensive search of Hart's home, a box of "Eley" No. 7 trapshooting cartridges was found; these, together with the Hendal and its ammunition and a double-barrelled Reilly shotgun, were part of a haul stolen from a Reading gun dealer on 4 November.

But it was at this point that an alarming discrepancy began to show in relation to the ballistics evidence. The pellets removed from the body of the victim were No. 7 *gameshot*; the cartridges found in Hart's possession were No. 7 *trapshot* (which is gameshot containing more of the hardening agent antimzyne). However, when the laboratory removed the contents from Hart's trapshot cartridges they were found to be gameshot. The enigma was quickly cleared up by the manufacturers, Eley Kynock of Birmingham; it transpired that, through simple human error, the wrong label had been put on a small batch of cartridges—the batch that was supplied to the raided gun-shop. Furthermore, the wads—the compressed board discs used to pack the shot—were both of a type unique to Eley, made from cardboard impregnated with paraffin wax and in use only since March 1976. The wads found in the victim's wound and those in Hart's cartridges were identical.

Even so, it was not until 20 January 1977 that Michael George Hart was taken into custody, and it was a further ten months before he appeared in court. In the meantime he had attempted to hang himself in his cell, and then confessed to killing Angela Wooliscroft "by accident." He had, so he said, tapped on the glass screen with the gun as Miss Wooliscroft had leant over to the right to fish money out of the drawer, and it had simply gone off. But it was too late for this kind of cynical deception. The scientists had done their job too well, and knew the wounds were just not consistent with such an explanation. When Michael Hart finally led police officers to the stretch of river from which they dragged the abandoned shotgun, the last piece of indelible evidence was slotted into its place.

On 3 November 1977, almost a full year after he had deliberately blasted away a young woman's life at close range, 30-year-old Michael Hart was convicted of murder and sentenced to serve not less than 25 years in prison.

UNITED STATES
MARK GARY GILMORE

"Let's do it!" *Having spent the greater part of his adult life in prison, Gilmore was sentenced to death for two separate robbery/murders in 1976. Despite every effort made to win* *him a reprieve, Gary Gilmore insisted on his own death, and was executed according to his wish, by firing squad.*

By the time he was paroled in 1976, Gary Gilmore had spent the greater part of his adult life in prison. In July that same year he senselessly shot and killed David Jensen, the 24-year-old attendant at a filling station in Oren, Utah. The following evening, Gilmore walked into the City Centre Motel, Provo, and murdered the young manager, Bennie Bushnel, before plundering the cashbox. Gilmore made no attempt to cover his own tracks, and was arrested that same night. He was tried, convicted and, according to Utah procedure, sentenced to death.

What elevated Gary Gilmore's case above his sordid murders was the obsessive determination with which he pursued the death penalty, despite considerable national outcry. At one point he threatened to dismiss his lawyers if they tried to win him a reprieve. It is not certain whether Gilmore was aware of the fact that his execution would be the first of a new era which would herald a renewed wave of judicial killing throughout the United States, but if he was it is unlikely that it would have made much difference.

Not noted for their sensational coverage of the minutiae of violent crime and punishment, even the *New York Times* on 17 January 1977 led with a wordy front-page headline: "Gilmore Faces Execution at Dawn; Two Appeals to Supreme Court Fail; Ten-year Death Penalty Moratorium Due to End." It was just six months previously, in July 1976, that the United States Supreme Court had ruled that the use of capital punishment was constitutionally permissible.

Gilmore himself, calm as ever, spent his last hours in the stark, windowless visitors' room with his aunt, uncle, cousins and his lawyers; at one point he spoke to his mother for the last time on the telephone to her home in Oregon. By all accounts Gary was relaxed and in good spirits; the only sign of tension was when somebody unwisely mentioned the word "reprieve," at which he became very angry, began using abusive language and had to be given a sedative. At no stage in the entire proceedings had Gary Gilmore relented in his determination to die for his crimes. He had become notorious for the philosophy "If you can get away with murder, do it; but if you get caught, don't cry about being punished." When earlier it had looked as though he might be reprieved anyway, Gilmore twice tried to take his own life.

About 7:45 a.m., in the half-light of the January morning, Gary Gilmore was transferred to the execution shed. The killing itself was to take place by firing squad in a warehouse formerly attached to the prison farm and used as a cannery; it was now a general store-room and had been specially cleared of stacks of paint cans and ladders for the occasion. Gilmore, wearing a black T-shirt and white trousers with tricolour red, white and blue tennis shoes, was escorted by guards to the leather-backed wooden armchair which had been raised about a foot off the ground on a small platform; almost like a stage set, the chair was bathed in light from above. Behind the chair was a plywood barrier half an inch thick, and between it and the concrete-block wall of the shed were piled sandbags and an old mattress—to soak up the bullets. Thirty feet away, down at the other end of the warehouse and directly in front of the chair, stood a bizarre-looking black cubicle. It had been fashioned of black muslin stretched over a wooden frame, and along the front five rectangular openings had been cut, about three by six inches. Inside, and out of sight of the condemned man, sat the firing squad. As they sat in their bunker, Gilmore sat loosely bound to the arms and legs of the chair.

When preparations were complete the score or so witnesses were ushered in and stood behind a line taped on the warehouse floor. The few people whom Gilmore had specifically requested to attend approached him and said their final few words—his uncle Vern Damico, Robert Moody, Ronald Stanger, and the literary agent who had bought the rights to Gary Gilmore's story, Lawrence Schiller. As the visitors walked back across the line to join the other witnesses, cotton wool was handed out to protect their ears. With the firing squad waiting anxiously, the prison governor stepped forward and asked the prisoner if he had any last message; looking first up to the roof and then straight ahead, Gilmore said, "Let's do it!" At that a black hood was eased over his head and a black target with a white circle was pinned over his heart. At a sign from the governor a volley of shots ripped into Gary Gilmore's body, filling the void of the warehouse with a deafening crash.

Two minutes later the doctor pronounced life extinct and the body was rushed to a nearby hospital where the corneas of Gilmore's eyes were removed for transplant.

On the afternoon following the execution a short memorial service was held at Gary Gilmore's request in Spanish Fork. The ceremony was attended by his lawyers and their families, the ever-loyal uncle Vern, literary agent Lawrence Schiller and half a dozen or so others. After the cremation, Gary's ashes were taken up in a light aircraft and scattered across the landscape around Salt Lake City.

UNITED STATES
GOD'S EXECUTIONER

Joseph Kallinger was the sort of eccentric of whom one might expect almost anything. Little surprise, then, that the man who lived in a twenty-foot-deep pit in the cellar of his house should also wear wedges in his shoes by which device he could adjust the list of his body to harmonise with his brain. It would have seemed strange if he had *not* received direct instructions from God—and from the Devil as well. Indeed it had become his conviction that God wanted him for a very special job—He wanted Joseph to annihilate mankind. For this prospective Armageddon Kallinger enlisted the help of his twelve-year-old son (the other son he had already insured for $70,000 and then drowned). Perhaps in preparation for their higher calling, Kallinger and son spent the years 1973-75 burgling, murdering and mutilating, evading capture more through good luck than smart planning. In 1976 their luck ran out, and Kallinger— still in contact with the Lord—faced his earthly judge. By now even his defence counsel was finding it difficult not to face the fact that his client was as mad as a hatter. Foaming at the mouth and gibbering in "tongues," Joseph the Cho-
(continued)

sen One was, incomprehensibly, judged to be able to distinguish right from wrong, enabling a jury to convict him and a judge to sentence him to a minimum of 42 years' imprisonment.

1977

UNITED STATES
DAVID BERKOWITZ, "SON OF SAM"

The so-called "Son of Sam" claimed to have been driven by the voices of what he described as "demons," and was sentenced to 365 years' imprisonment for a total of six murders. So great was the public interest in the case, and so much in demand did Berkowitz become to journalists and TV producers, that a new law—called the "Son of Sam Law" was introduced forbidding a criminal to make a profit from discussing his misdeeds.

At one o'clock on the morning of 29 July 1976 an eighteen-year-old medical technician named Donna Lauria and her friend, nineteen-year-old Jody Valente, a student nurse, were sitting in Jody's stationary car outside Donna's home in the Bronx. As they were about to call it a night and go home to bed a young man calmly walked out of the darkness towards the car, took a gun from a brown paper bag and started shooting; he left Donna Lauria dead and her friend wounded in the thigh.

The next shooting took place on 23 October in the middle-class Queens district. A young couple, Carl Denaro and Rosemary Keenan, were shot at as they sat in their car outside a bar at Flushing. Denaro had a small portion of his skull shattered but suffered no brain damage; his eighteen-year-old girlfriend was unharmed. Then a month later, at midnight on 27 November, Donna DeMasi and her friend Joanne Lomino were shot and wounded while sitting on the steps outside Joanne's home at 262nd Street in the same district of Queens. Donna made a complete recovery from her neck wound, but tragically the lower half of Joanne's body was paralysed by a bullet in her lower spine.

Meanwhile, ballistics experts had established that all three attacks had been carried out using the same weapon, a .44 Bulldog—giving the murderer the provisional name "The .44 Killer."

On 30 January 1977 another couple, John Diel and Christine Freund, were sitting in their Pontiac after a night out in Queens when suddenly the passenger window was shattered by bullets, one of which tore into Christine's skull; she died later in hospital but her fiancé was unharmed. A further senseless, random attack was made on 8 March, when nineteen-year-old Columbia University student Virginia Voskerichian was shot dead in the street. But things were about to take a new turn as an increasingly bold killer began to expose himself. The breakthrough came on 14 April 1977, when Valentina Suriani and Alexander Esau were both fatally shot as they sat in their car in the Bronx.

Police officers, members of the task force called "Operation Omega," established to investigate this series of killings, found a letter, presumably left by the murderer, lying near Alex Esau's car. It was addressed to the New York Police Department and read: "Dear Captain Joseph Borelli, I am deeply hurt by your calling me a woman-hater, I am not. But I am a monster." The killer also wrote a letter to flamboyant New York *Daily News* columnist Jimmy Breslin on 1 June: ". . . Not knowing what the future holds I shall say farewell and I will see you at the next job? Or should I say you will see my handiwork at the next job? Remember Ms. Lauria. In their blood and from the gutter, 'Sam's Creation' .44."

"Sam's Creation"? Now the *Daily News* had a new name for the killer: "Son of Sam." Breslin, through his column, replied to the letter, goading the killer into making another move; it was a dangerous game, and there were still more deaths to come.

On 26 June, in Queens, Salvatore Lupo and Judith Placido were wounded while they sat in a car. On 31 July, Stacy Moskowitz and Robert Violante became "Son of Sam's" last victims; shot in their car, twenty-year-old Stacy died in hospital and Robert Violante was blinded.

Like many criminals before him, the mystery killer called "Son of Sam" had just made his one fatal mistake. After the Moskowitz/Violante shooting he walked back to his yellow Ford Galaxie which had been parked blocking a fire hydrant, took a traffic violation ticket off the window and threw it in the gutter. This familiar scene was observed from her car by Mrs. Cecilia Davis, who might have thought no more of it had she not seen the same young man while she was out walking her dog later that night; this time he was carrying something up his sleeve that Mrs. Davis thought might be a gun. When the police were informed, they ran a check on the car that the ticket had been issued to and came up with the name David Berkowitz, resident of Pine Street in the suburb of Yonkers. When detectives found his car there was a loaded semi-automatic rifle on the seat and a letter, addressed to the head of Operation Omega and threatening another killing, in the glove box. They settled down to wait till Berkowitz came out of his apartment to claim them. No sooner had he settled himself behind the wheel, than Berkowitz was taken from the car and asked: "Who are you?" "I'm Sam," he replied with a smile. David Berkowitz went quietly to the police station where he made a full confession.

David Berkowitz had been born in June 1953, a bastard whose mother introduced him early to feelings of rejection when she put him up for adoption. Despite a protective bravado, Berkowitz was always uncomfortable in female company and as his paranoia grew over the years he began to entertain the notion that women despised him and thought him ugly. In 1974, so he later claimed, Berkowitz became aware of "the voices" as he lay in the darkness of his squalid apartment; the voices were telling him to kill. When police searched the Yonkers flat after his arrest they found the walls covered with scribbled messages such as "Kill for My Master." The source of the name "Sam's Creation" seems to have been Berkowitz's neighbour Sam Carr, whose black labrador kept Berkowitz awake at night with its barking. He began sending a series of hate letters to Carr, and in April 1977 shot and wounded the dog. With his generally peculiar behaviour and a fondness for sending anonymous letters to people he believed were intent on doing him harm, Berkowitz had already provoked complaints to the police, though such was his otherwise engaging charm that nobody seriously considered him a candidate for "Son of Sam."

An obvious paranoid schizophrenic, Berkowitz was nevertheless found fit to stand trial, though that process was pre-empted by his plea of guilty. On 23 August 1977 Berkowitz was sentenced to 365 years, to be served at the Attica Correctional Facility.

On 10 July 1979 Berkowitz was attacked by a fellow inmate who slashed his throat with a razor. Despite the fact that the wound was almost fatal, Berkowitz refused to name his attacker, saying only that it had some connection with his "occult past."

NORWAY
THE ORKDALE VALLEY MURDERS

Arnfinn Nesset managed the Orkdale Valley Nursing Home in Norway, and between 1977 and 1980 he murdered 22 of his elderly patients by the administration of the drug curacit (a derivative of curare, which is used by the natives of South America to tip their arrows). During a preliminary interrogation Nesset confessed to the killings, adding, "I've killed so many I can't remember them all"; at various times he gave different reasons for the murders, including euthanasia, pleasure killing, schizophrenia and a morbid need to take life. By the time he came to trial Arnfinn Nesset had retracted his confessions and pleaded not guilty. He was eventually convicted of 22 out of a final 25 counts of murder, plus charges of forgery related to the embezzlement of the deceased patients' money—not for his own use, he was

(continued)

quick to emphasise, but to swell the funds of missionary charities. Nesset was sentenced to 21 years' imprisonment, the maximum permitted under Norwegian law.

1978

GUYANA
REVD. JIM JONES

Revolutionary Suicide at Jonestown. *In which the charismatic Jim Jones was able to persuade no fewer than 913 of his cult followers to commit mass suicide by drinking a deadly cocktail of Kool-Aid laced with cyanide.*

James Warren Jones was born in 1931 in Lynn, Indiana—and it may or may not be significant that the town of Lynn was most noted for making coffins. His father was an alcoholic Klansman with a taste for religion, his mother a fantasist and self-declared mystic—which may account for young Jim turning out weird. Or at least that's the way his contemporaries remember him. They recall his funeral services for dead animals particularly, and one friend is on record as saying: "Some of the neighbours would have cats missing and we always thought he was using them for sacrifices." Jim was also a precocious preacher of the hellfire-and-damnation type so popular in the Midwest Bible-belt where he grew up. He made his first public sermon at fourteen, and after dropping out of Indiana University he and his new wife went touting door-to-door for the Methodist Mission. In the end Jim became a tad too peculiar for the conservative tastes of the church fathers, and in 1954 he was asked to leave. With characteristic stubbornness, Jim Jones bought his own church—a crumbling former synagogue in the predominantly black district around North Delaware Street, Indianapolis.

Now the fact is, a lot of what Jim Jones believed in

amounted to good Christian charity. True, he was a Communist; and true, he had strange notions—like seeing God travelling on a train—but Jim's ministry was among the poor and disadvantaged, the kind of people no other church wanted messing up their pews. His work for a multiracial community led to Jones being appointed by the mayor to the City Human Rights Commission, and he and his wife went as far as adopting eight Korean and black children. The so-called People's Temple was making its mark. Later they were to amalgamate with the Disciples of Christ, and Jones was ordained as a minister. The Reverend Jones took time out to lead a mission to Brazil, and on his return to the United States two years later he transported busloads of his congregation across country to Redwood Valley, California, buying another church in the rundown Fillmore district of San Francisco. Again the People's Temple became a refuge where the impoverished ethnic minorities could at least get food and care. Politicians were beginning to woo Jones for the enormous influence he had among the black voters, and in 1975 San Francisco's mayor George Moscone appointed him to the city housing authority.

With power came money. Soon the People's Temple had become an evangelical roadshow, and Revd. Jones bought a lease on 27,000 acres of Guyana rainforest where he intended to create his Utopia. The Temple could now lay claim to more than 20,000 followers, and power was beginning to control Jim Jones when once he had controlled the power. He began to lay extravagant claims to healing powers, and started to refer to himself as God. Jones introduced an unhealthy sexual element into his meetings and was now enjoying intercourse with a considerable number of his congregation.

But something more sinister than this Bible-thumping mumbo-jumbo was afoot. The People's Temple had a hidden agenda. Some years previously Jones had elected an inner circle of his most loyal and influential supporters, called the Planning Commission. In 1976 Jones began elaborating on a curious concept which he had developed years before: the use of mass suicide as an expression of political dissidence—''revolutionary suicide'' he called it. At a meeting on New Year's Day he put his followers' loyalty to the test and suggested the congregation drink a liquid which he said was poison. Some were quite prepared to do anything for the Revd. Jim, but others were less happy about their imminent self-sacrifice. The matter was resolved by an elaborate charade in which a plant in the congregation made as if to run away and was "shot." After everybody in the meeting had taken a draught of the liquid, Jim Jones announced that it was not really poison, but thanked them from the bottom of his big heart for their selfless gesture of loyalty. This was the first of several such meetings—called "White Nights"—at which the ritual suicide was rehearsed. Meanwhile work was going ahead apace down in Guyana, clearing the forest for the foundation of what was immodestly to be named Jonestown. An advance guard of some 300 faithful upped and left for Guyana to prepare the town for the expected exodus. In all about a thousand cultists invested their worldly possessions in the future Utopia, and the town began to fill out.

What most of the community hadn't realised was that this Utopia was a dictatorship, with Revd. Jim Jones as a supremo and a handful of powerful sycophants as minor lieutenants. Sex was all but forbidden to anybody but Jones and his cronies, and any follower suspected of entertaining lustful thoughts of a "non-revolutionary" kind (that is to say, sex for pleasure) was beaten. In fact all perceived misdemeanours—such as being inattentive during one of Jim's rambling sermons—were similarly punished with public beatings and torture. With such power Jones himself was becoming more than just unbalanced; he was on his way to becoming a card-carrying psychopath. One report stated that electrodes were attached to children who failed to smile at the mention of the Leader's name. And just in case anybody felt disillusioned enough to want out, Jones fabricated a story that a group of CIA gunmen were about to attack Jonestown, giving himself the excuse to post armed guards around the perimeter, more to keep people in than to keep them out.

Despite these elaborate precautions, news of such goings-on were bound to filter out sooner or later, and in August 1977 the San Francisco *Examiner* began to print decidedly unflattering reports on the state of affairs in Jonestown. The unease forced California congressman Leo Ryan, himself a seasoned human-rights campaigner, to raise the issue with the US State

Department. Ryan put together a formidable fact-finding team consisting of eight journalists and several parents of cult members, and on 14 November 1978 they flew to Jonestown.

To begin with Jones seemed amiable enough, welcoming his visitors and leading them on a guided tour of the complex. It certainly seemed impressive to the eye—even Congressman Ryan was moved to remark on how happy many of the people seemed. Then things began to fall apart. Jones almost attacked a reporter in his fury at being questioned over the heavy presence of armed guards. Several members of the cult passed messages to the team asking to return to the US with them; one lieutenant tried to stab Leo Ryan when he suggested that Jones should let those who wanted to leave go. Amid this general atmosphere of menace the fact-finding mission beat a hasty retreat in the direction of the airfield at Port Kaituma; they got as far as their waiting plane before the party was overtaken by a truck load of gun-toting cultists from Jonestown. In the massacre which followed, three of the departing journalists, one defecting cult member and Congressman Ryan were shot dead.

Meanwhile, back in Jonestown it was time for death, time to live out Jim Jones's dream of "revolutionary suicide." Now all the "White Nights" were to become a reality. Some of the faithful were mobilised into preparing large vats of purple Kool-Aid drink laced with cyanide; mothers fed their babies while children and adults were given paper cups of the liquid and told to drink. Those who exhibited a lack of enthusiasm were encouraged to do the required thing by armed guards. Then, their earthly duties to an end, the guards drank. Within five minutes more than 900 men, women and children lay dead where they fell. Jim Jones, his mission accomplished, put a gun to his head and pulled the trigger.

UNITED STATES
MURDER BY PROXY

The notion that money is the root of all manner of evils would have been enthusiastically supported by Mr. Franklin

(continued)

J. Bradshaw, late of Salt Lake City, Utah. Having made a
lot of money (over $60 million as a matter of fact) from
his own hard work, and believing in hanging on to what
he had, Bradshaw was frequently heard advising his family
that if it was money they wanted then they should take a
leaf out of his book. Youngest daughter Frances, however,
having twice failed to marry into money and left with a
family of her own to rear, was unenthusiastic about so monotonous and time-consuming a route to the riches to which
she felt entitled. Fortunately her teenaged son Marc was as
unscrupulous as herself, and in him Frances Schreuder
Bradshaw found a willing weapon. Although she had for
some time been receiving welcome, if modest, handouts
from Mrs. Bradshaw, Frances had already openly declared
that ''This family can't keep going much longer; not unless
somebody kills father,'' and on 23 July 1978 Marc was
despatched with a loaded Smith and Wesson .357 magnum
to take care of the job. After a protracted investigation,
Marc Schreuder stood his trial in 1982, when he freely admitted killing his grandfather for the simple reason that his
mother had asked him to do it as a favour. Frances Schreuder, who had never handled a gun in her life, was tried,
convicted and sentenced to life imprisonment for the shooting of her father, while the worthless Marc, whose finger
had been on the trigger, escaped with a token five years.

1979

UNITED STATES
THEODORE "TED" BUNDY

"Sometimes I feel like a vampire." *Sentenced to death for a series of kidnappings and murders of young women, Bundy spent much of his time between appeals against sentence co-operating with officers of the FBI Behavioral Science Unit in constructing psychological profiles of serial killers.*

In a classic prison interview with leading criminologists James De Burger and Ronald M. Holmes, Ted Bundy referred to a dimension of the killer's personality which he called the "Force": an unstoppable urge that makes a person kill repeatedly and which exists secretly alongside the personality of the kindly family man, or the good neighbour—the outward personality that ensures freedom from suspicion. Perhaps the most revealing observation to emerge from Bundy's discourse on the mind of the serial killer was summed up by Holmes: "Ted was able to talk about the classic characteristics of serial killers but not able to see the same in his own personality."

And this was perhaps the most remarkable thing about Ted Bundy. He seemed such an unlikely killer. Most sex murderers exhibit marked emotional repression and sexual inadequacy; but this was hardly true of Bundy. A well-educated, good-looking man, Ted Bundy's charm and wit made him an attractive companion, and he experienced no difficulty in his relations with women—except the need to kill them. Bundy's academic achievements alone placed him in a separate category, having been awarded, among other distinctions, a scholarship in Chinese studies at Stanford University. In 1972 he completed his college programme by receiving a BSc in psychology, and he had been employed as, ironically, an assistant director of the local Seattle crime commission. Later Bundy was successful in gaining entrance to the University of Utah to study law; it was to be noted later that when he moved to Salt Lake the mysterious spate of killings of young women in Washington State stopped and a new wave of disappearances began in Salt Lake.

Eventually Bundy was arrested and imprisoned for kidnapping an eighteen-year-old named Carol DaRonch; which was when officers investigating the murder of Caryn Campbell began to take an interest in him, proving eventually that Bundy had been at the location of Caryn's death on the day she was killed. An extradition order was issued, and Bundy removed to Colorado to face a charge of murder. In June 1977, while awaiting trial, he escaped, but was recaptured almost immediately. Six months later he escaped again, this time climbing through the ceiling of his cell, and carried out a further series of robberies, rapes and murders in the Florida area. It was February 1978 before Bundy was finally recaptured, and then by pure luck by officers investigating a minor traffic violation. Under interrogation, Bundy admitted that the number of his killings had reached more than 100. At his subsequent trial, Ted Bundy was sentenced to death, though the American system of appeals allowed Bundy to remain—prisoner 069063— on Death Row for a further ten years. It was not until 24 January 1989 that he was executed.

Clearly, a man who, over a four-year period, rapes and murders no less than 40 times over five States is not normal; but nothing in Bundy's background gives any clue to the frightening Jekyll-and-Hyde personality that developed. Utah State Prison psychologist Dr. Al Carlisle concluded: ''I feel that Mr. Bundy is a man who has no problems, or is smart enough or clever enough to appear close to the edge of 'normal' Ted Bundy himself claimed: ''Sometimes I feel like a vampire.''

FRANCE
THE DEATH INSTINCT

In November 1979 the life of Jacques Mesrine, France's "Public Enemy Number One," came to an end when he was shot down on a Paris street by the police he had evaded for so many years. There were few crimes in which this enigmatic gangster had not engaged—kidnap, robbery, bank raids, and murder. While serving a sentence in La Sante prison, Jacques Mesrine wrote his autobiographical memoir *The Death Instinct*—in effect, his confession to murder.

1980

UNITED KINGDOM
DAVID PAGETT

The Case of the Human Shield. *Accidentally shot dead by an armed policeman during a siege in Birmingham, Gail Kinchin became the pivot of a unique legal battle as to whether the captor using her as a "human shield" was guilty of murder by proxy.*

Like any other complex system, the law, and the agencies that enforce it, are subject to development if not exactly by trial and error, then by a process of learning from mistakes and closing loopholes as they are seen to appear. It is a great sadness that this gradual refinement so often results from deep personal tragedies. Such a tragedy was suffered by the Wood family of Birmingham in July 1980, but it was a decade before that the shortcomings that led to the death of seventeen-year-old Gail Kinchin resulted in improved police procedures in the matter of firearms use.

The background to this recent development was a unique siege situation which developed during the early morning of Thursday, 12 June 1980. Gail Kinchin had moved out of the home she shared with her mother Josephine and stepfather Eric Wood in the Kings Heath district of Birmingham and moved in with 31-year-old David Pagett in his council flat in Rugely.

Pagett turned out to be a thoroughly nasty bit of work—at least as far as Gail was concerned—much given to the pleasures of women and drink; he was also handy with his fists. With Gail now for all practical purposes in his clutches Pagett,

182

a man already known to be a bully, began to be driven by the blind belligerence that came with an increase in his dependence upon alcohol, and his behaviour towards Gail deteriorated into violence and paranoia.

Inevitably, Gail Kinchin became pregnant, and equally predictably, Pagett made her condition the excuse for further indignities, often forcing her to spend nights sleeping on the draughty floor. If she complained, or made to leave him, he made very believable threats to the life of Gail's mother.

If for no other reason than the safety of her unborn child, Gail Kinchin, with her mother's help, courageously made plans to flee the flat on the afternoon of 11 June 1980, travelling via her mother's home to that of a friend.

Pagett was furious, of course, and, the worse for drink, he loaded himself and a double-barrelled shotgun into his car and made for the Woods' home in Kings Heath. Here, shotgun raised, he smashed his way into the house to confront Eric Wood who, fearing for his own and his wife's life, made a life-or-death dash for the door to summon assistance. His bid for freedom was cut short by the blast of lead shot that tore into his limbs and felled him. Pagett now turned his violent attentions on Mrs. Wood, who was bundled at gunpoint, screaming and terrified, into the waiting car. All Pagett wanted now was an address.

When he had similarly snatched Gail from her "safe" house in Masefield Square, Pagett kicked and pushed her into the car to join her mother and drove off at a reckless pace towards Rugeley, skilfully evading the roadblocks set up by police in the wake of Eric Wood's wounding and his wife's kidnap. It was while Pagett was negotiating one of these that Josephine Wood, thinking quickly, managed to flee the madman's clutches. Not that Pagett seemed to care, even if he noticed; he got what he had come for, and the trembling, fearful Gail was back in his power. He would teach her a lesson she would never forget.

It was only minutes after David Pagett had reached the safety of his flat, barricading himself and Gail inside, that armed police officers began to surround the block.

Detective Sergeant Thomas Sartain and Detective Constable Gerald Richards, both carrying police-issue Smith and Wessons, entered the building. Hampered by the darkness imposed by broken landing lights, the two officers positioned themselves outside Pagett's door. Before long they heard a rattling of bolts, and in the flash of unaccustomed light from the now-open front door they could see the fugitive, a shotgun in one hand and Gail Kinchin grasped with the other as a human shield.

Obviously feeling securely above the law, Pagett rejected all appeals for him to surrender his weapon and, in total defiance, forced the two officers to retreat up the stairs behind them; to their horror the policemen found themselves trapped. Behind them was a solid wall, in front of them was a madman with a shotgun and a pregnant hostage. There was a momentary scuffle in the darkness below, and then with a deafening roar the shotgun exploded in a flash of fire. Miraculously the deadly spray of lead missed the crouching officers and in what they must at the time have considered their only means of self-preservation Richards and Sartain returned fire. Pagett loosed off the other barrel of his weapon and again the detectives returned his fire. This time, Gail fell bleeding on the floor, her baby inside her killed instantly by a bullet. Despite emergency treatment in hospital Gail Kinchin died before the month was out.

To sustain a murder charge against Pagett, it had to be demonstrated at his trial that he had used the girl as a shield in the full knowledge that when he first fired the shotgun at the detectives they were likely to shoot back and could maim or kill his hostage.

It was a complex and unique prosecution which divided the jury who eventually returned a verdict of manslaughter. On the lesser charges which Pagett faced—three of attempted murder (of Mr. Wood and the two police officers), and two of kidnap (Mrs. Wood and Gail Kinchin—he was found guilty). Sentencing Pagett to seven concurrent-twelve year terms of imprisonment, Mr. Justice Park observed: "The use of a hostage by a desperate armed man to achieve safety for himself—and by that use to cause the death of the hostage—is a very grave offence, falling only just short of murder . . ."

Nevertheless, the victim's family have remained far from happy with the way in which the police conducted the siege, a discontentment that was not relieved by the fact that due to the conduct of the trial much evidence concerning the shooting was never heard. It has been Mr. and Mrs. Wood's consistent view that the police should have been prepared to shoulder a great deal more the responsibility for the outcome of the incident.

Consequently, in 1990 Josephine Wood decided to sue the West Midlands Chief Constable at the time of the shooting, Sir Philip Knights, for negligence over the death of her daughter. In October the case was heard before the High Court at Birmingham, during which the Woods' counsel, Mr. Malcolm Lee, advanced the accusation that Gail Kinchin might not have died if correct police procedures had been followed. This fault in procedure, as outlined in the court, was that the two officers entrusted with the unenviable task of confronting Pagett were not senior enough to make the decisions required in such a potentially dangerous situation. Indeed, Mr. Colin Greenwood, a firearms expert and former police instructor, is reported as giving his opinion that the officer whose bullets hit Gail Kinchin: "Appears to have made command decisions he was not qualified to make. The entire command structure appears then to have failed." It must in fairness be added that former Detective Constable (now Sergeant) Richards defended his position vigorously, stating in support of his self-defence claim: "A shot was fired from the shotgun. I responded by firing four shots in all from my revolver."

Nothing will ever compensate Mr. and Mrs. Wood for the loss of their daughter and unborn grandson—least of all the small sum of agreed damages paid to the family. But perhaps they can console themselves that pressure such as theirs, and incidents like the tragedy that claimed the lives of Gail Kinchin and her child, have been instrumental in a wide reappraisal of the guidelines for the police use of firearms and the strict control by senior officers over the circumstances under which they are issued.

GERMANY
"THE AVENGING MOTHER"

Already a convicted child-molester, Klaus Grabowski was put on trial in March 1980 for the murder of seven-year-old Anna Bachmeier. Having sat through three days of the court hearing, the child's mother calmly rose from her seat, crossed the court, and fired seven bullets at point-blank range into Grabowski, killing him instantly. Frau Bachmeier—who became known as "The Avenging Mother"—was convicted of manslaughter in 1983 and imprisoned; she was released on parole two years later.

UNITED STATES
DEATH OF A CENTRE-FOLD

Dorothy Stratton's name had been Dorothy Ruth Hoogstraten before Paul Snider clapped his eyes on her. She was a waitress then, working in Vancouver, and Snider was one of those flashy, twilight figures whose eye is always on the lookout for a way of exploiting the fast buck. In Dorothy he saw star quality: "That girl," he said, "could make me a lot of money." In one sense at least Snider's instincts had been right on target—within a year Dorothy had become a celebrated centre-fold model for *Playboy* magazine. In 1978 she married Snider, and not long after won the coveted title "Playmate of the Year"; Dorothy Stratton was well on her way to a certain kind of stardom. In a classic tale of jealousy, Paul Snider came bitterly to resent Dorothy's success, the very success which he had created. After a brief separation Snider shot his "creation" dead at their home in Los Angeles in August 1980; then he killed himself. This modern *crime passionel* has subsequently become the subject of any number of bestselling books, magazine articles and films.

1981

UNITED KINGDOM
PETER SUTCLIFFE,
"THE YORKSHIRE RIPPER"

In November 1980, shortly after the brutal murder of Leeds student Jaqueline Hill, one national newspaper published its story under the headline "Did one man really do all this?" It seemed incredible at the time, and no less alarming in retrospect, that one man—Peter Sutcliffe—was able, over a period of five years, to bludgeon, stab and mutilate an admitted total of twenty women, thirteen of whom died from this savage treatment. These tragic victims, aged between sixteen and 46 with occupations between student and prostitute, had only one thing in common: they had been alone on the street after dark.

The investigation of the "Yorkshire Ripper" case was a story of determination and frustration, of a police force desperate to put a stop to one of the worst serial murderers in Britain's history, but seemingly powerless to stop the carnage. Above all, it is the story of a county in the grip of terror, its women fearful of being out of doors at night. Thirteen of them paid with their lives for that freedom.

Despite the largest manhunt ever mounted by British police, during which 250,000 people were interviewed and 32,000 statements taken, it was the very weight of all this paperwork that obscured the often obvious path through to Sutcliffe. He had been questioned on a number of occasions during the investigation, and as the result of one of these interviews a police officer had gone as far as to voice his suspicion that Peter

Sutcliffe was the Ripper; his report was overlooked. Another tragic complication of the case was the amount of time wasted by hoax letters, and by the tape recording sent to the police in June 1979, which was broadcast to the nation in the hope that the voice could be identified. Once again Sutcliffe's luck held out, and after yet another interview he was dismissed for not having a Wearside accent like the voice on the tape.

The five-year hunt for the "Yorkshire Ripper" ended in an anti-climax on 2 January 1981, when a routine police patrol became suspicious about a car parked in a dimly lit driveway. The owner, who gave his name as Peter Williams, was taken in for questioning; it was Peter Sutcliffe.

A multicide of the "evangelical" type, Sutcliffe's declared mission was to rid the streets of prostitutes. As he explained to his younger brother Carl: "I were just cleaning up streets, our kid. Just cleaning up streets." He had, so he said, first become aware of his mission while working as a municipal gravedigger in Bingley cemetery, when he heard the voice of God coming from one of the graves. There was, though, considerable doubt as to whether Peter Sutcliffe was truly psychotic or whether his "voices" were a clever device to support his defence of diminished responsibility. In the end, Peter Sutcliffe was put on trial and on 22 May declared guilty on thirteen counts of murder. He was sentenced to serve not less than 30 years in prison.

FRANCE

ISSEI SAGAWA

An Expression of Love. *The "Paris Cannibal" was confined to a French asylum for killing and cannibalising fellow-student Renée Hartvelt. Transferred to a mental hospital in his native Japan, Sagawa was quickly released under questionable circumstances.*

It all began in Paris in the summer of 1981 when two young women summoned the police to a spot in the Bois de Boulogne where they had seen a diminutive Oriental attempt to push two absurdly large suitcases into the Lac Inferieur. When he saw them coming the man scampered off as fast as his tiny legs would carry him, abandoning his luggage. Once they were reassembled, the contents of the plastic bags inside the suitcases were identified as 25-year-old Dutch student Renée Hartevelt. It was by way of the taxi driver who had transported the small man and his suitcases to the park that the police came to visit 10 rue Erlanger, where they found and arrested Issei Sagawa, a 32-year-old Japanese student, with his gun, his bloodstained carpet and a refrigerator full of human flesh. Sagawa, unmoved, unrepentant and under arrest, told how he had shot fellow student Renée Hartevelt after she had rejected his sexual advances and how he had then stripped the body naked and had intercourse. Then began the slow process of dismembering the corpse, pausing alternately to photograph his handiwork and to nibble on strips of raw human flesh. Finally Sagawa selected some cutlets to refrigerate for later and the rest of the body ended up in the Bois de Boulogne.

With the kind of back door chicanery that only money can buy, Issei Sagawa spent only three years in hospital in France before being returned to Japan where he was declared sane and released. It was not only the cynics who noticed how the Paris cannibal had been released from France at the same time as two large international companies—Kurita Water Industries of Japan and Elf Aquitaine of France—had signed a very lucrative business deal. It may be no coincidence that Issei Sagawa's father was the president of Kurita Water Industries. Following his discharge in September 1985, Sagawa claimed that the eating of Renée Hartvelt's flesh had been "an expression of love," the culmination of a lifelong desire to eat the flesh of a young woman. More disturbing still is the fact that he could not rule out the possibility that he might "fall in love" again.

The last that this author heard of Issei Sagawa added a final touch of almost unbelievable irony to a case already bizarre in the extreme. It would appear that Issei Sagawa is currently employed on the staff of a Tokyo newspaper—as a restaurant critic!

UNITED KINGDOM
THE CASE OF THE EXTRA INGREDIENT

As eternal triangles went this one had nothing very special going for it. Susan and Michael Barber had been married long enough to have produced three children, and the relationship had long since soured. Susan had worked her way through a succession of lovers and had left home twice, only to return for the sake of the children. In May 1981 Michael Barber returned home inconveniently early from a fishing trip and found his wife and his best friend, Richard Collins, in bed together. Furious, he beat his wife and threw Collins out of the house. The following day Susan made her husband one of his favourite meals, steak and kidney pie. This time it had an extra ingredient—a dose of weedkiller containing paraquat. Now paraquat is as lethal to human beings as it is to weeds, producing fibrosis of the lungs with symptoms identical to pneumonia and kidney disorder. On 27 June 1981 Barber died in Hammersmith Hospital, London. Fortunately for justice, the obligatory post-mortem was carried out by an observant pathologist named David Evans who, suspecting poison, removed samples from the organs for analysis before releasing the body for disposal. The results from the National Poisons Unit at New Cross Hospital confirmed that Michael Barber had been poisoned with paraquat. It was not until April 1982 that Susan Barber, now in possession of her husband's £15,000 insurance, was arrested and charged with murder. At Chelmsford Crown Court in November of the same year, Mrs. Barber was joined in the dock by Richard Collins; she received a life sentence for murder, he collected two years for conspiracy. But by now Susan Barber had a new lover, and in July 1983 she was briefly released from Holloway Prison in order to marry him.

1982

UNITED STATES
CHARLES YUKL

The Blood-Stained Casting Couch. *A typical product of a severely repressed childhood, Yukl grew up to be intensely shy in the company of women, almost fearful of them. The compensating fantasy of domination resulted in two murders.*

Emerging from a childhood characterised by rejection and punctuated by beatings from his Czech immigrant father, Charles Yukl developed into an isolated youth. Although to some extent he broke free from these early, repressive patterns by joining the United States Navy in 1952, Yukl was not long with the service, being dishonourably discharged two years later after no less than three courts martial. Thrown back into civilian life, Charles Yukl married in 1961, and after a succession of jobs began teaching music. (His father had been a musician, and an easy familiarity with music was probably the only thing he ever gave Charles.) Perhaps as a result of his childhood, he was still very shy, almost frightened of women, and knew very few.

In August 1966, an aspiring actress named Suzanne Reynolds enrolled with Yukl to take voice-training lessons. Instead, in October, he strangled her with his tie, sodomised her and slashed her body with a razor. In an attempt to divert attention from himself, Yukl dumped the body of his victim outside a vacant apartment in his own block and then called the police to report finding it.

It was his bloodstained clothing that gave the game away

191

for Charles Yukl, though it must be said that as the result of plea-bargaining a confession to manslaughter, coupled with good behaviour while in prison, Charles was paroled after serving only five years of a seven-and-a-half-year sentence.

In 1973 Charles Yukl returned to family life; but it was not long before the psychiatric disorders which the doctors had already discovered in pre-trial examinations began to manifest themselves in his fantasies. He began to advertise in the newspapers for actresses to star in some mythical film that he was about to produce, and entertained those who answered to lavish champagne suppers. On 19 August 1979, Yukl took one of his aspiring actresses, Karin Schlegel, and starred her in a re-run of his 1966 murder of Suzanne Reynolds. When they found the body on the roof of Charles Yukl's apartment, police officers could hardly fail to notice the identical form of strangulation with a necktie, the razor slashes on the body, the sexual abuse.

Yukl confessed again, pleaded guilty at his brief trial, and was sentenced to fifteen years to life. In August 1982, he hanged himself in the prison hospital.

1983

UNITED KINGDOM
DENNIS ANDREW NILSEN

"Killing for Company." *When Nilsen was arrested on 9 February, he confessed to an unbelievable "fifteen or sixteen" murders. Britain's worst serial killer of modern times, Nilsen lured young men to his flat, murdered and dismembered them, keeping some beneath the floorboards, some in a wardrobe.*

On 3 February 1983, residents of the flats at 23 Cranley Gardens, north London, were irritated to find that their lavatories were not flushing properly. It was not until five days later that a representative of the drain-clearage firm Dyno-Rod opened the manhole to the side of the house to check for blockages. Aiming the beam of his torch into the black hole, Mike Cattran could just make out a whitish sludge flecked with red. When he descended the twelve feet to the water line, he discovered lumps of rotting meat, some with hair attached, floating about in the slime.

Alerted by Cattran, the police made a fuller inspection of the manhole on the following morning. Although most of the flesh had been mysteriously fished out overnight, officers recovered fragments of flesh and bone later identified as being of human origin.

Among the residents of number 23, occupying the attic flat, was 37-year-old Dennis Nilsen, and when he arrived home from his job at the Soho Job Centre on the evening of 8 February it was to be met by three detectives. Nilsen expressed surprise that the police should be concerned with blocked

193

drains, and when told of the grisly finds replied: "Good grief, how awful."

It was an inspired guess, something that is as vital a tool to the experienced detective as any number of computers. Detective Chief Inspector Peter Jay rounded on Nilsen and said simply: "Don't mess around, where's the rest of the body?"

"In two plastic bags in the wardrobe. I'll show you."

When Nilsen had been cautioned he was driven back with the officers to Muswell Hill police station. On the journey, Detective Inspector McCusker turned to Nilsen and asked: "Are we talking about one body or two?"

"Fifteen or sixteen since 1978: three at Cranley Gardens and about thirteen at my previous address at Melrose Avenue, Cricklewood."

And so began the extraordinary story of Britain's most prolific serial killer. The police were at first flabbergasted by Nilsen's apparent frankness, his cold, matter-of-fact approach to the situation he found himself in, and the sheer enormity of his claims. They also found themselves in the bewildering position of having found their killer almost before the investigation had begun. Their task became one of, literally, piecing together the individuals whom Nilsen had murdered to determine when and where the crimes had occurred, and to find some answer to how such an orgy of killing could have gone completely unnoticed for so long.

However, thanks to Nilsen's uncannily clear recollection of the details, his crimes were soon a matter of record.

CHRONOLOGY OF A MASS MURDERER

23 November 1945. Dennis Nilsen was born, second of the three children of Betty Whyte and Olav Nilsen, a Norwegian soldier. The couple had been married three years earlier, but from the beginning the marriage was unhappy, with Olav frequently absent from home and usually drunk. The situation resolved itself in divorce in 1949. Mrs. Nilsen and her children went to live at 47 Academy Road, Fraserburgh, Aberdeenshire, the home of Mrs. Nilsen's parents, Andrew and Lily Whyte. The grandparents were the driving influence in the strict Presbyterian upbringing of the children.

• • •

31 October 1951. Nilsen's grandfather, Andrew Whyte, whom he idolized, died suddenly at sea at the age of 61. Nilsen was much affected by seeing the dead body of his grandfather laid out in the parlour.

1954. Betty Nilsen married Adam Scott, a builder, and the family moved to 73 Mid Street in nearby Strichen. Nilsen developed into a solitary child and disliked his stepfather.

August 1961. Nilsen enlisted in the Army Catering Corps at the age of fifteen to escape from home. He was trained at Aldershot for the next three years.

1964. Nilsen was posted to Osnabruck in Germany as a cook. It was at this time that he began to drink heavily and to discover his homosexuality. Over the next eight years he was relatively happy in the Army, being posted at various times to Berlin, Cyprus and Sharjah in the Persian Gulf.

October 1972. Nilsen decided to resign from the Army, partly because he was appalled by the way it was being used in Northern Ireland.

November 1972. Joined the Metropolitan Police, and was trained at Hendon before being posted to Willesden Police Station.

December 1973. He resigned from the police force, being unhappy both with the discipline and the restriction it put on his homosexual social life. He took a room at 9 Manstone Road, London NW8, and began work as a security guard protecting various government buildings in London.

May 1974. After resigning his job as a security guard, Nilsen was accepted by the Manpower Services Commission as a clerical officer at the Denmark Street Job Centre, in Soho. He continued in this employment until his arrest in February 1983. A large part of his work was to interview the unemployed, the down-and-out and the young rootless who hung about in Central London. At this time he was also regularly frequenting those public houses which attracted a homosexual clientele.

1974. Nilsen was evicted from his room in Manstone Road for entertaining male visitors late at night. He found new accommodation at 80 Teignmouth Road, Willesden.

1975. A young man named David Painter claimed that he had been attacked after rejecting Nilsen's sexual advances. Nilsen had met him at the Job Centre and invited him back to the flat. It was Nilsen who actually called the police after Painter had cut his arm in the struggle. Nilsen was interrogated for some time before being allowed to leave the police station.

November 1975. Nilsen met an unemployed man named David Gallichan at The Champion public house in Bayswater Road. After being invited back by Nilsen to his home, the pair decided to share a flat and moved to 195 Melrose Avenue.

May 1977. Gallichan left Nilsen, who felt humiliated and rejected by the sudden departure.

30 December 1978. Nilsen met a young Irishman at the Cricklewood Arms. After inviting him back to his flat to continue drinking, Nilsen strangled his guest with a tie during the night. The body was carefully undressed and washed before being stored under the floorboards, a procedure that became the pattern in Nilsen's subsequent crimes.

11 August 1979. Nilsen burnt the body of the Irishman in the garden. It had, until then, been stored in pieces in two plastic bags.

October 1979. Nilsen picked up a Chinese student, Andrew Ho, in The Salisbury public house in St Martin's Lane, and took him back to his flat. Ho offered sex and agreed to be tied up. Nilsen attempted to strangle Andrew, but he broke free and ran off to inform the police. Nilsen claimed that Ho had been trying to "rip him off" and the matter was dropped.

3 December 1979. Nilsen met a 23-year-old Canadian student, Ken Ockenden, at The Princess Louise pub in High Holborn; Ockenden was in London on holiday after graduating. This victim was also strangled in Nilsen's flat and placed under the floorboards. Nilsen tore up Ockenden's money "because it would be stealing to take it." Uniquely, Ockenden was missed, and his parents came to London and created considerable publicity over his disappearance, but to no effect.

May 1980. Nilsen's next victim was a 16-year-old butcher called Martyn Duffey; he took his place beside Ken Ockenden under the floorboards.

July-September 1980. 26-year-old Billy Sutherland, a Scot, went on a pub crawl with Nilsen and ended up with Duffey and Ockenden.

12 November 1980. Nilsen met Scottish barman Douglas Stewart at The Red Lion in Dean Street and took him back to Melrose Avenue. There he tried to strangle him, then threatened him with a carving knife, before deciding to let him go.

1980-1981. A succession of victims followed. A Filipino or Mexican was picked up at The Salisbury, followed by another Irishman, a building worker. There followed a half-starved down-and-out whom Nilsen had picked up in a doorway on the corner of Oxford Street and Charing Cross Road. He was burnt whole in the garden almost immediately because Nilsen was so horrified by his emaciated condition. Of the next victim Nilsen could remember nothing, except that he had cut the body into three pieces and burnt it about a year later. The ninth victim was a young Scotsman picked up in The Golden Lion in Dean Street, followed by another "Billy Sutherland" type. The next to fall prey was a skinhead who was heavily tattooed, including a dotted line round his neck, inscribed "Cut here." Nilsen obliged when dissecting him.

May 1981. Nilsen had a major body-burning session in the garden at Melrose Avenue.

17 September 1981. Malcolm Barlow was sitting against a garden wall in Melrose Avenue, complaining that he couldn't use his legs, when Nilsen found him; he phoned for an ambulance and accompanied Barlow to hospital. The next day, Barlow went back to Nilsen's flat to thank him, Nilsen cooked them both a meal, and strangled his guest when he fell asleep. Barlow was the last of the Melrose Avenue victims.

October 1981. As a sitting tenant, Nilsen was offered £1,000 to leave the flat in Melrose Avenue, so that it could be renovated. After a bonfire to remove the last vestiges of his murderous activities, Nilsen moved into the top flat at 23 Cranley Gardens, Muswell Hill.

25 November 1981. Nilsen met a homosexual student, Paul Nobbs, in The Golden Lion in Soho. Nobbs woke up next morning at Cranley Gardens with a worse than usual hangover; he went to University College Hospital for a check-up and was told that someone had tried to strangle him. Nobbs did not pursue the matter.

March 1982. Nilsen met John Howlett, a young criminal known as "John the Guardsman," in The Salisbury, and discovered that they had drunk there before, back in December 1981. Nilsen invited Howlett back to Cranley Gardens and tried to strangle him, but John put up a struggle and Nilsen had to bang his head against the bedrest before drowning him in the bath. This victim was quickly dismembered and portions of the body boiled in a pot because an old friend was expected to stay with Nilsen over the weekend.

May 1982. Nilsen picked up Carl Stotter, a homosexual revue artist known as "Khara Le Fox" at The Black Cap in Camden High Street. Nilsen tried to strangle Stotter and then drown him in the bath, but seems to have relented halfway through. Next morning Carl Stotter went for a walk in the woods with Nilsen, who hit him violently over the head, picked him up again and continued walking. The two agreed to meet again, but Stotter wisely avoided Nilsen from then on.

•   •   •

Late 1982. The next victim was Graham Allen, who was picked up in Shaftesbury Avenue. He was invited to the Cranley Gardens flat, and fell asleep while eating an omelette. Allen was dissected, some parts being put in a tea chest, some in a plastic bag, and others flushed down the lavatory.

26 January 1983. Stephen Sinclair, a 20-year-old punk and drug addict, was picked up in Leicester Square and taken to Nilsen's home. Stephen's body was left, covered by a blanket, for several days and Nilsen was in the process of dismembering it at the time of his arrest.

9 February 1983. Nilsen arrested.

12 February 1983. Remanded in custody for seven days by the Highgate Magistrates' Court. This became a regular weekly routine while police were investigating the case.

26 May 1983. Nilsen committed for trial at the Old Bailey on six counts of murder (Ken Ockenden, Malcolm Barlow, Billy Sutherland, Martyn Duffey, John Howlett, Stephen Sinclair) and two counts of attempted murder (Douglas Stewart, Paul Nobbs). The remains of Graham Allen were identified from dental records too late to be included in the first indictment. Likewise, Karl Stotter was traced too late for inclusion in the second, though his harrowing experience was used as evidence at the trial.

24 October 1983. The trial of Dennis Nilsen opened in Court No. 1 at the Old Bailey, Mr. Justice Croom Johnson presiding, with Mr. Allen Green representing the Crown and Ivan Lawrence QC, MP, defending. That Nilsen had committed the crimes was never disputed. The main thrust of the defence case was a plea for manslaughter on the grounds of diminished responsibility.

4 November 1983. After a day and a half's retirement the jury found Nilsen guilty by a majority of ten to two on all six counts of murder and two of attempted murder. He was sentenced to imprisonment for a period of not less than 25 years

and removed from the court to Wormwood Scrubs Prison, and
thence to Parkhurst on the Isle of Wight after he had been
slashed across the cheek with a razor by a fellow prisoner.

*Dennis Nilsen is at present serving his sentence at Albany
prison on the Isle of Wight, and it remains a matter of great
doubt whether society will ever feel it safe to release him.*

POSTSCRIPT

Such was the public fascination with this mild-mannered
"monster" that it was too much to expect the Nilsen case to
rest quietly for long. As well as the periodic books and magazine articles, there has been a string of more or less literate
television and theatre versions of aspects of the killings, and
in January 1993 the moment arrived, it seemed, that half the
nation had been waiting for. In a programme dealing with the
psychological profiling of serial killers made by Mike Morley
for Central Television, there, for all to see and hear, was
"Des," relaxed as you please, genially explaining his methods
of dismemberment. Whether or not we feel this added signif-
icantly to our understanding of the mind of the multicide is
debatable. However, the most remarkable aspect of the incident was its effect on the British Home Office and the deeply
unconvincing then Home Secretary Mr. Kenneth Clarke. Mr.
Clarke immediately sought and failed to get a High Court in-
junction preventing the programme from being shown. What
the publicity did succeed in ensuring, however, was that the
film was watched by a much vaster audience than would otherwise have bothered to stay up. The Home Secretary, smart-
ing from defeat, then entered into burlesque threats against the
programme-makers because, he contended, the words spoken
by Dennis Nilsen were Home Office copyright, and that copyright had been infringed—or some such nonsense.

1984

UNITED KINGDOM
THE HILDA MURRELL CASE

Fraught with conspiracy theories, it may just be possible that the murder of Hilda Murrell was a simple, sordid killing quite free from political intrigue.

A disturbing case that arose out of what seemed, at first glance, to be a straightforward, if unpleasant, murder.

The body of 78-year-old Hilda Murrell was found on 24 March 1984 at Moat Copse, some half-dozen miles from her home in Shrewsbury; she had been repeatedly stabbed and then left to die.

As well as being an internationally famous grower of roses, Miss Murrell was well known as a vociferous opponent of nuclear energy, and her murder began to appear the more sinister in light of the fact that although her house had been painstakingly searched, the only item stolen was the manuscript of a paper that Miss Murrell intended to present at the public inquiry into the construction of the nuclear-power station Sizewell B. Once the suggestion of a conspiracy was in the wind, other things came to light, such as Miss Murrell's possession of certain potentially embarrassing information (via a nephew in naval intelligence) on the subject of the *General Belgrano*, an Argentinian cruiser which had been controversially sunk by the British during the Falklands war of 1982.

Although there has been no shortage either of suspects or of theories, the death of Hilda Murrell remains a mystery.

UNITED STATES
THE FALL OF THE ACID KING

Seventeen-year-old Ricky Kasso, known on the street as the "Acid King," had become obsessed with black magic and Satanism to the point where fantasy and reality overlapped dangerously. At the beginning of June 1984, Kasso found himself several twists of "angel dust" missing and repeatedly accused another youth, Gary Lauwers, of having stolen the drugs. On 16 June Kasso, Lauwers and two companions hid themselves away in Aztakea Woods in Northport to partake of some mescaline, and during the course of subsequent reveries they renewed the dispute over the allegedly pilfered drugs. The result was a vicious attack by the dope-crazed Kasso on his companion, during which Lauwer's disinclination to embrace the church of Satan resulted in Kasso gouging out his eyes and hacking him to death as an unwilling sacrifice. On 4 July, following the discovery of Gary Lauwers's mutilated corpse, the Acid King was arrested and thrown into jail, where two days later he hanged himself.

JAPAN
NOBODY'S PERFECT

For the third time in a single year a prisoner on Japan's death row was freed by a court after being cleared of the charges on which he had been imprisoned. Yukio Saito had spent almost 27 years wrongfully incarcerated for the murder of a family in Matsuyama. In July 1983 Sakae Menda was released after 32 years, and in March 1984 Shigeyosh Taniguchi was released after 34 years.

1985

UNITED KINGDOM
JEREMY BAMBER

The White House Farm Murders. *In one of the most cynical crimes of the twentieth century, Bamber shot his family to death and made the murder of his sister appear like suicide in order to lead the police to the conclusion that it was she who committed the murders.*

On the vast majority of occasions the work of the police scenes-of-crime team is impeccably carried out and provides the inquiry with the support it needs to bring a case to a successful conclusion. However, nothing can be perfect as long as it contains the possibility of human error—and this includes police work; indeed, we can learn a great deal from those few cases where errors have been made.

In the early hours of an August morning in 1985, the station officer received an agitated telephone call from a young man giving his name as Jeremy Bamber and claiming to be anxious about the safety of his parents. He told the policeman that a few minutes earlier his father had telephoned to say that his daughter Sheila—Jeremy's sister—was at their Essex farmhouse home going berserk with a semi-automatic rifle, there had been the sound of a shot and the line went dead.

When an investigating team arrived at White House Farm they found the battered and shot bodies of Nevill and June Bamber, the "insane" daughter Sheila Caffel, and her own twin children Daniel and Nicholas. From the state of the bodies and the story of his sister's mental instability enthusiastically related by Jeremy it looked like a clear case of murder followed by suicide—the young woman, a bullet through her brain, was still holding the .22 Anschutz.

This was the one insurmountable psychological disadvantage to the police inquiry: the "killer" had already been named, and it was with this misinformation at the forefront of their minds that investigating officers found themselves, in effect, looking for clues to fit the story of the young woman's mad rampage, in the process misinterpreting what did not fit the murder/suicide theory.

Information was there for the looking, and even if no other suspect came immediately to mind, then at least all the evidence indicated that Sheila Caffel *could not* have committed the murders. It was later learned that she suffered impaired hand-eye co-ordination anyway, and had no experience whatever of handling firearms. Nevertheless, she is supposed to have fired 25 accurate shots into her family, stopping twice to reload the gun. It might have seemed inconsistent, even to the untrained eye, that such extensive ballistic activity could have been carried out without the slightest damage to the "killer's" perfectly manicured fingernails, and leaving her hands free of oil and powder deposits. What was more, the soles of her feet were found to be as clean "as though she had just stepped out of a bath"—despite having run around the house on a bloody massacre.

Nobody thought to ponder how this slim, five-foot-seven woman had bludgeoned her healthy, sturdily built, six-foot-four father with the rifle butt, which broke under the impact, without suffering injury herself. Incidentally, because of their assumption of her guilt, the real killer, Jeremy Bamber, who probably *was* bruised and marked in the struggle, was not examined by the police for four weeks.

The pathologist's report revealed that Sheila Caffel could not possibly have killed herself; either one of her wounds would have been instantly fatal, and besides, detailed examination had shown that while one of those wounds had been inflicted with a gun in its normal state, a silencer had been used during the other shot—even the most inexperienced officer might have felt that this represented an unusual extravagance for a suicide. Besides, she would have needed much

longer arms to have shot herself in the head with a gun length-
ened by a silencer.

Ignoring the clues offered by this victim's body was not the
only area of the investigation that proved wanting. Fingerprinting procedure was, by all reports, rather lackadaisical, and
many were surprised when experienced scenes-of-crime officers moved the murder weapon with bare hands. Not all of
the bodies were fingerprinted at the time, and the cremation
of the victims so soon after the crime rendered the situation
unsalvageable. Ironically, the police took the real killer's prints
six weeks after the shooting. By now Jeremy had developed
an almost theatrical display of filial grief. Blood was obligingly washed off the farmhouse walls, and bloodstained bed-
ding and carpets removed and burned.

One week later the inquest on the victims opened before
the deputy coroner. In evidence, a Detective Inspector outlined
the scenario as seen by the police, and emphasised once again
that the official view was to regard the young woman as guilty
of the murders.

Rather less happy with the outcome were the surviving
members of the Bamber family, in particular two of Sheila's
cousins. David Boutflour and Christine Eaton were convinced
that she was incapable of killing anybody, least of all the twins
she adored. In more practical terms, they knew that Sheila's
bad co-ordination made pouring a cup of tea without spilling
it difficult enough. How could she manage to shoot her whole
family? Adding a certain ''Miss Marple factor'' to this already
bizarre scenario, the amateur detectives visited the farmhouse
and retraced the steps of the police search. They entered the
study where, as the police had done before them, they found
the gun cabinet. To the police it had contained nothing significant; to David Boutflour and Christine Eaton it contained
a bloodstained gun silencer of a type that fitted the murder
weapon. They lost no time in alerting the police to this vital
piece of evidence they had missed the first time round. And
vital it most certainly was, for the silencer provided indisputable evidence that their suspect could not have shot herself.
The blood that had seeped into the silencer's baffles was her
own—which made it rather difficult to explain how it got into
the gun cupboard if she, the last to die, had killed herself.

Although the information was not revealed until the trial, the silencer, when it came into police possession, had a single grey hair adhering to it. This hair, presumably from the head of either of the elder victims, was lost by police while in transit to the forensic laboratory for testing.

The true perpetrator of this brutal and cynical act of familicide turned out to be the very young man who had so unashamedly pointed the accusing finger at his own sister. But when Jeremy Bamber stood in the dock he was not the only person to find himself on trial. Fairly or not, the whole of the initial police inquiry came under scrutiny in court. The judge himself remarked that the examination by officers at the scene of the crime "left a lot to be desired"; and the Deputy Chief Constable of the force concerned added that "with the benefit of that perfect science, hindsight, the judgement made at the scene of the crime . . . was misdirected." Finally, the then Home Secretary called for an urgent report on police handling of the murder inquiry.

UNITED STATES
THE DEATH OF ANA MENDIETA

Did She Fall, Or Was She Pushed? *In September 1985 Ana Mendieta fell to her death from the 34th floor of the Greenwich Village apartment block where she lived with the famous sculptor Carl Andre. But how?*

The name of Carl Andre is more familiar in the elevated world of contemporary art criticism than in the average bar or front parlour; his one claim to notoriety in Britain—the purchase by the Tate Gallery of his sculpture "Equivalent VIII" (the "Bricks") in 1976—being long forgotten by all but the most deeply cynical. That Andre finds himself in such company as Dennis Nilsen is due to a mystery that even lengthy investigation has failed to solve.

In September 1985, 35-year-old Cuban-born artist Ana Mendieta fell to her death from a window on the 34th floor of a Greenwich Village apartment block. Such was the impact that her head made a dent in the rooftop below. The case was a classic of the "did she fall or was she pushed?" genre. Ana

Mendieta was Mrs. Carl Andre.

Andre and Ana had met in 1979; he was already an established artist, she was in town for the opening of her first solo exhibition in New York. Over the next five years, despite bitter quarrels and frequent separations, the couple remained emotionally close. In January 1985, in Rome, they married. By June, the familiar problems were haunting their marriage, and within three months friends were reporting that Carl and Ana were getting along as well as they ever did—which meant a lot of squabbling punctuated by periods of genuine and deep affection.

The night of Saturday, 7 September 1985 the Andres spent at home, Ana retiring to bed some time between 1 a.m. and 3:30 a.m. At 5:30 a.m. Edward Mojzis, a doorman, heard a woman's scream followed by a huge bang. Ana Mendieta had landed on the roof of a Chinese restaurant. As to what led up to this sudden, tragic death we have only the testimony of Andre himself, though his statements to the police just after the incident are confused and contradictory. He claimed that he became anxious when he went into the bedroom at 3:30 a.m. and found his wife missing; he spent twenty minutes looking for her, and then called the police. In fact, his call was logged as being an hour and a half later. When police entered the apartment they found the bedroom in disarray. There were four empty champagne bottles in the lounge (Ana Mendieta's blood had twice the ''legal'' alcohol content), and there was one scratch on Andre's face and another on his arm—received, he maintained, while moving some furniture. Andre was also inconsistent on the subject of the state of his relationship with Ana that night; to one officer he said there had been a quarrel, to another that there had been no animosity. On the Sunday evening, Carl Andre was charged with murder. At his subsequent trial, he was acquitted of the charge, and we have no reason to doubt the court's judgement.

Why then, did Ana Mendieta die? She had been drinking heavily, and on that humid summer night all the windows in the apartment were wide open; even so, it is difficult to fall accidentally from a window the ledge of which is hip high. Suicide was a popularly entertained theory, and there was some evidence that the relationship was entering a particularly

bitter phase, despite Andre's claim that they had no more problems than "any other couple." But suicide was not, her family
emphasised, Ana's way; indeed, her sister claims that Ana had
spoken of divorce only the day before she died. Furthermore,
Ana Mendieta's artistic career was on an upward spiral, her
ambitions were being fulfilled in the direction that was the
most important in her life—would she throw that away in a
drunken or desperate moment? It seemed unlikely to all who
knew her well. So how did Ana Mendieta come to die?

GERMANY
MICHAEL WOLPERT

The Girls in the Woods. *Not only did the 1980s witness a
huge rise in the rate of serial killers in the United States, the
disease had also spread, with alarming effect, to the mainland
of Europe.*

Between 8 May 1980 and 26 November 1983, eight young
women were murdered within a ten-mile radius of the city of
Frankfurt.

The first attack took place in Langen, and left 23-year-old
Gabriele Roesner lying dead in a wood. She had been found
with her underwear ripped off and according to the post-
mortem report she had been raped and manually strangled.
One month later, Regina Barthel, aged fourteen, was raped and
stabbed to death about a mile from the site of the first murder;
her jeans and underwear had also been torn off.

Twenty-eight-year-old prostitute Annedore Ligeika was
found strangled at her home in Offenbach, and on 7 February
1981, another prostitute, Fatima Sonnenberg, was found strangled in her apartment in the Rodgau district of Frankfurt. Both
these victims had recently engaged in sexual intercourse, presumably with a killer who was posing as a client.

Five days before Christmas 1981, sixteen-year-old Beatrix
Scheible was found stabbed to death and raped in Frankfurt
city park, and on 9 May the following year Regina Spielmann
was stabbed and raped in the Heusenstamm Forest. The pattern
of the knife-wound on her body matched those of Regina Barthel. Although they now knew they had a serial killer on the

loose the German police had not at this stage associated the two prostitute murders with the series.

On 3 November 1983, Simone Newin was attacked while jogging in the Offenbach city park; she was raped and strangled with her own trousers. The next victim was Ilke Rutsch, 21, who was found raped and stabbed to death in a forest near Barbenhausen on 26 November. Again forensic tests proved the knife-wounds in this attack were consistent with those in previous cases.

Three days after the murder of Fraulein Rutsch, a 25-year-old electrician named Michael Wolpert was arrested for the attempted rape of a schoolgirl, and during questioning made oblique references to "the girls in the woods," particularly the Heusenstamm Forest. Under further interrogation, Wolpert eventually admitted all eight murders. He had a previous record for minor sex crimes, but was unable to give any more satisfactory explanation for his actions than that he had an exceptionally high sex drive. He was sentenced to life imprisonment on 24 May 1985.

1986

UNITED KINGDOM
THE SUZY LAMPLUGH CASE

Who Was Mr. Kipper? *Although the disappearance of estate agent Suzy Lamplugh remains officially unsolved, it has been suggested—to the satisfaction of Suzy's family at least—that a man subsequently imprisoned on another charge may have been responsible for her death.*

Some homicide cases seem to transcend their inevitably sordid circumstances and by their very tragedy leave an indelible mark on society's collective consciousness. In some instances the catalyst is injustice; for example, who failed to be moved by the release of poor Stefan Kiszko after sixteen years' imprisonment for a horrific murder which he could never have committed, and to know that there was scientific evidence available at the time of his trial which would have *proved* his innocence? More recently still the frightful murder of two-year-old James Bulger created shock-waves of anger throughout the nation, not merely because of the age of the victim—child murders are sadly no rarity—but because of the age of James's alleged killers: just ten years old.

There can't be many, either, who do not remember the name of Suzy Lamplugh. Indeed the case seems so fresh in our minds that it is difficult to believe that it was as long ago as 1986 that the 25-year-old estate agent kept that fatal appointment with a bogus client. It cannot simply be the mystery of an unsolved disappearance—thousands of people go missing in Britain every year; it cannot simply be because Suzy was young, attractive, intelligent and so unlikely a victim of violent crime—though she was all of those things. Perhaps what we remember most of all, however subliminally, is the way in which, in the face of such unimaginable grief and bewilderment, the Lamplugh family refused to allow Suzy's case to be confined to some dusty file lying on a long-forgotten shelf. Suzy's mother, the redoubtable Mrs. Diana Lamplugh, actively perpetuated the story in order to keep the investigation fresh in the public's mind, and later used the publicity in order to launch the Suzy Lamplugh Trust, a body committed to spreading an awareness of the very dangers which robbed her of a daughter. The case will never now be just the Suzy Lamplugh story, but the Diana Lamplugh story as well.

The following chronology of the landmarks in the Suzy Lamplugh investigation has been assembled from contemporary media reports.

CHRONOLOGY OF THE SUZY LAMPLUGH CASE

1986

28 July. London estate agent Susannah Lamplugh keeps a 12:45 p.m. appointment with a prospective client calling himself "Mr. Kipper." The arrangement to view a house at Shorrold's Road, Fulham, was made by telephone. The resident of a neighbouring house witnessed the meeting at 1:15 p.m., and is able to help a police artist create a visual impression of the enigmatic Mr. Kipper. Suzy Lamplugh, a former beautician aboard the *QE2* liner, was using an office car which is found unlocked at ten o'clock that night parked in Stevenage Road on the other side of Fulham—though witnesses have suggested that it may have been there since before 5 p.m. Ms. Lamplugh's purse was still in the vehicle when it was found.

29 July. Convinced that Suzy Lamplugh was abducted by Mr. Kipper, police investigators, led by Detective Superintendent Nicholas Carter, issue descriptions of both the victim and the possible kidnapper: Ms. Lamplugh, who lived in a flat in Disraeli Road, Putney, is 25 years old, had shoulder-length blonde hair and blue eyes. When she disappeared she was wearing a peach-coloured blouse, grey skirt and black jacket. The man police wish to interview is described as being aged between 25 and 30, about five feet seven inches tall, medium build, with neat, dark, swept-back hair, wearing a dark lounge suit. Meanwhile police frogmen search the stretch of the River Thames which runs parallel to the road in which the car was found abandoned.

4 August. Despite more than 1,000 calls from the public, and the emergence of a number of "Mr. Kippers" (one of them actually engaged in looking for property in the Fulham area), police are no nearer finding the missing woman. In the hope that it might jog the memories of possible witnesses, police stage a reconstruction of Ms. Lamplugh's last known movements. Dressed in identical clothing to that worn by Suzy Lamplugh when she disappeared, Police Constable Susan Long left the Fulham Road office of estate agents Sturgis & Co. at 12:40 p.m. and drove to the house in Shorrold's Road for a 1 p.m. appointment with Mr. Kipper, here played by Detective Sergeant Christopher Ball. After a few moments in the house, the couple leave in Ms. Lamplugh's white Ford Fiesta (registration number B396 GAN) and drive to where the car was parked in Stevenage Road. Police officers along the route of the reconstruction question residents and stop motorists who may have remembered seeing the incidents the previous week.

20 August. Scotland Yard issue a new photofit portrait of Mr. Kipper based on witness accounts giving an entirely new picture of Susannah Lamplugh's last hours. Police now think it possible that she had lunch with her client after showing him around the Shorrold's Road property. A witness claims to have seen a man holding a bottle of champagne with Ms. Lamplugh outside the house. Furthermore, an acquaintance of the missing woman saw the couple driving along the Fulham Palace Road in a white Ford Fiesta at 2:45 p.m. Various other recent witnesses add to the description of Mr. Kipper that he was wearing an "immaculate" charcoal-grey suit and light-coloured shirt and tie.

September. As public interest begins to wane, the Lamplugh family—in particular Suzy's mother Diana—begins to make opportunities to keep the case in the news by talking to the press. It is a hint of things to come when Mrs. Lamplugh officially launches the Suzy Lamplugh Trust.

12 November. Suzy Lamplugh's house in Disraeli Road is sold by her parents to the couple with whom Suzy was negotiating the deal before she disappeared.

14 November. Diana Lamplugh and her family take the stage at the Royal Society of Medicine seminar to announce the foundation of the Suzy Lamplugh Trust: "I suppose it began as something just for myself, to pull something worthwhile out of the most horrendous experience. But now I've talked to so many people, I can see that even if Suzy walked back through the door tomorrow, the Trust would have to go on."

4 December. Press conference held in London to announce the Suzy Lamplugh Trust. Its aim is to raise £450,000 and by means of videos, newsletters and courses it hopes to "encourage women to be self-aware and to be aware of others—both to reduce their vulnerability and to increase their effectiveness at work."

1987

15 January. Scotland Yard officers fly to Antwerp to interview a man whose car was found abandoned in north London. The blue BMW is registered in Belgium to a man named Kiper.

16 January. Police checking the clue of the car registered to Mr. David Kiper were told by his family that the vehicle had been stolen the previous summer. Thirty-nine-year-old Mr. Kiper himself, a diamond merchant, is on business in the Middle East. The car, which was found in Queen's Grove, St. John's Wood, has been checked by forensic experts and no connection has been found with the missing Suzy Lamplugh.

26 January. Police issue a statement clearing Belgian Mr. David Rosengarten of any connection with the Lamplugh case. Mr. Rosengarten became implicated because his mother's maiden name is Kiper, and his uncle, to whom the car belongs, has that surname.

11 March. Following an odd clue given by a London accountant, Thames Valley Police search historic Denham Place in Buckinghamshire. Officers leading the search for Suzy Lamplugh had been told she was being held in the house.

30 March. A new theory is being tested by the police, that Ms. Lamplugh was "moonlighting" as a private beautician with a select group of clients including men, who she visited in their homes. A qualified beautician, she once worked aboard a cruise liner.

6 May. A female estate agent is lured by a bogus purchaser to a house in Margate, Kent, where he attacks her. Police on the Lamplugh case deny there is any connection between the incident and their inquiry.

July. On the first anniversary of Suzy Lamplugh's disappearance, after one of the most exhaustive police inquiries, the team is no nearer a solution to the enigma than in the first weeks of the investigation. All that seems to have been resolved is the conviction on the part of the police and the Lamplugh family that Suzy is no longer alive.

[*8 October.* Mrs. Shirley Banks disappears while on a shopping trip in Bristol. The search for her abductor will throw up connections between this case and the disappearance of Suzy Lamplugh.]

[*29 October.* John Cannan arrested in Leamington Spa.]

[*23 December.* Cannan charged with murder of Mrs. Shirley Banks.]

1988

[*4 April.* The body of Mrs. Banks is found floating in a stream.]

23 September. Assistant Commissioner Paul Condon of Scotland Yard issues a statement defending the reputation of Suzy Lamplugh after a book by *Observer* newspaper journalist Andrew Stephen suggests that she had numerous lovers and was obsessed with men. The Lamplugh family had already failed in their attempt to prevent Faber & Faber publishing the book. In response the publishers emphasise that it was originally the family which wanted an independent account, and the book was based to a large extent on correspondence and taped interviews with members of the family.

14 October. Despite having dissociated themselves from *The Suzy Lamplugh Story,* both the family and the Trust have been unable to revoke the publishing contract under which a percentage of the book's royalties went to the Suzy Lamplugh Trust. The Trust's chairman says that under trust law they are obliged to accept the money.

1989

[*6 April—28 April.* Trial of John Cannan on charges of murder, rape, abduction and assault results in him being convicted on all counts and sentenced to several terms of life imprisonment. Free from the restraints imposed by the court proceedings, the Press once again reopen the question of John Cannan's connection, if any, to the Lamplugh case. Police interviews with Cannan fail to provide any further evidence and Cannan consistently denies ever having met Ms. Lamplugh.]

11 May. Publication of Diana Lamplugh's book *Survive the Nine to Five,* which outlines ways in which women can avoid potentially dangerous situations at work.

1990

8 May. Publication of the Lamplugh Trust conference report *Working With the Sex Offender,* echoing current demands for dramatic change in the way the criminal justice system treats sex offenders.

[*23 July*. John Cannan's appeal is heard and rejected.]

September. Detectives studying the Cannan–Lamplugh connection have a mass of circumstantial evidence, none of which is sufficient to bring charges. Senior officers are publicly cautious, and state that in the absence of a body, forensic evidence, eyewitnesses or a confession, John Cannan must be considered, as he himself claims, innocent. However, Suzy Lamplugh's mother has stated that she is convinced the man who killed her daughter is now in jail.

IS JOHN CANNAN MR. KIPPER?

So what is this mass of circumstantial evidence which is supposed to make the connection? The main points are outlined below, though no matter how convincing, no single factor or any combination of them *proves* that Cannan is Mr. Kipper.

1. The Identikit picture of Mr. Kipper bears a strong resemblance to John Cannan, who was known by his fellow-prisoners in Wormwood Scrubs as "Kipper."
2. Cannan was released from prison on 25 July 1986, three days before Suzy Lamplugh disappeared. He had told friends he was dating a girl from Fulham.
3. John Cannan was living in a parole hostel in Fulham, just four miles from where Ms. Lamplugh worked and where Mr. Kipper claimed he was looking for property.
4. It is thought that Mr. Kipper drove a BMW car—John Cannan did drive a BMW car.
5. One newspaper report claimed that Cannan visited two bars known to have been frequented by Suzy Lam-

plugh—The White Horse, and the Crocodile and Tears.

6. Cannan was fond of impressing women with champagne; there were reports of Mr. Kipper carrying a beribboned bottle of champagne when he met Ms. Lamplugh at Shorrold's Road.

7. Cannan had previously used the ploy of posing as a house-buyer in order to lure women.

8. Gillie Page, a girlfriend of Cannan's, recalled him discussing bodies in concrete while talking about the Lamplugh case.

9. A woman visiting Cannan in prison reported that he mentioned Suzy Lamplugh and said he knew who killed Shirley Banks, Suzy Lamplugh and another woman [Sandra Court?].

10. Suzy Lamplugh had spoken of having a boyfriend in Bristol, where John Cannan abducted Shirley Banks and which he looked upon as his "home town."

11. Cannan was reputed to be obsessed by numerics, and when he put false number plates on Shirley Banks's Mini he chose SLP 386S—it has been suggested that this represents a code for Suzy Lamplugh and the year of her disappearance, '86.

After interviewing John Cannan, a police spokesman for the Lamplugh investigating team said: "He [Cannan] is a clever and convincing liar. When the dust has settled and he has had a chance to consider his future behind bars we hope he will be able to help us. We are paying close attention to the *modus operandi* of his abductions. The fact that we believe Suzy Lamplugh knew her attacker may also be important." He confirmed that the file on Ms. Lamplugh would be reopened and extra officers assigned to the investigation. Police have also said that the evidence linking Cannan with Ms. Lamplugh, while circumstantial, is "overwhelming." It should, nevertheless, be added that through his solicitor, John Cannan still denies the connection: "My instructions are that he has never met the lady. What the police position may be I can't say."

UNITED STATES
THE PRINCE OF DARKNESS

Dr. Jay Smith, Principal of Upper Merion High School, Pennsylvania, had acquired the nickname "Prince of Darkness" on account of his eccentric behaviour. In June 1979 the body of Susan Reiner, a teacher at Upper Merion, was found naked in her car, and she was later discovered to have taken out huge life-insurance policies benefiting one of Smith's henchmen, Bill Bradfield, who was also on the staff of the school. In 1981 Bradfield was arrested and convicted of theft by deception. Two years later he was charged with the Reiner murder and found guilty. Meanwhile Jay Smith had been in prison on other indictments and when he was released in 1986 faced charges arising out of the death of Susan Reiner. He was convicted, and sent straight back to prison. Thus a man who was already known to be involved in drugs, swindling and Satanism also achieved star billing as a killer.

UNITED KINGDOM
MAHMOOD HUSSAIN

Sweet Revenge Grows Harsh. *Arson is one of the most difficult crimes to hide from the skills of the forensic chemist, and when that fire itself tries to mask multiple murder, it is all but impossible to escape the hand of justice.*

Murderers frequently display a certain naivety—or at least a suspension of common sense—when it comes to covering their tracks. There is always the conviction that they can, literally, get away with murder, despite all evidence to the contrary. With the scientific techniques available today, it is an unwise killer who would seek to mask homicide with arson.

At 9 p.m. on Monday evening, 2 March 1987, a fire crew were called to fight a blaze in Christchurch Street, Preston. The routine fire was, in a very short time, to become what was later described as one of the most serious crimes Lancashire police had experienced.

When firemen entered the burning building, a Victorian terrace house broken up into single bedsits, they found the badly charred bodies of three young men, each apparently poring over his college textbooks, each stabbed to death and each doused with paraffin before being set alight. It was clear even to the most inexperienced fire officer that the fire had been a deliberate, clumsy attempt to disguise murder.

Immediately, armed police were put on standby, and scene-of-crime officers began a minute search of the area immediately around Christchurch Street in an attempt to locate the murder weapon. Meanwhile, detectives and forensic experts began to unravel the background to a sadistic multiple murder.

The victims were subsequently identified as 21-year-old Tahir Iqubal and 23-year-old Ejaz Yousaf, both students at Lancaster Polytechnic, and Peter Mosley, who was on a sandwich course at British Nuclear Fuels at Salwick. To all appearances, the attacks had been carried out with a precision that indicated an assassin possessed of a high degree of military training, and investigating officers were beginning to build up a profile of their suspect as "an SAS-style killer," because of the stealth and speed with which the attacks would need to have been carried out without the victims having a chance to put up a struggle. As Detective Chief Superintendent Norman Finnerty, in charge of the case, stated: "He knew the vital areas of the body to strike at, exactly what to do." Consequently, a search was begun through Army records for any clues to disturbed or disaffected soldiers.

In fact it took the police a bare 48 hours to make their arrest, and on 5 March, Mahmood Hussain was remanded in custody by Preston magistrates on a triple murder charge.

But the 24-year-old from Birmingham who faced the bench at Preston Crown Court the following July was far from the "highly trained SAS-style professional assassin" of the police profile; he was not even a Middle East-trained terrorist. Hussain, who fully confessed his crimes, had acted on a passion to kill that was untaught in any military academy. As prosecuting counsel Mr. John Hugill explained to the jury, Hussain's girlfriend, Dionne Gonga, had become friendly with Peter Mosley, and Hussain's jealousy grew into an uncontrollable monster that destroyed not only his imagined rival but two innocent lives as well.

On 2 March, Hussain hired a car, stole a knife from a Birmingham shop and bought a can of paraffin. When he arrived at the house in Preston, he repeatedly stabbed Peter Mosley in the back after a quarrel; he then called Tahir Iqubal into the room and stabbed him to death as well. Ejaz Yousaf was chased around the house before he too was stabbed to death in a frenzied attack. Hussain then set fire to the bodies.

As he serves his three life sentences he will have at least

twenty years to ponder whether, as the Bard of Avon cautions, "Sweet revenge grows harsh."

UNITED STATES
THE BABY FARMER

Gary Heidnik was a psychotic sex killer who picked up women around Philadelphia and kept them in chains in a damp, cold cellar. The members of this "harem" were subjected to daily beatings, were raped and forced to engage in oral sex; in an attempt to render himself inaudible to the women, Heidnik perforated their eardrums with a screwdriver. By 23 March 1987, Heidnik's sex slaves numbered five; two had already died, partly as a result of the sparse diet of oatmeal and bread. On 24 March Josefina Rivera escaped and alerted the police; on 1 July of the following year, Gary Heidnik was found guilty on two counts of murder and sentenced to death.

BAHAMAS
IN SUSPICIOUS CIRCUMSTANCES

Diana Carson, wife of the British defence attaché in the Bahamas, was found drowned in her swimming pool in October 1987. When bruising was discovered on her head, Captain Christopher Carson, her husband, immediately fell under suspicion. Carson was recalled to Britain after the Bahamas government allegedly indicated that his presence was "no longer acceptable." However, despite the unsubstantiated suspicions, the cause of Mrs. Carson's death remains "accidental."

1988

UNITED KINGDOM
JOHN FRANCIS DUFFY "THE RAILWAY KILLER"

Known throughout the long investigation into his three murders as "The Railway Killer," Duffy was the first criminal in English legal history to be identified by the procedure known as psychological offender profiling (POP).

A petty criminal described variously as "weak," "immature," "lazy," "lying," "insignificant," and "almost invisible," John Duffy nevertheless compensated for his inadequacies by throwing a blanket of fear over the activities of young women around north London and parts of the Home Counties. And far from describing him as "insignificant," Duffy's wife told an Old Bailey jury how he had become "a raving madman with scary, scary eyes" (he was also nicknamed by the Press "The Man with the Laser Eyes"), who used to tie her up before sex and frequently bragged that "Rape is a natural thing for a man to do."

The first attack that has been linked to Duffy was a rape in 1982, during which two men attacked a 23-year-old woman in Hampstead, close to the North London Link railway line. It was the first of a four-year series of rapes, in eighteen of which Duffy worked with a so-far unnamed and uncharged accomplice. In July 1985 there were three violent attacks in a single night and the police, frustrated by lack of progress, launched "Operation Hart," which was to develop into the most comprehensive manhunt in Britain since the search for the Yorkshire Ripper (see page 187), and which involved officers from four forces—Scotland Yard, Surrey, Hertfordshire and the British Transport Police.

In the following month, August, John Duffy was arrested and charged with offences involving violence, but quite unconnected with the "railway rapes." Against police recommendations, Duffy was released on bail. Nevertheless, due to the nature of the crimes, he was routinely entered on the suspect file of Operation Hart.

Shortly after his release, Duffy attacked another young woman in north London, though in her confused "rape trauma" condition she was unable to bring herself to identify her attacker until December of the following year. By that time he had killed three times.

On 29 December 1985, John Duffy dragged nineteen-year-old secretary Alison Day off an east London train and took her to a squalid block of garages in Hackney where he garotted her with what is known as a "Spanish Windlass," a kind of tourniquet favoured in the carpentry trade (which Duffy once followed) for holding wood tightly together. Seventeen days later Miss Day's body was recovered from the River Lea.

The connection with the "Railway Rapist" was not finally made until three months later, when a fifteen-year-old schoolgirl, Maartje Tamboezer, was killed on her way to the shops in West Horsley, Surrey. Duffy had tried to remove clues by burning his victim's body, but left semen traces and a set of uncommonly small footprints (it later transpired that Duffy had always been sensitive about his diminutive five feet four inches). At this point information on the two murders was included in the computer-based files of Operation Hart, and the hunt was accelerated.

On 18 May 1986, Mrs. Anne Lock, who worked for London Weekend Television, disappeared on her way home from the studios; her body was not found until July.

In the meantime, forensic scientists had been working on eliminating suspects from the Operation Hart file by matching blood samples from Maartje Tamboezer's body with those on the suspect list. The register of more than 5,000 was thus reduced to 1,999 men, of whom John Duffy was number 1505. Duffy was interviewed in July but refused (as was his right) to provide a blood sample, and after bribing a friend to "mug" him, put himself voluntarily into a psychiatric hospital to recover from the trauma.

In 1986, psychological profiling was a relatively unknown factor, in Britain at least, in the arsenal of weapons being made available by the rapidly emerging science of forensic psychiatry. Increasingly concerned by their own lack of progress, the police enlisted the professional help of Professor David Canter, an expert in behavioural science and professor of applied psychology at Surrey University. Canter carefully built up a projectural profile of the "Railway Killer" based on statistical analysis of police witness statements. From these reports, Professor Canter was able to make deductions such as that the killer lived in the Kilburn/Cricklewood area of northwest London, was married, childless (this turned out to be a particular source of anguish to Duffy), and surrounded by domestic disharmony. In all, Professor Canter's profile was to prove accurate in thirteen out of its seventeen points; he explained: "A criminal leaves evidence of his personality through his actions in relation to a crime. Any person's behaviour exhibits characteristics unique to that person, as well as patterns and consistencies which are typical of the subgroup to which he or she belongs."

While the police were awaiting David Canter's report, Duffy struck again. This time the victim was a fourteen-year-old girl who was blindfolded before her ordeal. During the struggle this mask slipped and she caught a glimpse of her attacker; why Duffy did not kill the girl is inexplicable on the basis of his former *modus operandi*. When the psychological profile was run alongside the computer file of Operation Hart it came up with the name that officers had been waiting years for: John Francis Duffy. After a short period of intensive surveillance, Duffy was arrested at his mother's home where scene-of-crime officers recovered sufficient forensic clues to build a watertight case against him.

John Duffy's trial took place during the first two months of 1988. He offered a weak and unsuccessful defence of amnesia, and on 26 February Mr. Justice Farquarson, who described him as "little more than a predatory animal who behaved in a beastly, degrading and disgusting way," sentenced Duffy to seven life sentences, adding the recommendation that he serve at least 30 years. His Lordship added: "You should not depend on that being the total amount of time you will serve."

In the case of Anne Lock, Mr. Justice Farquarson directed the jury to return a verdict of not guilty on account of insufficient evidence.

UNITED STATES
JEFFREY LYNN FELTNER

The Man Who Had to Confess. *When Jeffrey Feltner phoned the police to confess to multiple murder, they just wouldn't believe him—in fact they locked him up for making malicious phone calls. Following his release he began to confess again . . .*

In 1988 police and local crisis centres began to receive a series of anonymous telephone calls from a man claiming to have committed multiple homicide at the New Life Nursing Home at Melrose, Florida. When questioned over the telephone he would add nothing further. The caller, later picked up and identified as Jeffrey Feltner, insisted that he had been responsible for the deaths of three women and two men at the home.

There had been one sudden death at New Life on 10 February 1988, when Mrs. Sara Abrams had been found with some minor bruising around her mouth. The case was looked into, but the conclusion was that Mrs. Abrams had not died in suspicious circumstances. As a result, Feltner was prosecuted for making malicious telephone calls and spent four months in prison. During this time he was diagnosed as suffering from AIDS.

Following Feltner's release from jail the telephone calls resumed; furthermore, Feltner started telling his friends that he was a multiple murderer. At the time Feltner was employed by the Clyatt Memorial Center, Daytona Beach, and after investigation by the local police force, he was arrested and charged with the murder of 83-year-old Doris Moriarty at the Clyatt Center on 11 July 1989. In custody Feltner described how he had climbed upon Mrs. Moriarty's chest as she lay in bed and covered her nose and mouth with his rubber-gloved

hands until she was dead. He claimed it was the same method
he had used to kill Sara Abrams. In addition Feltner was laying
claim to four other murders at Melrose and one at the Bowman
Medical Center. He was charged with just the Abrams and
Moriarty deaths.

In his defence, Feltner insisted that his motive was entirely
altruistic—that he felt compassion for the elderly sick who
could look forward to nothing but pain and suffering. While
awaiting trial Feltner attempted suicide and this was used by
his attorney as the basis for a defence of "unfit to plead."
The judge ruled that Feltner was perfectly competent to stand
trial and Jeffrey Feltner was arraigned first for the murder of
Mrs. Abrams at the Palatka courthouse in January 1989. The
prosecution emphasised Feltner's own admission to no less
than seven murders, and played the court a tape recording of
his confession. Following this Feltner changed his plea to
guilty and he was sentenced to life with a minimum of 25
years before parole. Feltner appeared subsequently to plead
guilty to the second-degree murder of Mrs. Moriarty and was
given a concurrent sentence of seventeen years. Given his
medical condition, it is unlikely that Jeffrey Feltner will leave
prison alive.

1989

UNITED KINGDOM
ROBERT SARTIN

The Man in Black. *A great admirer of the mass killer Michael Ryan, Sartin tried to copy the Hungerford massacre with his own shooting spree around the northern seaside suburb of Monkseaton. Unlike Ryan, Robert Sartin left most of his victims alive to tell the tale, and did not commit suicide.*

It seemed a relatively idyllic life, a happy contented landscape. But underneath a very dark river had flowed unsuspected for years. That river broke through and burst into terrible reality in that quiet community. What caused it we may never know.

(David Robson QC, at Robert Sartin's trial)

The date was 30 April 1989, a quiet Bank Holiday Sunday in the seaside suburb of Monkseaton, Tyne and Wear. Kenneth Mackintosh, the father of two young children and an enthusiastic member of the local St. Peter's congregation, was delivering church leaflets along Windsor Road. From the opposite direction the slight figure of a young man with dark glasses and a ponytail approached, dressed entirely in black with a combat knife strapped to one thigh and a shotgun held straight out in front of him. As Mr. Mackintosh looked up, the assassin fired off both barrels of the weapon, sending his victim reeling to the pavement. Reaching up his hand, begging the gunman for help, for mercy, Mackintosh heard the words "No, it is your day to die!" before the contents of two more cartridges blasted their way into his chest from point-blank range. He was dead before the man in black had turned and walked on.

It was only later that the story of Robert James Sartin's twenty-minute rise to notoriety was fitted into the context of what became known as the Bloody Sunday Slaughter.

Early on that dry, sunny morning, Sartin had been served breakfast of sausage and egg in bed by his parents before they left their house in Wentworth Gardens to visit friends. Robert had taken his time dressing in his favourite black—the devil's colour, he liked to think—aware, as he often was, of the voices in his head and of one voice in particular, the voice of "Michael." Putting on the dark glasses that kept the thoughts inside, Sartin loaded his father's shotgun into the back of his beige Ford Escort and pulled slowly away from the front of the house. At 11:55 a.m. he was seen parking the car and walking along Pykerley Road. Seconds later Judith Rhodes, driving her car in the opposite direction along the street, found herself looking into the twin barrels of Robert Sartin's gun, too late to avoid it. The first shot shattered Mrs. Rhodes's windscreen; as she slammed on the brakes and flung herself under the dashboard a second blast sent burning pellets into her left hand. Reloading the gun, Sartin fired a shot defiantly at the sky before turning on his heel and walking back down the street, "Looking sharp, not nervous," as one witness recalled. "He was turning left and right and pointing his gun."

William Roberts was at his garden gate exchanging Sunday chitchat with Lorraine Noble when the madman in black bore down on them. "Oh God," Roberts shouted, and flung himself to the ground as the shotgun's barrels levelled. There was a deafening explosion and Mrs. Noble collapsed, seriously injured, to the ground.

Thirty-nine-year-old Robert Wilson, hearing the sound of shooting and fearful for the safety of his girlfriend, who was out walking the dog, had just stepped out of his front door when the rain of shot tore into his face and left side of his body. As Wilson fled, heedless of his own injuries, in search of his girlfriend, Sartin took a pot shot at neighbour Kathleen Lynch, looking out of her bedroom window at the growing scene of carnage. The next victim was at this very moment cycling towards Sartin when he saw what he thought was an airgun in his hands; two blasts that threw him from his bike and all but robbed him of his life told Brian Thomas that this was no toy. In acute pain, and trailing blood behind him, Thomas made the effort that saved him and dragged himself to the security of a nearby house.

All the time The Voices. Michael's voice. A gunman out of control.

A car approached, the driver negotiating around Brian Thomas's bicycle abandoned in the middle of the road. The car's three occupants—Robert Burgon, his wife Jean and their daughter Nicola—drove through a hail of shot as Sartin opened fire, seriously injuring Mr. Burgon and his wife, before turning his murderous weapon on to Ernest Carter and another motorist whose car careered out of control into a wall. As the windscreen shattered the sound was met by the explosion of another shot and Jean Miller was hit in the stomach as she stooped to weed her front garden.

Madness taking him over. The Voices.

"What the hell is going on?" Elderly Vera Burrows had heard the noise of shooting and was confronting Sartin for disturbing her Sunday peace.

"It's me—I am killing people. I am going to kill you."

The gun raised like slow-motion . . . aim . . . The Voices . . . the weapon lowering again . . . "Oh, you are old. I am not going to kill you . . ." Turning . . . walking away . . . back to the car . . . driving off . . .

Robert Sartin sat in a seaside car park as an unarmed police constable placed him under arrest. It was early evening already; and one person lay dead. Fourteen others were wounded.

By later that same day, with Robert out of mischief in a police cell, his heartbroken parents Brian and Jean struggled against their disbelief: "There was our gentle, quiet son who loves kids and animals; he loves people. He is so gentle. It must have been something inside him."

It was The Voices that were inside him . . . one voice in particular . . .

But for every neighbour to whom 22-year-old Robert Sartin was "everyone's favourite son," there was a schoolfriend who remembered the "weirdo," the boy who liked to drop the "r" from his surname so that it sounded like "Satan," and who always wore black clothes.

Exactly one year after he had turned Monkseaton into a blood-bath, on Monday, 30 April 1990, a jury was empanelled to assess the evidence as to Robert Sartin's sanity. In the Crown Court at Newcastle upon Tyne, Mr. David Robson QC, for the prosecution, instructed the jury in their duties. He emphasised that Sartin's fitness to plead went beyond whether or not he could say "guilty" or "not guilty," but whether his mental state permitted the defendant to understand the charge that was made against him, instruct his legal counsel and, if necessary, give evidence on his own behalf: "You are not here to decide the issue of guilt or innocence. The whole of justice is held in the balance. On the one hand there are the victims of crime and the public interest that they should be protected; on the other that real justice is done and a man is not put on trial when he has no ability to defend himself."

Mr. Robson went on to describe the schizophrenia that had been developing over a number of years, and Sartin's conviction that his mind was being controlled by another. He recalled for the jury Sartin's statement to the police when he was taken into custody: "I know I was arrested because I shot people, but I wasn't thinking about it . . . I don't feel anything for them now. I remember hearing people scream, I wasn't bothered if I hit them . . . I was not taking proper aim at anybody. Every time I fired I think I was shooting both barrels—the cartridges would just eject and I would put in the next ones. *It was as if it was not me inside myself.*"

Then the jury discovered who it was that possessed Robert Sartin, the voice that made him kill. It was Michael. From childhood, Sartin had been obsessed with the macabre, with the occult, to such an extent that other children went in fear of him. In youth this unhealthy preoccupation found expression in Satanism and a morbid fascination with Moors Murderers Ian Brady and Myra Hindley, and the mad poisoner Graham Young. Eight months before his own rampage, Robert Sartin had visited the scene of Michael Ryan's Hungerford

Massacre. Above all there was the influence of Michael. Michael Myers.

Home Office psychiatrist Dr. Marion Swann explained to the court: "He hears more than one voice, and one of them is Michael. Initially he didn't know who this person was, but then he watched the video of [the film] *Halloween* and came to realise Michael's [Myers, the film's teenage psychopath who hacks his family to pieces] was the voice he had been hearing. He describes the ability to actually see Michael and many of the drawings he had were of Michael..." In conclusion, Dr. Swann argued: "He is so sick and mentally disturbed that he needs treatment for this condition as a matter of urgency."

Robert Sartin was not in court to hear this most intimate evaluation of his psyche; he had been confined to Moss Side Special Hospital, near Liverpool. The jury, predictably, passed the only humane and just verdict possible—the verdict of "unfit to plead." Whether Robert Sartin will ever be considered well enough to stand trial is doubtful.

CANADA
THE MAN WHO HATED FEMINISTS

In a senseless mass shooting, Marc Lepine shot up a class of female students at the University of Montreal. In a three-page letter Lepine explained that he "hated feminists"; it is thought that the incident, in which fourteen women were killed, may have been sparked off by Lepine's girlfriend insisting on her right to have an abortion.

1990

UNITED KINGDOM
DAVID LASHLEY

The Long Memory of the Law. *Lashley was put on trial for the murder of Janie Shepherd thirteen years before. Although he was interviewed as a suspect at the time of the killing, police eliminated him from their inquiry; it was only when Lashley boasted to a fellow prisoner that he was the killer that he was brought to trial.*

Statistically, Janie Shepherd was a very unlikely victim. She was the stepdaughter of Australian businessman John Darling, and had left the family home in Sydney in 1971. In 1977 she was living with her cousin Camilla and Camilla's husband Alistair Sampson in a luxury apartment in Clifton Hill, north-west London. Like many girls born into the wealthy middle-class, Janie was in receipt of a generous allowance from her father, and worked because she chose to rather than needed to; in her case it was at the Caelt art gallery, a specialist dealing in modern unknown artists, with premises in London's Westbourne Grove. When she left the gallery on the evening of Friday, 4 February 1977, Janie drove back to the flat in St John's Wood, changed quickly, threw a few "essentials" into her red shoulder bag and by 8:40 p.m. was back behind the wheel of her dark-blue Mini Cooper. She had planned to spend the weekend with her boyfriend Roddy Kinkead-Weekes. He had telephoned the gallery earlier that evening and suggested they spend a quiet evening together at his flat in Lennox Gardens, Chelsea. She offered to pick a snack up on the way over and stopped in at the Europa Supermarket in Queensway.

When Janie had not arrived by 9:30 p.m. Kinkead-Weekes checked with her cousin. He rang again at 10 p.m. and at regular intervals until midnight. Then Roddy Kinkead-Weekes and Camilla and Alistair Sampson between them rang around the local hospitals to see if Janie had met with an accident. All the replies they received were comfortingly negative, but with increasing alarm both the Sampsons and Kinkead-Weekes reported Janie missing to their respective local police stations.

At 3:15 a.m. on 5 February, Janie Shepherd became an "official" missing person, and her description and that of her car were prepared and circulated.

Just four days after her disappearance Janie Shepherd's car was found spattered with mud and with a collection of parking tickets under the windscreen wiper on a yellow line in Elgin Crescent, Notting Hill. The parking tickets dated back to the morning of 7 February, but witnesses were found who would testify to seeing the car parked there as early as 1:10 a.m. on Saturday 5th—even before its owner had been reported missing.

The state of the car left police with little optimism for Janie's safety; it was clear that a fierce struggle had taken place in the vehicle resulting in two deep slashes in the soft sunroof. The girl's boots had been left in the car, as was the red satchel bag—without its usual contents, but with two recent till receipts. One was from a petrol station where Janie had topped up the seven-gallon fuel tank of her car. Given the amount of petrol left in the tank, police scientists estimated that the car would have been driven on a roughly 75-mile round trip. The journey had been through muddy countryside, as was obvious from the state of the tyres and bodywork, but exactly where within that 45-mile radius around Notting Hill was anybody's guess.

The hunt for Janie Shepherd was relentless. Police helicopter teams made aerial searches over the area that may have been covered by the car, and for the very first time in a British murder inquiry dogs trained to sniff out dead bodies were used in the ground search. The customary "Appeal for Assistance" posters were distributed, asking the general public for sightings of Janie or her car, while the Press carried descriptions and photographs of models in similar clothing to that worn by her when she disappeared. In addition, more than 50 officers under the direction of DCI Roger Lewis were engaged in similar intensive routine searches.

Back at Scotland Yard, Detective Chief Superintendent Henry Mooney had begun the painstaking task of searching records at the Yard and at Notting Hill police station for similar offences against women, and discovered that in July 1976 a young women had been raped and murderously attacked in her own car less than half a mile from where Janie Shepherd's Mini had been abandoned in Elgin Crescent. The woman survived her ordeal to give a description of her assailant and to help construct an Identikit portrait of a black man with a noticeable scar on his face. Although police routinely searched their files for possible suspects, they dismissed the most likely one because his record made no mention of a scar. The man's name was David Lashley, a van driver who in 1970 had been convicted of a series of five rapes of young women in cars, and sentenced to twelve years' imprisonment. At the time of the Chesterton Street offence Lashley had recently been released on parole.

If his predecessors had overlooked the obvious connection it did not escape Henry Mooney, and on 17 February 1977 Lashley was picked up at his current address in Southall and taken in for questioning on the Chesterton Street rape and the disappearance of Janie Shepherd. At an identity parade "Miss A," the Chesterton Street victim, positively identified David Lashley as her attacker—he had the distinctive scar on his cheek. Mooney was equally certain that Lashley had abducted and murdered Janie Shepherd.

It was not until 18 April, Easter Monday, that Janie Shepherd's rustic grave was discovered by ten-year-old Neil Gardner and eleven-year-old Dean James, on the common known as No-man's-land, near Wheathampstead in Hertfordshire. As soon as the body had been found and the preliminary on-site examination and photography had been carried out, the sad remains of Janie Shepherd were removed to the St. Alban mortuary for forensic post-mortem. In charge of the medical examination was pathologist James Cameron, Professor of Forensic Medicine at the London Hospital Medical School.

The body of Janie Shepherd was fully clothed in her jeans and striped socks (the boots she had left home wearing were found abandoned in her car), and a black sweater with bright green cuffs and a scarlet neck. Beneath the clothing Cameron found a ligature around the left ankle and a mark on the right that indicated the feet had been bound; there were also ligatures on the upper arms. Extensive bruising on the upper part of the body suggested that Janie had put up a courageous fight for her life. Cause of death was established as asphyxia on account of congestion of the heart and lungs, and Professor Cameron gave his opinion that Janie Shepherd had died from "compression of the neck."

Identity was established by Bernard Sims, a forensic dentist experienced in the identification of badly mutilated human remains by means of dental features. Using a post-mortem dental chart and comparing it with that kept by Janie Shepherd's dentist, Sims was able to prove the uniqueness—almost like a fingerprint—of the victim's teeth.

At the inquest on Janie Shepherd's death, the jury returned the only verdict they could, that of murder "by person or persons unknown."

The case file, it seemed, was all but closed, and the officers actively pursuing the murder drastically reduced. In December 1977, David Lashley was sentenced to fifteen years' imprisonment for the attempted murder of Miss A. About Janie Shepherd he would say nothing—to the police that is. When he did decide to talk it was by way of an arrogant boast to a fellow inmate named Daniel Reece—not his real name as it turned out, but the one which he had been given, along with a new identity, after giving evidence as a "supergrass" in an armed robbery case and had put his safety at risk. His own crimes included a thirteen-year sentence for rape and buggery.

The Shepherd inquiry was reactivated in July 1988, when Detective Superintendent Ian Whinnett of the Hertfordshire force assembled a team of seven officers to reassess the evidence and make further inquiries. It is possible that the imminent release of David Lashley in February 1989 led senior police officers to make every attempt to keep the man with an undisguised hatred of women and policemen, and who had spent the whole of his eleven-year term as a Category A (dangerous) prisoner, on the inside for as long as possible.

It is at this stage that the police are believed to have become aware of David Reece's claim that Lashley had confessed to the Shepherd murder. Both Lashley and Reece had been fanatical body-builders while in Frankland Prison, and spent much of their free time weight-lifting in the prison gymnasium. This and perhaps their mutual commitment to rape and violence, threw the two men as close together as such bizarre personalities ever can be. Lashley, according to his confidant, had boasted of grabbing a "nice looking blonde" in her Mini car (he even recalled the "For Sale" notice that Janie Shepherd had recently stuck on her rear window), threatening her with a knife and slashing the sun roof to show that he meant business. Then Lashley said he had driven her to a secluded part of Ladbroke Grove where the rape and murder took place. At this point Lashley began to reveal details that could only have been known to the police and the killer; Lashley demonstrated to Reece, for example, exactly how he had killed Janie, holding her neck in one hand and pressing the fist of his other into her windpipe: as Professor Cameron had observed, she died of a "crushed throat." Another detail that had puzzled the earlier investigation was why Janie Shepherd's body had been found dressed in her *spare* set of clothes. This Lashley obligingly explained, saying he had slashed the clothing she was wearing with the knife, and had needed to redress the body in order to drive it out of town, strapped into the passenger's seat, to where it was dumped. Reece decided that Lashley was a menace to womankind and too dangerous to be released—hence his brief moment of good citizenship in reporting Lashley's conversation to the prison authorities. And without Reece's testimony in court it is very unlikely that the police, new inquiry or not, would have been able to make out a watertight case against David Lashley for the murder of Janie Shepherd.

On the morning of 7 February 1989, David Lashley was released from Frankland Prison. He was a free man for just half a minute before being placed under arrest and charged with the Shepherd murder. By the time Lashley had worked his way through the magistrates' hearings and their consequent remands in custody, others of Lashley's fellow prisoners had begun to tell tales: tales of his confessions to killing a woman in a car and dumping her body in some woods. One of them was Robert Hodgson, who had shared a cell in Wakefield Prison with Lashley; Hodgson was later to give evidence at his cellmate's trial.

Thirteen years to the month after Janie Shepherd left her home in London never to return, her killer was finally brought face to face with justice. On 7 February 1990, David Lashley stood in the dock of St. Albans Crown Court; he pleaded not guilty to murder. Daniel Reece appeared as chief witness for the Crown, and as a final piece of hard fact, the prosecution was able to introduce a piece of forensic evidence impossible to imagine when Lashley first came to the notice of the Shepherd inquiry team. In the rear of Janie's abandoned car, scene-of-crime experts had found a semen stain. In 1977, technology had not been sufficiently advanced to be able to make identifications from these body fluids, but the sample had been kept. The intervening years had seen the development of DNA profiling—the genetic analysis of body secretions—and from the stored sample it was now possible to identify the source as an A-secretor. David Lashley was an A-secretor.

The jury retired to consider their verdict on 19 March. After two hours and fifteen minutes they returned with a unanimous verdict of guilty. Amid cheers of delight that the court usher had difficulty subduing, Mr. Justice Alliot, the trial judge, began to address the prisoner, and in sentencing Lashley to life imprisonment, remarked: "In my view you are such an appalling, dangerous man that the real issue is whether the authorities can ever allow you your liberty in your natural lifetime . . . The decision is such that whoever is responsible must have careful regard before you are allowed your liberty again."

David Lashley is now confined in a British prison which has not been named to ensure his personal safety.

UNITED STATES
CHRISTIAN BRANDO

The Messenger of Misery. *When the son of America's most famous movie star commits murder, that's news! Brando, much the worse for drink, shot his sister's lover in Marlon's Hollywood home, and thanks to some skilful plea-bargaining by the best lawyer money could hire was given a controversially light sentence of ten years.*

The case began as a simple, sordid story of violent death American-style—a fatal cocktail of domestic dispute, booze and guns. As a movie script it would hardly have got past Reception, but this drama had a head start: it starred "America's greatest living actor."

By the time the cops drove up to Marlon Brando's rambling mansion in the Hollywood Hills it was all over. It was late on the night of 16 May 1990, and they had been summoned by the Great Man himself. There on a sofa in the TV room slumped the victim, 26-year-old Dag Drollet, a small round wound on his face where a bullet fired at almost point-blank range from a .45 had ripped through flesh and bone, leaving the skin tattooed with a peppering of burnt powder before exiting at the base of the neck. The officers were to recall afterwards how neat it all was; there was no sign of a struggle almost as if the dead man had simply fallen asleep. That was the weird part, because the other leading player in this family drama, Marlon's 32-year-old son Christian, had already told his father and the police that there had been a fight and he had accidentally shot Dag.

Normally only Marlon would have been found rattling around the two-acre estate, but he had invited his common law wife Tarita Teriipia and their daughter Cheyenne to stay. Cheyenne had brought along Dag Drollet, son of a leading Tahitian politician and the father of her unborn child. Cheyenne and Christian had always been close, and on the evening of 16 May they had dined out together. It must have been during the meal that Cheyenne confided to her half-brother that things were not exactly a bed of roses with Dag, and that he had started beating her up. Now, there is no shred of evidence to support this extravagant claim, but it convinced Christian. When the pair returned to the house on Mulholland, Christian, much the worse for drink, went hunting for Dag with a .45 SIG-Sauer semi-automatic.

Later, in police custody, Christian made an incoherent statement during the course of which he recounted the story of the life-and-death struggle which followed: "We got into a fight and the gun went off in his face. I didn't want to hurt him; I didn't want to kill him." This maudlin whining was followed by a more aggressive claim: "You know, we got in a struggle ... I'd been drinking ... I didn't go up to him and go *Boom!* in my dad's house. If I was going to do that I'd take him down the road and knock him off." Later in the interview, Christian seemed to get back his old arrogance: "If I was going to do something devious like this [murder], I would have said [to Drollet] "Hey, let's go out, you know, check out the mine shafts on the Mojave." You know, or something like that. Whoops! He fell down a hole. Couldn't help it. "See you later sucker!" You know, I mean, all delicately laid— take him out to Death Valley with no clothes on, and give him three gallons of water "Get a suntan.""

Next day a woebegone Christian stood, handcuffed and unshaven, and wearing prison-issue grey, in the dock of the Los Angeles county court. William Kunstler, Marlon's lawyer, entered a plea of not guilty and added: "The weapon was fired accidentally during a struggle. There was no intent to harm anyone. This was not murder by any means." In other words, he was going for a reduced charge of manslaughter.

Predictably the Brando family closed ranks, and even Christian's ex-wife whom he had once threatened to kill was emphatic that "He's no killer ..." At the bail hearing five days later Marlon himself put in an appearance. This was what the media wanted—who was interested in some dipso kid with an itchy trigger-finger, who described his occupation as "self-employed welder"? Here was the *real* news. And Marlon didn't disappoint them; standing there on the steps outside the courthouse he broadcast to the waiting cameras his belief in Christian's innocence, and as though he were back there on the set of *Julius Caesar* intoned: "The Messenger of Misery has come to my house . . ."

Cheyenne, for her part, made only the briefest of statements to the police, but it was to the effect that Christian had "just walked in and killed Dag." She was prevented from making any more damaging observations by the simple expedient of flying her back to Tahiti. There, far from the clutches of the District Attorney's office, she gave birth to the late Dag Drollet's child.

Despite the court refusal to admit Christian's statement made in custody because of a legal technicality, and then its ruling that Cheyenne's statement that Christian was angry with Drollet was inadmissible, it did concede that "there is no doubt there has been a killing; there is no doubt that the defendant pulled the trigger"—in short, Christian was going up for trial.

In the meantime moves were afoot to flush Cheyenne out of her Tahitian retreat to give evidence, though the extradition application became purely academic anyway when Cheyenne tried unsuccessfully to take her own life. When she eventually emerged from a coma, Cheyenne was judged by a French court in Tahiti to be incapable of looking after herself and was placed in the care of her mother on the island. And so, faced with the unlikelihood of getting their star witness into court, the State of California decided to cut their losses and agree to a reduced charge of voluntary manslaughter in exchange for a plea of guilty.

When Christian Brando appeared before the sentencing hearing on 26 February 1991, his lawyer had already entered into a plea-bargain with the prosecutor's office. True to expectation, at the hearing Marlon, though clearly hating every minute of the limelight on which he had turned his back for so long, took the witness stand on his son's behalf and courageously exposed the family skeletons of Christian's unsatisfactory early life. Batted backwards and forwards like a tennis ball between his separated but still-warring parents Christian found himself sometimes in the custody of an absentee film-star father for whom displays of affection came hard, and sometimes in the custody of his mother, Anna Kashfi, who was gradually losing herself to drink and drugs

Education was spasmodic, and after dropping out of private school at the age of eighteen, there followed for Christian a period as a California beach bum, a broken marriage, and the development of an unhealthy interest in drink, drugs and guns. In many respects, it might have been more surprising if Christian had *not* got drunk someday and shot someone.

After all the media ballyhoo and legal tub-thumping had died down, Christian was sentenced to ten years' imprisonment. It was, as everybody had predicted, an affair from which only the lawyers gained. For Marlon there was the unwelcome intrusion into his jealously guarded privacy; for Cheyenne a further jolt to an already unsettled mind; for the Drollet family the loss of a son; and for Dag the ultimate loss. But perhaps the most haunting figure in this script where life tried hard to imitate Hollywood is Christian Brando himself.

1991

UNITED STATES
ERIK AND LYLE MENENDEZ

Life Imitates Hollywood. *The murder of super-rich parents by their offspring has become such an epidemic in the United States that it has its own special term—the "West Coast Syndrome."*

According to their own story, Erik and Lyle Menendez went to see the popular *Batman* film for a second time on the night of 20 August 1989. Then, again according to evidence that they gave to the police, they kept up the happy atmosphere by taking in a wine and food festival in Santa Monica before arriving for a supper appointment with a friend back in Beverly Hills.

It was approaching midnight when the brothers reached home and found their parents in the den. José Menendez had been shot eight times at point-blank range before the shotgun was forced into his mouth and a final cartridge blew the back of his head away. His wife Kitty had been shot five times. At 11:47 p.m. Beverly Hills police logged an hysterical telephone call from Lyle Menendez: "They killed my mom and my dad." According to neighbours, Erik was out on the porch sobbing as though his heart would break.

The case made headlines, not just in Los Angeles, not just in California; the Menendez killings were world-wide news—from a country with more than 20,000 homicides the same year. But then, the Menendez family were not exactly ordi nary. For a start they were rich, very rich. And they lived in Hollywood; in fact they lived in the reputedly $5-million mansion once the home of a succession of rock superstars such as Elton John and Michael Jackson. José Menendez himself had been big in the entertainment business. A refugee from Fidel Castro's revolution Cuba, 45-year-old Menendez had risen to executive positions in a number of companies, and at the time of his tragic death was on the board of directors of Carolco, the company which made the blockbusting series of *Rocky* films; Sylvester Stallone was a fellow board member. José was also chief executive of Live Entertainment, a major music and video company. And now he was dead in what at first was thought to be a Mafia execution—the hit carried out quickly (there was no sign of forced entry or a struggle at the scene of the shootings) and cleanly (whoever pulled the trigger had also been meticulous in picking up the spent cartridge cases).

When, in March 1990, the Menendez brothers Erik and Lyle were arrested and charged with parricide it was a media dream come true; real life was imitating Hollywood. And now at least four television "docudramas" were in the making, a film or two, and the usual clutch of books about these, the latest "celebrity" murders.

But just wait a minute! All these storylines assumed that Erik and Lyle are guilty; there wouldn't have been much of a plot otherwise. *But* the Menendez brothers have not even been put on trial yet. True, they have been held for some time without bail; true, police and prosecution have released enough tasty morsels of evidence to keep the public's interest in the boys' guilt going. *But* whatever happened to the concept of being innocent until proved guilty?

There are many, not least of the immediate family, who have been vociferous in their belief that 22-year-old Lyle and 19-year-old Erik Menendez could never have killed their own parents. One uncle is reported as believing that "The whole situation with the kids is something the police have fallen into for lack of a better lead."

Could it possibly be as he says?

It is true that the police did take a long time—more than six months—to press charges against the brothers for murder. It is also true that out of sympathy neither boy was checked for forensic evidence. Detectives had disposed fairly early of the "Mafia hit-man" theory, partly because there was no evidence to suggest that José Menendez was in the grip of the Mob, or had ever had any dealings, wittingly or not, with gangsters, and partly because it is not characteristic of "execution-type" assassins to create a bloodbath—the professional does not need to loose off a shotgun fourteen times to make his point.

Of course the Menendez brothers had been routinely questioned, and may even have been routinely considered suspects in the weeks of the investigation. But it was not until the heartbroken youths had begun to spend, spend, spend, that they once again came under official scrutiny. By the time the brothers—sole benefactors under their father's will—had taken delivery of the first instalment of the $400,000 insurance policy on his life. Erik's first step was to shelve plans to enter university and instead hire an expensive tennis coach in the hope that his already promising talent could be brought up to professional standard. Meanwhile Lyle was at the Porsche showrooms selecting a new car, and was soon to move into the apartment he had bought in Princeton where he attended university. For good measure he also bought a restaurant in town. But what really attracted attention was the way Lyle Menendez had taken to being chauffeured around in a hired limousine flanked by bodyguards—protection, he claimed, against those disgruntled business associates who had robbed him of his parents. Further revelations kept the media ball rolling during the latter part of 1989, when it was learned that two years previously, in collaboration with his pal Craig Cignarelli, Erik Menendez had written a screenplay. The script was called *Friends,* and told the story of an eighteen-year-old named Hamilton Cromwell who murders his parents for the $157 million inheritance. It contains this chilling passage: "The door opens, exposing the luxurious suite of Mr. and Mrs. Hamilton Cromwell Sr. lying in bed. Their faces are of questioning horror as Hamilton closes the door gently." Kitty Menendez typed the manuscript for her son; we will never know what she made of such a plot.

The most significant, and the most controversial, piece of evidence gathered by the police investigators was a tape recording allegedly of the boys confessing murder to their psychologist Jerome Oziel. The existence of the recording had come to official attention in a most bizarre way. Another of Oziel's patients claimed she had been sitting in the waiting room when she heard the conversation through the wall. It was subsequently established that such a feat would be virtually impossible, but that did not prevent officers seizing a number of tapes from Mr. Oziel's consulting rooms and making application for them to be accepted as evidence in court. It is normally considered that what secrets pass between a doctor and his patient are sacrosanct, but according to California state procedure, such information *may* be revealed if the psychiatrist considers the patient to be a serious threat to himself or others. The content of the tapes has not yet been made public, but at the preliminary hearing a judge ruled that the tapes could be used by the prosecution as evidence: "Dr. Oziel had reasonable cause to believe that the brothers constituted a threat, and that it was necessary to disclose those communications to prevent the threatened danger." It was a decision strongly opposed by the Menendez defence counsel, who have referred the ruling to a higher court.

On Thursday, 8 March 1990, Lyle Menendez was arrested on suspicion of murdering his father and mother; three days later Erik returned from a tennis tournament in Israel and was taken into custody at Los Angeles airport. Both young men have pleaded not guilty to charges that could carry the death penalty.

When this entry was being prepared for publication in early 1993, it looked as though the Menendez case would never get to trial—years of pre-trial squabbling between counsel had kept it out of the courts until, in June 1993, it was announced that jury selection was about to begin. The delay had given Erik and Lyle's attorney, Ms Leslie Abramson, time to abandon the plea of not guilty and substitute one of self-defence: "Our clients believed themselves to be in danger of death, imminent peril or great bodily injury." Not danger in the ordinary sense of the defence, but the culmination of years of child abuse! This, of course shows the relevance of psychiatrist Dr. Oziel's tapes in a new light; they will help corroborate the fact that the killings were carried out "out of hatred and a desire to be free from their father's domination.'' Meanwhile the judge, Mr. Stanley Weisberg, was wrestling with his own dilemma—whether to have one jury only, or two, so that the evidence against one brother would not sway verdict against the other.

UNITED KINGDOM
JOHN TANNER

The Case of the Mysterious Stranger. *The cynical murder of student Rachel McLean by her boyfriend John Tanner appeared the more awful by his televised pleas for information on her whereabouts and his enthusiastic participation in the reconstruction of her last known movements.*

In April 1991, nineteen-year-old student Rachel McLean disappeared from her lodgings in Oxford. Young, intelligent, attractive, she was destined for the same extravagant media attention as Suzy Lamplugh had been five years previously (see 1986). From Rachel's flatmates police learned that her steady boyfriend was John Tanner, like herself a student, originally from New Zealand. Over the succeeding days Tanner was interviewed by detectives and gave his account of the last time he saw Rachel. It had been on the evening of Monday 15 April. They had spent the weekend together at Rachel's flat in Argyle Road, and she had gone to see Tanner off at Oxford railway station. While they sat in the buffet waiting for John's train, a friend of Rachel's came up to them, chatted, and offered Rachel a lift home when she had said her goodbyes. Tanner's description of the man was later turned into an Identikit likeness—long dark brown hair, clean shaven, aged between eighteen and 22, five feet eleven inches tall, and "scruffily dressed" in a bomber jacket, faded blue jeans and baseball boots. Nevertheless, apart from prompting some people to remark that the person it most resembled was John Tanner himself, the face staring out from every newspaper and television screen in the country jogged no memories. On 29 April a reconstruction of the farewell was enacted on Oxford station with a policewoman posing as Rachel, a student as her friend, and Tanner enthusiastically playing himself. Prior to the reconstruction, Tanner had appeared at a press conference, calm but concerned, with the hint of a sob in his voice, speaking of his conviction that Rachel was still alive somewhere: "I would appeal to anyone who knows where she is . . . to come forward and tell us, out of consideration to her mother and father and to myself."

Although thorough searches had already been made at the house in Argyle Road, it was not until the evening of 2 May that, with the help of architectural plans, police officers began to strip down any cavity in the building which might conceal a body. Rachel's remains were found beneath loose floorboards in a recessed ground-floor cupboard under the stairs. Within hours of the discovery, John Tanner was arrested in a public house near his home in Nottingham. It was not until the following December that Tanner appeared at Birmingham Crown Court charged with murder; he pleaded not guilty to murder but admitted manslaughter. He had, according to his own defence, become involved in a quarrel with Rachel when she confessed to being unfaithful and wanting to leave him. As the row escalated he lost all control and found himself strangling her. After concealing Rachel's body he returned home and later concocted the story of the long-haired stranger at the station. As he sat alone on Oxford station that Monday, he wrote a letter to Rachel as part of his elaborate and cynical sham; he thanked her for the wonderful weekend, and signed "your devoted John."

After a retirement of four and a half hours, the jury returned a majority verdict 10–2 of guilty of murder. John Tanner is currently serving a life sentence.

1992

UNITED STATES
AILEEN WUORNOS, "THE DAMSEL OF DEATH"

Highway prostitute Aileen "Lee" Wuornos, a confirmed man-hater and recent lesbian, killed and robbed seven of her clients. According to the FBI Lee Wuornos is the first of a new breed of female serial killer.

Since the end of 1989, the Florida State Police had been taxed by a series of unsolved murders around Marion County that looked as though they followed a pattern. All the victims had been white males, middle-aged or older, and all had been shot dead with a .22-calibre handgun; some of them were found naked. When the victims had been identified it was further learned that they had all been travelling alone by road along one or other of Florida's Interstates, and the stolen cars had later been found abandoned. Twelve months later, the Marion County Sheriff's Office task-force investigating the deaths were convinced that a serial killer was stalking the highways—not difficult to believe in view of the fact that an estimated 100 serial killers are at large in the United States at any given time. What was unusual in this case was that it was beginning to look as though the murderer was a woman. This was consistent with the fact that some of the victims were naked, and that their cars were found with condoms on the floor and long blonde hairs on the upholstery. It would also account for how the killer could get so close to the victim without arousing suspicion. The most probable explanation was that their suspect was a prostitute working from the road-side.

The first victim grouped with the series was 51-year-old Richard Mallory. His badly decomposed body was found in some woods in December 1989; he had been repeatedly shot with a small-calibre gun. Over the first few months of the new year five more bodies were found in similar circumstances. Finally, in June 1990, a 65-year-old missionary named Peter Siems left his home in Jupiter, Florida, bound for Arkansas along the Interstate 95 coast road through Daytona Beach; he never saw either his home or Arkansas again. Indeed, Siems's bodily remains have never been located. However, on 4 July his grey Pontiac Sunbird was involved in an accident at Orange Springs. Witnesses running to the scene were just in time to see the two female occupants of the car flee from the wreck and disappear over the fields; from their descriptions police artists were able to compile a pair of likenesses which were broadcast nationwide. It was not long before detectives came up with the names of Tyria J. Moore, a 27-year-old sometime hotel maid, and her lesbian lover Aileen "Lee" Wuornos (alias Camie Greene, Lori Grody and Susan Blahovec). With co-operation from Ty Moore, who was to turn state's evidence, undercover officers were able to stake out the bars and clubs around the Daytona Beach area, hoping to get a sighting of Aileen Wuornos. At a seedy, single-storey brick shack which called itself the Last Resort, they got lucky.

Aileen Wuornos had been born in Detroit, Michigan, in 1956; when she was six weeks old her teenage mother deserted Aileen, her brother and a psychopathically violent father who regularly beat his wife and anybody else who happened to be in his way. Aileen and Keith found themselves abandoned to the care of an elderly, well-meaning grandmother and a brutal, alcholic grandfather, whose ill-treatment of the children, according to Aileen, made their every day a living nightmare. By the age of twelve, Aileen had already succumbed to the family weakness for alcohol; at thirteen she was pregnant, and supplementing the booze with drugs. After her baby had been given away for adoption, Aileen dropped out of school in tenth grade and began to sell her favours on the streets in order to finance a growing habit. Over the coming years, she would work her way through a succession of dead-end jobs. As she hitched around America, Aileen claims to have been raped more than a dozen times, and beaten more often than she can remember. It was in 1976, when she was twenty, that Aileen arrived at Daytona Beach, Florida. She formed a succession of unsatisfactory relationships with men and after one particularly acrimonious separation she tried to commit suicide by shooting herself in the stomach. It was just the first of several unsuccessful attempts over the years.

Aileen met Tyria Moore in 1986, in a bar called the Zodiac. In the beginning, at least, a close and intense affection existed between the two women—though by all accounts heavy drinking resulted in frequent bitter arguments. If we can believe Aileen's subsequent stories, she was utterly devastated by Ty's desertion, and for her it marked the end of her world. Throughout their love affair Aileen continued as a highway hooker—but the strain was beginning to unhinge her already unstable mind. Although Aileen claimed to have up to a dozen clients a day, there were some who wouldn't pay, and some who would beat her up, just for the heck of it. If she hadn't already hated the whole of the male gender, she certainly did now. In 1989 she picked up a .22 revolver—an equaliser. Shortly after this the killing spree began.

The trial of Aileen Wuornos, by now dubbed the "Damsel of Death," opened at Deland, Florida, on 12 January 1992. Although she had made a videotape confession to seven killings, there was only one charge on the indictment—the first-degree murder of Richard Mallory, her first victim. According to State Prosecutor John Tanner, Aileen had been plying her trade when she was picked up by Mallory at an overpass near Tampa. They drove along Interstate 4 to Daytona Beach, where Mallory pulled the car off the road into some woodland where they had sex before Aileen shot Mallory dead and hid his body. This much she was prepared to admit. But she insisted that the killing was self-defence. In Aileen's version of things, Mallory had tied her to the steering wheel of the car, raped and sodomised her, and threatened to kill her if she kept struggling. She just managed to pull her gun from her purse as Mallory, so she said, lunged forward at her. Through her attorney Aileen protested that Mallory was drunk and had been smoking marijuana. "What happened was bondage, rape, sodomy and degradation." What's more, she was convinced that Mallory wasn't going to pay her.

It was a defence that attracted ridicule from the prosecution: "She was a predatory prostitute," John Tanner told the court. "She killed out of greed—no longer satisfied with the ten, twenty, thirty dollars, she wanted it all. It wasn't enough to control his body, she wanted the ultimate—his car, his property, his life."

Giving evidence against her former lover, Tyria Moore said that on the evening of 30 November, Aileen had come home a little the worse for drink, driving a new car. Later Aileen announced she had just killed a man. Moore said: "I didn't believe her." Cross-examined, Ty Moore was adamant that her partner made no mention of being raped or beaten, nor seemed particularly upset about anything. Tanner's implication was clear: here was a cold-blooded, emotionless killer who, far from suffering the trauma of "rape, sodomy and degradation," had simply shot one of her clients for his car and the contents of his wallet.

It was clearly the explanation favoured by the jury who, on 27 January after a 95-minute retirement, found Aileen Wuornos guilty as charged. As she was led from the dock, Wuornos turned on the jury, screaming "Scumbags of America!" before being hustled out. Two days later, acting on the jury's recommendation, Judge Blount sentenced Aileen Wuornos to death. In May 1992, Wuornos was tried and convicted of three more of her seven admitted killings. After Judge Thomas Sawaya sentenced Wuornos to death she yelled: "Thank you, I'll go to heaven now, and you will rot in hell."

RUSSIA
ANDREI CHIKATILO, "THE ROSTOV RIPPER"

In April 1992, news reached the West via the news agencies that in the southern Russian port of Rostov a 56-year-old grandfather and former schoolteacher was about to stand trial accused of torturing, butchering and cannibalising no fewer than 53 victims, many of them children, and some, it was said, his own pupils. Andrei Chikatilo insists he has claimed at least two more victims, though so far no tangible evidence had been found to support legal charges. One fact is certain: Chikatilo has earned his place as one of the most brutal and prolific multiple killers in the criminal history of the world.

Andrei Romanovich Chikatilo was born in 1936, in the shadow of the Stalinist purges, in the town of Novocherkassk, north of Rostov on the southeastern corner of what was the USSR. Although his youth was reportedly disturbed by feelings of inadequacy, particularly in the company of women, Chikatilo was bright enough to earn a good degree in Russian literature from the University at Rostov. He remained a studious and rather serious young man throughout his military service, usually preferring books to bars. In 1966, when he was 28 years old, Andrei Chikatilo married, and shortly afterwards fathered a son and, in quick succession, a daughter. The marriage was to all recollection a happy one, and in his spare time Andrei became not only an active member of the Communist Party, but was elevated to chairman of his regional sports committee.

It was probably around 1975, during the early months of Chikatilo's post as lecturer in Russian literature at the nearby school of Novo Shatinsk, that his sexual envy and frustration became uncontrollable; perhaps it was, as one journalist suggested, being surrounded by eager young women experimenting for the first time with new adolescent emotions, but for whom he could never be more than a schoolmaster. Shortly afterwards, Rostov would be thrown into a twelve-year reign of terror by an unknown assassin whose young victims had been subjected to unspeakable torture and mutilation before death, and against whom the police seemed utterly powerless.

The first victim, a teenaged girl, was found dead in a wood in 1978. The horror of the crime was avenged with swiftness and finality when a known child molester was successively arrested, tried, convicted and executed for the killing. The police were still slapping each other on the back when the next bodies were found. The wrong man had faced the firing squad.

Over the succeeding years the list of those who disappeared grew longer, the discovery of mutilated remains punctuated the normally quiet life around the port with increasing regularity; in one year alone there were eight deaths in a single month. The killer's approach was always the same. With the uncanny sixth sense of the natural predator, he could pick out the weak and vulnerable on the edges of society's groups. Trawling the streets and railway stations for the homeless drifters who were unlikely to be missed, he singled out the solitary child on his way to school. Years later the monster who had become known as the "Rostov Ripper" would himself explain: "As soon as I saw a lonely person I felt I had to drag them off to the woods. I paid no attention to age or sex. We would walk for a couple of miles or so, then I would be possessed by an awful shaking sensation." The savagery of the attacks have rarely been matched in the history of violent crime. First the killer cut out the victims' tongues to ensure they did not cry out; then he gouged out the eyes and spiked through the eardrums. While the mute and struggling bodies were still alive, the "Ripper" carried out his surgical operations, sometimes raping, always hacking at the genitals with his knife and cannibalising the flesh. The awful remains were buried where they lay, in the woods alongside the railroad tracks, a characteristic that earned the monster his second nickname, "The Forest Strip Killer."

Despite an extensive manhunt that stretched from Rostov to Siberia and was led by experienced detectives seconded from Moscow, the police still seemed helpless in the face of a catalogue of carnage. It had spread to the neighbouring states of Ukraine and Uzbekistan when schoolmaster Chikatilo changed his job to become head of supplies at the Rostov locomotive repair shop, a post which enabled him to travel all over the south of the USSR. But if anybody had even hinted that the quiet, kindly ex-teacher with his white hair and thick spectacles was the Rostov Ripper the whole of Novocherkassk would have laughed out loud—the very thought was absurd.

On one occasion the police did arrest a suspect; he committed suicide while in prison awaiting his trial. And still the death toll rose.

In 1979 another man had been picked up in an isolated wooded area, but persuaded the police that he was simply an innocent hiker; after taking his name and particulars he was allowed to wander on his way. Five years later the same man was picked up close to the scene of one of the murders and this time was found to be carrying a length of rope and a knife in his briefcase. When he was subjected to a blood test and it was proved by the laboratory that the man's blood group differed from that of the semen samples recovered from the bodies of some of the victims, the suspect was immediately released. His name was Andrei Romanovich Chikatilo.

What the Russian police, with their rather primitive grasp of forensic procedures, did not learn until many years and many murders later is that in extremely rare cases secretions from different sources in the body can have different serological groupings. Andrei Chikatilo is one of those rare cases.

Early in 1990 the police investigation team, still no nearer to stopping the Ripper's reign of terror, co-opted the expertise of psychiatrist Alexander Bukhanovsky who, using relevant data contained in the case files on each of the murders, and relating it to his experience of human behaviour patterns and predictability, built a psychological profile of the Rostov Ripper which proved to be remarkably accurate. The fact that initially so many murders had been committed in such a restricted geographical location indicated a fundamental requirement of the home-based serial killer—social respectability. The killer needed to be known as a loving family man, a trusted employee, cooperative neighbour, loyal friend, and so on: the kind of man of whom nobody could believe ill.

The killer had been able to approach and lure children, many of whom might have been expected to view an elderly stranger with mistrust, even fear, into the woods. The fact that there were never any consistent reports of misconduct against an individual suggested to Bukhanovsky that his suspect might be a schoolteacher, a person used to putting children at their ease and feeling at ease with them, a person capable of generating trust. The savage nature of the mutilation and the areas of the body chosen for it were consistent with a violent repressed sexuality and a resentment of other people's physical sexuality.

It was in November 1990 that the net began to close around the Rostov Ripper, the Forest Strip Killer. On 6 November a police officer routinely stopped Andrei Chikatilo in the street, reportedly after spotting a bloodstain on his face. When shortly afterwards another body was found in the woods the officer reported the incident of the bloodstain to his superiors, and Chikatilo was put under heavy surveillance. On 20 November police saw Chikatilo approach a young boy at a railway station; he was immediately taken into custody, where under questioning he readily confessed to an unbelievable 55 brutal murders, though, as Chikatilo is the first to admit, "there may be more."

To sophisticated Western eyes, the trial of Andrei Chikatilo presented a spectacle almost as bizarre as his crimes were dreadful. The process took place in Rostov's own very unceremonial court. Chikatilo was tried by a chairman—a professional judge named Leonid Akubzhanov—and two "people's representatives," who have no legal qualification at all; there was no jury.

In the centre of the threadbare court a huge iron-barred cage had been built around the dock. Inside sat the prisoner, chained liked a wild beast. Around the cage were the baying crowds of his victims' families, screaming for his blood, demanding that the Ripper be handed over to the mob for the dispensation of instant "justice." There were to be many occasions during the trial when the first-aid team on duty were called upon to revive spectators faint from overtaxed emotions.

As the trial opened on 14 April 1992, it took two hours to quieten the crowd sufficiently to read the two-volume document listing the charges against Chikatilo; they consisted of 35 child victims—eleven of them boys—and eighteen young women. In all it was anticipated that scores of witnesses and upwards of 200 documents would be brought as evidence to support the charges. Although he had previously been described as a quiet, retiring family man, Andrei Chikatilo sat in the cage now with his shaven head lolling rhythmically from side to side, and with wild, rolling eyes. He inflamed the court into further outrage by holding up pages of photographs of naked women torn from pornographic magazines and jeering back at the crowd. If he was not mad before, he was certainly giving an impressive performance as a madman now.

Not surprisingly, Andrei Chikatilo has been subjected to extensive psychiatric evaluation since his eventual arrest late in 1990. Although it is clear that he falls broadly into the category of serial "lust" killers—that is, his motivation to kill is determined by his need for sexual gratification—his basic requirement for sex has been interwoven with other, far deeper fantasies. According to the published theories of psychiatrist Alexander Bukhanovsky, it is likely that his patient's deep sense of his own worthlessness originated in the arrest of his father on political charges during the Stalinist regime. The grievance that he nurtured against the world for this injustice triggered his self-protective delusions of grandeur, the pivot of which was his fantasy of being able to dominate women. In reality Chikatilo's sexual inadequacies soon gave lie to the delusions, and it became clear that he could only ever exert domination by exercising the power of life and death over his victims. As to the cannibalism, Dr. Bukhanovsky says Chikatilo refers constantly to an episode during a famine in the 1930s—as yet unconfirmed—when a group of starving peasants killed and ate his brother.

Towards the end of the first week of his trial, Andrei Chikatilo insisted on addressing the court, and in addition to confirming once again his guilt, he gave the court a self-pitying account of the early privations of his home life and of his "dreadful" childhood. He also referred again to the eating of his brother by hungry Ukrainian peasants who, he claimed, had been deprived of food as a result of Stalin's collectivisation of private farmland. Chikatilo concluded his speech: "I am a freak of nature, a mad beast."

There was never any likelihood of Andrei Chikatilo being found not guilty of the crimes with which he was charged—after all, he not only confessed in detail, but he led police searchers to forest locations where many of his victims still lay buried. What is in dispute is his sanity, and therefore his culpability. If, as the prosecutor claims, Chikatilo was sane at the time of his killings, then he faces death in front of a firing squad. On 15 October 1992, the three judges decided: "The court cannot but sentence this man to what he deserves for his terrible crimes—that is, to death.''

At present, Audrei Chikatilo awaits execution in the squalid surroundings of Cell 33 in Novocherkassk Prison.

Alphabetical
Index of Cases

TRUE CRIME
AT ITS SHOCKING BEST